Saudade in Brazilian Cinema

Saudade in Brazilian Cinema
The History of an Emotion on Film

intellect Bristol, UK / Chicago, USA

First published in the UK in 2017 by
Intellect, The Mill, Parnall Road, Fishponds, Bristol, BS16 3JG, UK

First published in the USA in 2017 by
Intellect, The University of Chicago Press, 1427 E. 60th Street,
Chicago, IL 60637, USA

A catalogue record for this book is available from the British Library.

Copy-editor: MPS Technologies
Cover designer: Emily Dann and Aleksandra Szumlas
Production manager: Mareike Wehner
Typesetting: Contentra Technologies

Print ISBN: 978-1-78320-763-3
ePDF ISBN: 978-1-78320-764-0
ePUB ISBN: 978-1-78320-765-7

Contents

Acknowledgments

In my research on cinema and saudade over the past decade, I have received essential assistance from many corners. Regarding my archival and library visits in Brazil, I extend special thanks to Christina Ravanelli at the Museu de Imagem e Som in São Paulo, Erica Resende at the Universidade Federal Rio de Janeiro (Campus Praia Vermelha library), Marcia Carvalho at the library of the Pontifícia Universidade Católica in Rio de Janeiro, Anna Paes at the Museu de Imagem e Som of Rio de Janeiro and Caio Brito at the Cinemateca of São Paulo. Petra Costa and Li An Costa were inspirational in their filmmaking and in several conversations about my project. Their assistant at Buscavida Filmes, Quelany Vicente, was also very helpful in acquiring some images for the book. I thank Lúcia Murat and Consuelo Lins for lending me their ears and helping me to flesh out some of my ideas about saudade in film with filmmakers and scholars in Brazil. Conversations with Salgado Maranhão about saudade in a broader context of Brazilian poetry, song lyrics, literature and culture were also essential. At Intellect, I thank Amy Damutz, Jelena Stanovnik, May Yao, Jessica Mitchell, Tim Mitchell and Mareike Wehner for their encouragement and logistical support at various stages of the publishing process. I am very thankful to the University of Missouri Research Board for both a grant supporting the earlier stages of my research on saudade in 2007, and a publication subvention for this book in 2016. Chapter 6 is a longer, revised version of a chapter originally published in *Migration in Lusophone Cinema* (Palgrave Macmillan, 2014). I thank the editors Cacilda Rêgo and Marcus Brasileiro for their work on that invaluable collection, and for their organization of the *Diasporas and Brazilian Cinema* panel at the Brazilian Studies Association Congress of 2012, where I first presented some of my research for *Saudade in Brazilian Cinema*. Finally, I give my utmost gratitude to my dear family, especially Jamila, Ruby and Aurelio, for their love and encouragement. Whenever we are apart, I learn again what saudade truly is.

Chapter 1

Introduction - Rethinking Saudade and Cinema

The cinematic frame becomes a window on the past when a filmmaker wishes to explore memory or history. In the case of Brazilian cinema specifically, the incorporation of the emotion of saudade in filmic narratives has often provided emotional colouring to these windows, influencing our perception of the landscapes, characters and other imagery visible through them. As a complex emotion related to nostalgia, saudade takes on diverse and subtle hues over the course of the more than 60-year period spanned by the films analysed in the following chapters. Often the emotion is mirrored, refracted or heightened by frames within the frame, other windows on the past, static or moving, which emphasize the sentiment's liminal essence, such as windows of vehicles from truck to train to plane, or other kinds of glass (reflective or transparent), televisual or cinematic screens, or even bodies of water such as rivers or oceans. The viewer is more or less encouraged by these varied vistas to identify with, or to reflect upon, a sense of longing for a person, place or era that can appear tantalizingly close, just beyond the window frame, but always out of reach. The evocation of saudade, we will see, imbues the Brazilian nation with an affective charge (including its urban and rural landscapes and its people) to varying effects, including an emphasis on neo-Romantic, satirical or postmodern imaginaries, perceived from subject positions that range from powerful (hegemonic) to marginalized (subaltern).

Saudade is a powerful 'sister emotion' of nostalgia that has received much attention, at times celebratory and at times more critical, from artists and other intellectuals in the Lusophone world. Over the course of many years of research, I have sought to synthesize, clarify and refine the large body of art and cultural criticism featuring saudade. I have concluded that the affective structure of the sentiment can be best understood as a tripartite 'feeling blend' (Rosenblatt 1999), involving a fusion of two emotional components of love and grief that are always mediated through the third structuring element of memory. While this conclusion can be considered to fall within the tradition of thought on this emotion, there are several areas in which I seek to make significant strides beyond or outside of the tradition in what follows.

The first innovation I develop with regard to the philosophical and artistic tradition is to bring to bear the analytical framework of the field of emotion studies. In Part 1 of this introduction, I place my own and others' insights on saudade in dialogue with studies of emotion and affect. The fact that saudade has not yet been brought under the umbrella of emotion/affect studies is a shortcoming not only in thought on saudade, but in the field of emotion studies itself. Both fields can mutually inform each other. On the one hand, thinkers of saudade anticipated various insights in emotion studies avant la lettre, while the example of saudade as an emotion complicates a number of more general philosophical, cultural and affective-physiological theories of emotion. On the other hand, scholars of emotion/affect studies in recent decades have developed a number of interdisciplinary analytical tools and approaches that have a clear potential to lead to new insights, even into an emotion that has already been the object of many centuries of contemplation. In Part 1, I outline several theoretical approaches from emotion/affect studies that in some ways grow out of the genealogy of thought on saudade, but also break free of some of the limitations of previous thought and serve to expand the fields of emotion and affect studies themselves, simultaneously contributing to a revision of our broader understanding of the history of western thought related to subjectivity and affect.

In Part 2 of this introduction I analyse saudade with respect to ideology, hegemony and subalternity. To do so, I first demonstrate the canonical thought on saudade to be problematic in its failure to articulate clearly the ideological, political nature of expressions of the sentiment in cultural production. While saudade has been presented at times as a learned, social emotion (DaMatta 1993) or a national mythology (Lourenço 1999), these more critical approaches are rare and they do not even adequately distinguish artistic expressions of saudade from the experience of the emotion in everyday life. Here we can find some theoretical support for a more thorough exploration of saudade's relationship to power not only in emotion studies, but also from thinkers more focused on ideology and hegemony such as Ernesto Laclau, Judith Butler and Slavoj Žižek. Moving from hegemony to its constitutive exclusion of subalternity, and making use of examples from twentieth- and twenty-first-century Brazilian cinema, I also highlight the existence of alternative saudades that grow out of the unique standpoints of various subsets of the global Lusophone population. I make this final departure from saudade's intellectual tradition in order to assert that it has tied the emotion too strongly to a timeless, universalist national identity, obscuring regional, class, gender, racial and historical variants. While various thinkers have attempted to make distinctions between Portuguese and Brazilian modes of the emotion (e.g. Orico 1940), the question of corresponding saudades developing out of other kinds of subnational or transnational, differential subject positions has been left largely unexplored. These differential emotional discourses, as represented in Brazilian cinema since the 1950s from an array of subjective perspectives, will then be introduced in the chapter summary and analysed in detail in the remainder of the book, as counterpoints to more traditional, hegemonic feeling subjects.

Part 1: Saudade Thought and The Field of Emotion Studies

As we begin to bring the theoretical field of emotion studies into focus for the purposes of filmic analysis, we can get a sense of its value as a tool for understanding saudade at the same time that we discover the incorporation of the history of saudade thought into emotion studies as an effective move to enrich that field itself. I understand emotion studies as an emergent field of cultural studies and thus as an inherently interdisciplinary, culturalist and social-constructionist approach to the study of emotion. The interdisciplinary nature of this field will become clear as we proceed; however, we can consider for a moment in more detail what comprises a culturalist analysis. Jennifer Harding and E. Deidre Pribram pose the following questions as key to a culturalist approach to emotions:

> To what uses are emotions put? What meanings have they accrued that make possible those uses? How do they circulate in the social formation? [They continue:] To this end, we understand emotions as cultural practices which help to give various social formations their meanings and power. We conceptualise emotions as both cultural practice and as constitutive of the possibilities for cultural practice.
>
> (2009: 4)

With regard to the social-constructionist theoretical framework inherited from cultural studies, Deborah Lupton emphasizes 'the lived experience and social relational dimension of emotion, including the role played by such factors as gender and power relations in emotional experience' (1998: 38). Lupton also advocates in this context for a 'poststructuralist perspective on subjectivity that sees it as dynamic and shifting, and as constituted, rather than distorted or manipulated by, sociocultural processes' (1998: 38). These culturalist and related social-constructionist analytical approaches of emotion studies are useful models for theoretical innovations in studies of saudade. Incorporating these innovations into an analysis of saudade in Lusophone cultures sheds new light on age-old debates about this emotion and can provide us with the architecture of a subfield we could call 'saudade studies'. Saudade studies can provide additional confirmation and further enrich the conclusions already arrived at in emotions studies about the relationship between emotion and culture.

At the same time, saudade studies can expand emotion studies' understanding of the relationship between emotion and memory greatly, revealing the particular feeling blends associated with memory and how memory itself is shaped through various discourses addressing the past in the ideologically contested cultural spaces of the nation in both colonial and postcolonial historical contexts. With this book, I am answering the call of Harding and Pribram to 'investigate how specific emotions are formed and function as part of the historical, cultural, and political contexts in which they are practiced to reproduce, and potentially to resist, hegemonic relations' (2004: 865). I overturn a number of commonplaces with regard to saudade, as noted above, but also more broadly with regard to the perception of emotion and affect. Firstly, the history of thought on saudade supports a vision of the subject that is less self-enclosed and more open to affective exchange in his or her social environment, both with the beloved and with other desiring subjects. An analysis of the emotion in this framework supports the work of thinkers attempting to question or dismantle the transcendental feeling subject in its historical and contemporary guises (e.g. Ahmed 2004; Brennan 2004; Probyn 1996; Sedgwick 2003; Terada 2001; Tomkins 1995). Secondly, manifestations of saudade in cinema and other arts break down the affect/emotion divide in the ambiguous feeling blend that comprises the sentiment, supporting the work of scholars who demonstrate significant overlap between affect and emotion (Harding and Pribram 2004; Probyn 1996; Terada 2001). Finally, as I explain further in Part 2 of this chapter, the study of saudade offers to emotion and affect studies a history of nostalgia and of mourning alternative to the dominant Hofer-Freudian paradigm, which has pathologized both of these emotions (Freud [1917] 1957; on Johannes Hofer, see Boym 2001).

Emotions and Cultural Authenticity

Various cultural studies thinkers have emphasized that emotions can be powerful markers of the authenticity of a given identity, be it individual or collective (Harding and Pribram 2009). Since at least the work of Raymond Williams (1977), cultural critics have argued that emotions help to (re)produce culture itself. Williams' concept of the structure of feeling is an early representative of emotion studies from a culturalist perspective. According to Williams, the emotional discourses and dispositions of a given generation should be understood as a fundamental and often overlooked element of a nation's culture in that generation's historical era. A generation's structure of feeling is what gives that historical group a unique, authentic identity and way of life. Saudade itself can be considered a structure of feeling that periodically reappears and evolves over many generations in the Lusophone world, helping to reproduce that social world and its various subcultures. From the perspective of saudade, the human world takes its shape through affective interconnections and memories, linking Lusophone national, transnational and subnational communities across space and time. Such a perspective is beautifully expressed, for instance, in Luiz Gonzaga and Hervé Cordovil's song 'A vida do viajante' ('The Life of the Traveller'):

> Minha vida é andar (My life is to wander)
> Por este país (Through this country)
> Pra ver se um dia (To see if one day)
> Descanso feliz (I rest happily)
> Guardando as recordações (Storing up memories)
> Das terras por onde passei (Of the lands through which I passed)
> [...] E dos amigos que lá deixei. (And of the friends I left there)
>
> ([1953] 2000)[1]

For Lila Abu-Lughod and Catherine Lutz, emotion should be seen 'as about social life rather than internal states' ([1990] 2009: 100). Accordingly, various scholars of culture have also demonstrated how emotions can help to produce nationalism as well as social hierarchies within a given society. For instance, Harding and Pribram argue that 'loyalty and pride are operative in the construction of nationalism and patriotism' (2009). An analysis of saudade confirms and deepens such insights from emotion studies. It is undeniable that saudade, too, has been operative in constructing both Portuguese and Brazilian nationalism over many centuries. Both the Portuguese and Brazilian Romantics saw saudade as essential to valorizing their respective nations, as can be seen in the writings of Almeida Garrett, Gonçalves Dias and José Alencar among others. The Portuguese then proceeded to transform this association of saudade with love of country into a mystical, millenarian 'religion of saudade' in the Saudosista movement of the early twentieth century, exemplified in the philosophy and poetry of Teixeira Pascoaes and Fernando Pessoa (see for instance Pascoaes [1913] 1976). This devotion to saudade imagined an era of redemption for the Portuguese nation and later the Lusophone world as a whole in the thought of philosophers from Dalila L. Pereira da Costa to Agostinho da Silva (Costa and Gomes 1976; Henrique 1998).

With regard to social hierarchies, Judith Butler demonstrates their relationship to emotion in her analysis of grieving. For Butler, the key question related to the politics of grief is: 'What makes for a grievable life?'. A given society/culture determines that certain lives are more grievable than others, establishing a 'hierarchy of grief' (2004: 393). The deaths of the least privileged, most subaltern members of society are considered unworthy of public grieving. Thus, emotion both reflects and reinforces the unequal distribution of power and citizenship rights in a society. This kind of contextualization of emotion in a political-ideological struggle is helpful in understanding saudade as well. The key question in this light related to saudade is: 'How does saudade discourse make certain objects of desire more saudade-worthy?'. Over the history of art and thought representing the emotion of saudade, various objects have been selected and privileged as the most worthy of being ennobled by the aura of saudade. These objects of saudade include family, lovers, country and of course the Portuguese and Brazilian nations as noted above. The inverse of this valorization through saudade is the underprivileging or marginalization of certain objects as unworthy of saudade. Perhaps more significant for our purposes is the marginalization of certain forms of saudade itself, not allowing them to represent the emotion of saudade in a more universal sense. Saudades incorporating the standpoints of women, underdeveloped regions and their populations, and non-white racial groups have been sidelined in favour of nationalist, patriarchal, Euro-Brazilian or Portuguese saudades in much of the mainstream discourse on the emotion. Some of these subaltern saudades will be discussed further below with examples from Brazilian cinema in Part 2.

Desire and the Philosophy of the Subject

Judith Butler also raises many important insights on desire that have bearing on saudade in her discussion of the French Hegelian tradition of thought on the desiring subject. For instance, she remarks upon intentionality in her discussion of Kojève's appropriation of Hegel: '[T]he subject *is* its desire for its object or Other; the identity of the subject is to be found in the intentionality of its desire' (Butler 1987: 67, original emphasis). Recent scholarship in the philosophy of emotions has tended to confirm the significance of intentionality in the creation of our sentiments (Hatzimoysis 2003; Solomon 2004). Kojève in particular places desire – directed at a particular object – at the very core of the subject's identity, and the tradition of art and thought on saudade tends to support the application of these conclusions about desire to saudade itself. It is safe to say that the latter emotion, which involves a certain fusion of desire with other emotions and memories, very often serves to define the subject by the object for which he or she feels saudade. As the saudoso[2] recalls a lost object, not only is a full emotional range of sadness and joy revealed but also the subject's own limitations and weaknesses as well as other factors that separate him or her from the saudado. Thus, one could certainly imagine that some of the great artists or thinkers of saudade such as Luís Vaz de Camões or Joaquim Nabuco would have agreed that the intentionality of saudade reveals much about the identity of its subject – indeed, such a revelation has often been at least part of the intent behind artistic representations of saudade.

Butler's thoughts on Jean Paul Sartre's philosophy of desire are also very relevant here. Firstly, she discusses Sartre's special focus on the imaginary as an expression and sublimation of desire. The manner in which Butler describes the functioning of the imaginary bears a striking resemblance to artistic representations of saudade:

> The imaginary provides a tentative satisfaction for desire, because it effects a momentary denial of the factic; it creates its own temporality, it renders fluid the facticity of matter; it shapes contingency with the authorship of the human will.
>
> (1987: 95)

Sartre's imaginary resonates with saudade firstly, because it is so closely tied to artistic production, and secondly, because it is an attempt to reach a 'tentative satisfaction' through a mutation of temporality. Although it may be going a step too far to qualify the saudoso as satisfied, the emotional process of saudade certainly involves an attempt to compensate for what is hoped to be temporary distance and isolation from the beloved. In this sense, the emotion 'renders fluid the facticity of matter' in a myriad of ways in order to give a sense to the saudoso of being closer to the saudado than empirical reality would indicate. Sartre's rather constructionist view that '[t]he subject of desire [...] is manufactured through the labor of desire, articulated as an imaginary being [...]' can extend this discussion beyond what the subject of desire does to the very constitution of that subject (Butler 1987: 97). Here I would suggest that in much the same way, the labour of saudade (including artistic representations thereof) produces the subject of saudade (saudoso) through its own enactment. This is an important point to stress because traditionally, saudade discourse has painted an aura of inevitability around the desire/love for the saudado, thus placing the desired object in a more active role and the desiring subject in a more passive one. Accordingly, the object is sometimes said to 'possess' the subject of saudade. However, if we accept that saudade itself consists of an emotional process *through which* the saudoso is produced, it makes little sense to insist on a passive/active duality between a subject and object that come into being simultaneously.

Sartre also ties desire to the subject's place in the social world, a connection that is evident in the expression of saudade as well. Desire is 'a way of finding and refinding a tentative identity within the network of the social world' (Butler 1987: 99). We can go even further with saudade in this case and argue that saudade helps to establish and maintain social networks and thus to (re)produce the Lusophone social world across space and time. The sum of one's attachments to other people, places, eras etc. also plays a large part in defining who one is, well expressed in the aforementioned 'Life of the Traveller'. Rather than seeing himself as an abstract bourgeois individual with no emotional ties to anyone, the singer of 'Life of the Traveller' emphasizes that his entire life has been about travelling and making emotional connections with people everywhere he goes.

The point at which the philosophy of the subject engages the Freudian tradition of psychology and psychoanalysis reveals an essential aspect of saudade. The emotion centres around a notion of lost plenitude that finds significant resonance in the Lacanian view that a split away from an original plenitude (prior to individuation) is constitutive of the subject. As Butler describes it, the subject is 'founded as a necessary defense against the libidinal fusion with the maternal body' (1987: 187). Elsewhere, Butler states that the subject is 'predicated on what it refuses to know, it is separated from itself and can never quite become or remain itself' (1997: 10). So in the Lacanian-Freudian view, the saudoso in art is representing a condition of existence and desire that is fundamental to every subject, a primal urge towards merger with the mother blocked by the basic incestual taboo. Artists and thinkers of saudade could be said to be imagining a utopian moment of redemption in which some approximation of that original plenitude or unity could be regained. Indeed, when Butler critiques Lacan for developing a 'religious dream of plenitude' in his formulation of the forbidden desire constitutive of the subject of language, she could just as well be describing a typical representation of saudade in Luso-Brazilian art or philosophy (1997: 203). The impossible return to a state prior to individuation is the psychological equivalent of a return to Eden. This metaphor of exile from an Edenic state or place of origin is developed by countless artists of saudade, from poets Luís Vaz de Camões and Gonçalves Dias to popular musician Luiz Gonzaga. Returning to Sartre's notion of the imaginary, we can now understand its importance in envisioning an impossible return to this Edenic state: 'the imaginary [e.g. artistic production], as a postulated presence, relieves consciousness temporarily of its estrangement from plenitude' (Butler 1987: 158). Slavoj Žižek ([1989] 2008) stresses the temporariness of this relief, arguing that Lacanian desire involves a search which ultimately produces the object that causes it. Thus, the subject itself is continually reproduced in this movement towards an impossible moment prior to subjectification, just as saudade is ever renewed in the countless imaginative artistic attempts to recover its lost object.

Considering Butler's critical analysis of the subject a bit further, the emotion of saudade can be understood as implicated in the process of subjectification itself. First of all, Butler determines that the socialization of the subject involves the fabrication of 'the distinction between interior and exterior life' (1997: 19). Thus, rather than being a given, a priori quality of the self, the subject's interiority is produced as he or she comes to know the social norms of a given society. In this context, we can understand saudade discourse to be taking part in the formation of the interior world of the subject, along with its differentiation from the exterior. One has only to refer to the inclusion of a chapter on saudade in Alceu Amoroso Lima's *Meditação sobre o mundo interior* (*Meditation on the Interior World*) (1955) to realize that theorists of saudade have duly recognized the emotion's important role in producing the interiority of the subject. Not only does saudade help to shape and express the interiority of the subject in the Lusophone world, but the emotion also adds an aura of authenticity to this interior as noted above. With regard to saudade, this authenticity is generally expressed as a certain level of emotional and experiential profundity belonging to the saudoso.

The discussion of the sublime in the philosophy of the subject also has relevance for a deeper understanding of saudade. In particular, it is revealing to consider Slavoj Žižek's discussion of the sublime object. According to Žižek, there is nothing particularly sublime in the nature of this object, indeed it can appear as 'an ordinary vulgar object' if we get too close to it ([1989] 2008: 192). This object simply stands in for 'the impossible-real object of desire' ([1989] 2008: 221) – in itself a 'positive fullness without lack' ([1989] 2008: 192). Here we can clearly note the similarities between the sublime object and the saudado or object of saudade. The particular saudado, such as a distant lover, one's homeland or memories from childhood, is interchangeable in the sense that each of these different objects can produce a similar emotion that longs for the radical state of plenitude which the tradition of thought on saudade has invoked as the saudoso's universal object. Thus, the sublimity of any given saudado stems from its ability to point towards an impossible limit of plenitude, which itself can be imagined in theological or psychological terms as noted above, or indeed in philosophical terms as a manifestation of the sublime. The sublime is an appropriate concept for understanding saudade in another sense, in that the sublime object invokes both displeasure and pleasure. Displeasure because of its inadequacy to the impossible plenitude of the 'Thing-Idea', but pleasure because it references 'the true, incomparable greatness of the Thing, surpassing every possible phenomenal, empirical experience' ([1989] 2008: 229). The greatness of this impossible Thing-Idea, suggesting the final redemption from existential exile, paradoxically sheds light on the imperfection of any particular object of saudade once it is grasped in some way. A wonderful example of such a disappointing experience can be found in the poetry of Gilka Machado, who once wrote 'by your side, my love, / what saudade for saudade!' ('ao teu lado, querido / que saudade da saudade!') (quoted in Orico 1940: 70). Note that in this moment of dissatisfaction with the saudado, the poet writes of her desire turning in upon itself. This reflexive 'saudade da saudade' can be considered a natural consequence of the inadequacy of the sublime object, when grasped, to truly represent saudade's imagined plenitude.

Michel Foucault's key insight with regard to desire is that '[d]esire is created by the repressive law itself [...]' (Butler 1987: 218). From this starting point we could consider to what degree power and powerful agents produce saudade. What kind of historical events and causes could be considered the work of a 'repressive law' that evokes saudade through its consequences? Over the course of the last 600 years, Portuguese dreams of empire have been dashed, northeastern Brazilian peasants have been exiled from their region, individual lovers have been separated by a variety of circumstances and Portuguese and Brazilians alike have experienced various forms of exile from their homelands. It is fair to say that in many of these cases, saudoso subjects have experienced their desires being repressed by some combination of destiny, ill fortune and a variety of less mystical economic and political forces beyond their own control. It is undeniable that these enforced separations from the beloved have produced many saudades. Thus, the emotion of saudade follows the negative logic of Foucault's analysis of desire fairly closely. The many versions of a prohibition experienced by the saudoso in this long historical period have all served to (re)produce and strengthen the saudades of both individuals and groups.

Part 2: The Ideology, Hegemony and Subalternity of Saudade

Sara Ahmed warns us against the all-too-common 'erasure of the history of [emotions'] production and circulation' (2004: 11). One of the key stumbling blocks for saudade studies I want to circumvent in the concluding section of this introduction is the traditional notion of emotions as interior and involuntary passions, a notion that relies upon the erasure of the real conditions of production and circulation in affective economies. Emotion studies analysis blows open the western conception of emotion that opposes it to public reason, in which ideological discourses are clearly acknowledged. Alison Jaggar ([1989] 2009) provides a clear example of the social, learned nature of emotions when she explains that children are very much taught to feel – that is, they are taught what it is appropriate to feel in various contexts and they also learn from adults and other children, sometimes on a less conscious level, how to appropriately express their emotions. One has only to consider the various examples of children's books,[3] stories and even educational curricula that feature saudade narratives to understand that Jaggar's insight applies to saudade in Portugal and Brazil. Furthermore, saudade narratives have brought emotion into the public sphere to represent the nation for centuries, though admittedly these narratives have often deployed some more traditional conceptions of emotions as interior, involuntary passions.

Yet, as Jaggar points out, this kind of framing of emotions typically makes them all the more effective ideologically: '[E]motions are often useful in attaining their goals only if they are interpreted as passions rather than as actions' ([1989] 2009: 55). The consequence of this fact is that saudade and other emotions, while very much part of the social world and implicated in ideological discourses and actions as noted above, are often represented through a performance of interior, involuntary passion. Paradoxically, then, the appearance of emotions can be natural, involuntary and authentic while their essence is far more socialized and ideological, and thus 'artificial' from a traditional standpoint. In what follows, I explore this dual nature of emotional representations with a focus on saudade, arguing that even as they are produced and authentically felt within individuals, emotional discourses can 'establish, assert, challenge or reinforce power or status differences' (Abu-Lughod and Lutz 1990: 108).

Because of this ideological function of emotions like saudade and their involvement with power and resistance, we can get a more accurate picture of the diversity of emotional discourses and their politics if we consider them through theories of hegemony and subalternity. Ernesto Laclau defines the hegemonic relationship as one 'by which a particular content becomes the signifier of the absent communitarian fullness' (1996: 43). He labels the transformation of the particular into a universal signifier a 'secular incarnation' and also compares the substitution of the part for the whole to the representation of universal exchange value by the particular precious metal of gold (1996: 25). In the development of feelings of saudade, typically some beloved lost object comes to represent the emotion itself for the saudoso and by extension, the audience of the saudoso artist or intellectual. Often as these authors represent saudade, certain iconic figures such as the home country, the lover or the mother come to stand in for saudade per se and thus point towards universally accepted narratives in which the emotion can be situated. However, part of the value of Laclau's theory is its emphasis on the exchangeability of the particular content with regard to representing the universal, itself essentially empty of particular content. As in Laclau's theorization of the political subject, the particular saudoso and its saudado attempt to represent, in an essentially ideological manoeuvre, the universal ideal of saudade. Within the canonical tradition of saudade going back all the way to King Duarte I of Portugal in the fifteenth century, thinkers and artists of the emotion have always attempted to represent what they consider to be the universal process of feeling the emotion and the related valuation of its appropriate objects. This manner of framing saudade should be understood along the lines of Laclau's theory of a historical subject's attempt to represent the universal through his or her own particular representation of the relationship between saudoso and saudado.

Moving on to consider alternative, non-hegemonic representations of saudade, we can begin with Raymond Williams' contention that a structure of feeling can reveal the 'tension, blockage [or] emotional trouble' within a given society ([1979] 2009: 49). Harding and Pribram suggest that we consider plural 'structures of feeling' in a given society rather than Williams' more monolithic, nationalist framework for the concept. Nevertheless, they rightly emphasize that the 'class-linked' and 'periodizing' elements of Williams' theory of emotion and experience are very revealing and should continue to be a focus of emotion studies (2004: 867). A focus on the variety of lived experiences in a certain historical era is directed specifically towards emotions in Alison Jaggar's work, who deploys the concept of 'outlaw emotions' to designate the possibility of subcultures that develop and experience alternative structures of feeling. Jaggar sums up the potential for highlighting the existence of outlaw emotions as follows:

> When certain emotions are shared or validated by others [...] the basis exists for forming a subculture defined by perceptions, norms, and values that systematically oppose the

> prevailing perceptions, norms, and values. By constituting the basis for such a subculture, outlaw emotions may be politically because epistemologically subversive.
>
> (Jaggar [1989] 2009: 61)

Considering the emotion of saudade, there is certainly ample evidence of outlaw, subaltern saudades that have not been sufficiently explored by the tradition of saudade thought. My own analyses of representations of saudade are in full agreement with Jaggar that such subaltern emotions can subversively reveal much that is overlooked about the power relations within a given society or national cultural context. Considering feelings more broadly, Laura Marks argues that embodied memories, integrating sensorial and emotional experiences, are an important source of cultural knowledge for minority and diasporic communities, constituting 'some of the most important registers of global shifts in power and the emergence of new subjectivities' (2000: 200). Finally, within emotion studies itself, another way of looking at subaltern emotions has been through the concept of disenfranchisement. This concept has been most notably applied to grief – an instance of disenfranchised grief is defined as one in which one's own culture does not recognize one's right to grieve (Rosenblatt 1999).

These related concepts of outlaw and disenfranchised emotions, and their connection to remembrance, imply a certain hierarchy of emotions and memory with respect to the social acceptability or status of the objects towards which emotions are directed. In her study of grief and grieving already noted above in the section on emotions and cultural authenticity, Judith Butler (2004) explicitly argues that within a given sociocultural context, one encounters a hierarchy of grievable objects. Persons, places or things that are higher in status are more able to be remembered and grieved publicly and thus accepted as legitimate objects of grief that have left behind survivors worthy of sympathy from the larger community or nation. Butler provides the example of the subaltern grief of a Palestinian citizen of the United States who wished to publish, in a San Francisco newspaper, obituaries for two Palestinian families killed by Israeli troops in the Occupied Territories. The newspaper ultimately denied the request to publish the obituaries or even statements 'in memoriam', arguing that the deaths of these individuals were too controversial for publication. Because of the contested status of the objects of grief, the survivors' emotions and memories were disenfranchised, in the sense that they were left unrecognized by the media and, by extension, the larger public. Here we can see a clear example in recent US history of Ahmed's point, addressed in the previous section, that less-privileged subjects are often too marginalized to be able to successfully mobilize narratives of injury in the public domain.

In European history especially, nostalgia has been disenfranchised since its very inception as a recognized emotion. Swiss medical student Johannes Hofer coined the term 'nostalgia' in the late seventeenth century to identify the sentiment as a disease, pathologizing a feeling of homesickness felt by Swiss mercenary soldiers as they travelled outside their mother country (Boym 2001; Davis 1979). In the late 1700s, the mental disease of pyromania was even associated with nostalgia. Young, live-in domestic servants who had set fire to their employers' homes were described as having been overcome by nostalgia for their own families, wishing to destroy the workplaces that kept them away from their familial abodes (Zwingmann 1959). Later, the Freudian tradition took up the pathologization of nostalgia by emphasizing that proper, healthy mourning involves decathecting or detaching oneself from the beloved object of one's love/longing after a traumatic loss and replacing the lost object with a new, accessible beloved (Freud [1917] 1957). A prolonged attachment to a lost love would lead to chronic melancholy, itself pathologized in this Freudian paradigm.[4] More recently, one reviewer of Fred Davis's (1979) wide-ranging sociology of nostalgia in US society referred to the emotion as 'commonly stigmatized as ephemeral, self-indulgent, and conservative' (Panelas 1982). On the other hand, nostalgia's sister emotion saudade never experienced the same pathologization or stigmatization in the traditions of Portuguese and Brazilian thought on the sentiment. As discussed above, the case was quite the opposite – saudade has tended to be celebrated as a unique sentiment, and indeed it is precisely the fact that the sentiment was not pathologized in the same manner as nostalgia that gives it much of its special aura in Luso-Brazilian philosophy and art. However, despite the unique valorization of the emotion, thinkers of saudade have nevertheless disenfranchised non-national expressions and representations of the emotion, not including them in the canon or pantheon of celebrated saudoso literature and art. In fact, at least one important philosopher of saudade, Dalila L. Pereira da Costa, has acknowledged a hierarchy of saudados. In her theological schema, the highest form of saudade would be one directed at God as the infinite, ineffable saudado (Costa and Gomes 1976). One's native country (in this case Portugal) seems close to God in this hierarchy, while more profane objects rank lower. Leaving aside Costa's more limited theological discussion of saudade, her acknowledgment of this saudade hierarchy is important in its own right. No doubt dominant perspectives vary to some degree between historical and cultural contexts as to which forms of saudade are most esteemed; yet, the fact remains that the existence of a hierarchical system necessarily involves a hegemonic model for representations of saudade that either excludes, devalues or undervalues non-hegemonic, subaltern variants of the emotion.

Chapter Sketches: Saudade's Evolution Across Sixty Years of Brazilian Film

In the development of his affection-image theory, Gilles Deleuze finds in the cinematic image the possibility of transformation beyond the powers of language alone ([1983] 2013: 87–101). Deleuze focuses on the face as a visual trope for artistic, cinematic expression of affect beyond words.[5] In this vein, the specific examples of Brazilian cinema I will discuss below also go beyond language to evoke emotion through image, sound and a variety of bodily senses. Further, psychologist Sylvan Tomkins specifically stresses that the importance of art (as well as ideology) with regard to affect goes beyond mere expression:

> [...] the world created by words, most notably in art and ideology, involves something more than an expression of affects. It is a world in which affects can be extraordinarily modulated and amplified, enriched and deepened. Imagination, aided by words, has created worlds which have completely captured the minds of men, *evoking and creating rather than expressing affects*, and binding the evoked affects to possibilities which are eventually actualized just because men were inspired to dream and then to act.
>
> (1995: 96, emphasis added)

Cinematic theory gives us a crucial alternative example of art which can also evoke and create affects but without reliance upon the power of words alone (music would be another artistic form of this kind, also incorporated in cinema itself).

The multisensorial, bodily and linguistic narratives of cinema are uniquely positioned to represent the disenfranchised saudades of various historical eras analysed closely in this book. These subaltern saudades are analysed in conjunction with the saudade of subjects in more privileged positions, with whom they find themselves in a dialectic. The chapters follow a loose chronology by decades, but in cases that I found it particularly revealing to develop a diachronic analysis, they are more oriented by theme, such as Chapter 4's focus on televisual representations and Chapter 7's on childhood. By no means does the book exhaustively explore the cinema of each decade, but rather analyses representative films of the latter half of the twentieth and first decades of the twenty-first centuries. The late works of Humberto Mauro and those of the Vera Cruz Studios provide a starting point, involving key filmmakers who helped establish two key paradigms for Brazilian film production that would influence the representation of saudade by later generations in various ways, as we shall see.

One further clarification regarding temporality in the book's analytical approach relates to the common temporal duality of modernity and tradition, so often present in analyses of Latin American art and culture. Rather than placing modernity and tradition in opposition, this book analyses diverse filmic responses to a process of modernization (which sometimes rely on an invention of tradition). This process encompasses economic development as well as related social reform/revolution/reaction on local, regional, national and international levels. Two early examples in the book are the spatial and temporal liminality of films in the 1950s, which tend to produce saudade for a given landscape, era and/or system of social relations. These liminal, emotional perspectives are not just connected to national history but often to personal affect and the biographies of characters and filmmakers, and more recently are connected to a shift to storylines in transnational spaces. The object of saudade (saudado) can be perceived in this context as a fetish[6] to be conserved or renewed. This variance in orientation to the saudado, ranging from a more fixed to a more fluid fetishized object, in turn, produces a more rigid or flexible notion of tradition and its relationship to modernization.

Firstly, let us consider Humberto Mauro's series of films from the 1950s, all set in the rural environs of Volta Grande, Minas Gerais, and analysed closely in Chapters 2 and 7.

In making these films, Mauro was returning to his native region after establishing himself as one of Brazil's premier directors while working in the cultural capital of Rio de Janeiro. The emotional tone set in the various fictional and documentary films he made during this decade (consisting of one fictional feature and several short films) is very much characterized by a saudade for rural Brazil, mirroring the director's own homecoming to rural Minas Gerais. Throughout these series of films, Mauro frames the rural as a space for memories of a free, innocent childhood experienced in the loving embrace of the natural landscape. In this way, Mauro grounds his work firmly within the Brazilian Romantic tradition, even adapting to film a famous, saudoso Romantic poem by Casimiro de Abreu entitled 'Meus oito anos' ('When I Was Eight') (Mauro [1945, 1954–56] 2002). As in the poem, Mauro establishes the saudoso subject as a Euro-Brazilian male, though in this case rather than being set in a coastal plantation in Rio de Janeiro state, the man gazes across the cattle-raising landscape of the Volta Grande region. He reminisces over his childhood memories that are then featured in a flashback sequence accompanied by a lyrical melody. Thus, Mauro marshals poetry, music and cinematography as well as synesthetic references to sense memories like the smell of flowers in order to express saudade in a multisensorial way, no doubt aiming to evoke the same sentiment in his viewers.

These iconic memories are to some extent embodied from a relatively privileged perspective, reflecting the director's traditional, paternalist attitude towards his region and its workers, and also Mauro's own family's status as part of the rural elite in the region. Yet ideologically speaking there can still be found a critical, subaltern edge to the director's narratives represented in this film and the others of the same era. After all, in the 1950s, the hegemonic national narrative in Brazil was one of progress qua urban developmentalism, culminating in the construction of the new, ultramodernist capital, Brasília, towards the end of the decade. Mauro's pedagogical project in his films of the 1950s, for which he was able to procure state funding due to his close ties with the National Institute of Educational Cinema (INCE), goes counter to the prevailing urbanism and uneven development of the time. Using the Volta Grande region as a symbolic setting, Mauro seeks to remind the contemporary audience, particularly young people and schoolchildren who might view the films, of the continued importance of regional, rural cultures throughout Brazil even as a mass exodus of workers from rural regions was ongoing throughout the decade, including in the state of Minas Gerais itself (Portes and Santos 2009: 2).

Saudade is put to work here generating fond memories, respect and indeed love for Brazilian rural lifestyles and popular culture, as Mauro represents everything from agricultural pursuits to rural folktales in his 1950s films. What in the past had been a relatively dominant perspective amongst the plantation elites could now be considered a countercultural stance on Mauro's part. Clearly, Mauro himself was fully cognizant of the ideological implications of his work, since he was explicitly attempting to insert it into the educational curriculum of Brazilian children, particularly those in urban areas who would more likely have access to a cinema or at least a projector. Part of this education was a sentimental one, privileging saudade as an emotion appropriate for both adults and children with respect to Brazil's rural regions and history. On a more specific economic and cultural level, Mauro had founded his own Rancho Alegre studios in Volta Grande in order to produce these films, and thus was promoting economic development and cultural production outside of the established, hegemonic cultural and media centre of Rio de Janeiro. The implications of producing rural Brazil as saudado for his audience went far beyond a conservative desire to slow cultural and economic change, seeking rather to martial the love of the rural on behalf of a more equitable development across Brazil's diverse and far-flung regions. On the other hand, another film analysed closely in the chapter, *Sinhá moça* (*The Landowner's Daughter*) (Payne [1953] 2005), looks to the historical moment of abolition in order to portray an idealized, hierarchical, multi-racial family as an object of saudade that promotes a history of racial harmony after 1888.

More than a decade after these films of the 1950s, the Cinema Novo director Joaquim Pedro de Andrade would reach the point of parodying not only urban developmentalism, but also rural (neo-)Romanticism in his masterpiece *Macunaíma* ([1969] 2006), discussed in Chapter 3. For Andrade, rural workers (and even less so rural elites) could no longer be considered as legitimate objects of a saudoso gaze, as they were in Mauro's 1950s films and even some of the Cinema Novo films of the early 1960s like Nelson Pereira dos Santos's *Vidas secas* (*Barren Lives*) ([1963] 2005) or Anselmo Duarte's *O pagador de promessas* (*The Given Word*) ([1962] 2005) (also considered in Chapter 3). Andrade's *Macunaíma* is a satirical romp through rural and urban landscapes of Brazil, criticizing both rural backwardness and urban violence and political repression during the military dictatorship. Nevertheless, the film reappropriates Brazilian culture like that of the *chanchada* musical comedy films of the 1930s–1950s, considered kitschy and outmoded by 1969. In the general vein of the Tropicália art movement, Andrade provides an example of a somewhat ironized saudade, produced out of a camp aesthetic that nevertheless privileges certain Brazilian popular cinema and culture as saudados. Thus, for example, the film includes on its soundtrack a Brazilian Portuguese version of the song 'By a Waterfall' from a 1933 Busby Berkeley musical number. The song itself is a lyrical, romantic story of love in a natural landscape, played on the soundtrack when the characters in *Macunaíma* find a spring gushing from the earth. The song indicates respect and saudade for a popular tradition within Brazilian cinema, but the sentiment is ironized by a reference to racial hierarchies and historical white supremacy in Brazil. The characters discover that the fountain is magical and rush to bathe themselves in its rapidly diminishing waters in order to magically transform their own racial identity from black or indigenous to white. The character of Macunaíma is played by a famous black actor, *chanchada* star Grande Otelo, in itself a reference back to that popular film form. Macunaíma succeeds in transforming from black to white thanks to his bath in the magical fountain and rejoices at the prospect of his new racial identity. While here clearly recognizing the real, often overlooked problem of racism in Brazilian society, the saudade directed towards *chanchadas* emphasizes a creative tradition of appropriating and adapting foreign culture to reform and strengthen Brazilian art forms (a process often referred to in Brazil as *antropofagia* or cultural cannibalism since theorized by poet Oswald de Andrade in 1928).

Macunaíma is also a story of Brazilian rural–urban migration, and in this context the film specifically cites the northeastern country (*forró*) song 'Respeita Januário' ('Respect Januário'). This song tells the story of an internal migrant's (and musician's) life and refers to his ties back to the traditional culture of the northeastern rural interior (sertão). On the film's soundtrack, the lyrics implicitly resonate with the migration of the protagonist Macunaíma to Brasília, and they foreshadow his return to his primitive rural abode at the end of the film. While evoking this traditional saudade of the rural–urban migrant (typically depicted as male) for his simpler rural roots and the loved ones he has left behind, the film at this very moment also contextualizes the song and the migrant character in a ridiculous situation in which a bird is defecating on his head, ironizing this figure who had been posed as an ideal subaltern subject by earlier films of the Cinema Novo movement. Thus, in this reference to the rural–urban migrant, as well as the various references to *chanchadas* and other Brazilian popular culture in *Macunaíma*, we can identify a dynamic which Linda Hutcheon has identified with nostalgia, namely, that saudade is framed through irony in order to make it more 'palatable' to sceptical audiences or even for the director himself ([1997] 2000: 207). In this sense, Andrade and other artists of the Tropicália movement anticipated, thanks to their rethinking of the by-then established 'non-aligned' or Third Cinema perspective, what would later become a postmodern emotional paradigm steeped in irony. Nevertheless, the emotion of saudade in *Macunaíma* maintains, in circumscribed form, its impact of a positive affective aura bestowed upon the saudado, thus continuing a tradition common in Brazilian art since the Romantic era.

Over the course of the remaining middle chapters in this book, covering films of the 1970s through the 2000s, the reader will witness the expression and relevance of saudade going through a variety of transformations, reflecting grand historical changes, while periodically continuing to echo the emotional discourses of previous eras. Chapter 4, for instance, examines the impact of the expansion of mass-media penetration across Brazilian territory on expressions of, and the framing of, saudade in film. As television has become an increasingly common part of all Brazilians' lives, cinema's framing of the medium has developed from a saudade for pre-TV-era popular culture to an embrace of television as a medium for expressing national-popular saudades. Specifically the two road-movies analysed in the chapter, *Bye Bye Brasil* (Diegues, [1978] 2007) and *O caminho das nuvens* (*The Middle of the World*) (Amorim, [2003] 2004), move from saudade for travelling circus troupes in the northeastern interior to a celebration of saudade on television in the pop-rock performances of Roberto Carlos. Thereafter, Chapter 5 focuses on two feature films of the 1990s, one by the well-known directorial team of Walter Salles and Daniela Thomas, and another by Salles alone. Saudade features prominently in both films, and I explore how the emotion is deployed cinematically in a way that mirrors canonical, traditional representations of saudade in Brazilian literature in *Central do Brasil* (*Central Station*) (Salles, [1998] 1999), but takes on a more melancholy, European Portuguese tone, responding to the critical state of the nation, in *Terra estrangeira* (*Foreign Land*) (Salles and Thomas, [1995] 2005). *Terra estrangeira*, too, establishes many ties to the historical discourse of saudade in the Lusophone world due to the postcolonial

Luso-Brazilian-African socio-economic context of the narrative. The chapter also explores the increasing usage of epistolary discourse by Salles in his films of the 1990s, tying Salles's film letters to a common affective association between letter writing and nostalgia in diasporic and exilic cinema as explored by Hamid Naficy (2001). In the book's sixth chapter, two twenty-first-century films are explored to reveal a postnational, postmodern shift in representations of saudade. *Budapeste* (Carvalho, 2009) and *Um passaporte húngaro* (*A Hungarian Passport*) (Kogut, 2001) reveal how the emotion seems to be shifting its object away from the more traditional national context in this century. The films explore new transnational or postnational saudades that call into question the previous linking of the emotion to national and regional identities or even to the Portuguese language.

Petra Costa's documentary feature *Elena* ([2013] 2014), explored further in Chapter 7, provides a contemporary example of alternative saudade. In the same vein as a variety of other Brazilian films of this century, Costa's narrative frames saudade in a transnational context that stretches beyond the historical transatlantic spaces of Portuguese colonization. Specifically, *Elena* represents saudade as an emotion that ties a young, increasingly alienated immigrant to New York back to her family in Brazil. The diasporic narrative of this film toes the line between autobiography and fiction, representing the struggles of the director Petra Costa herself to learn more about her sister Elena Andrade's life leading up to her suicide in 1990, when Petra herself was just seven years old. With recourse to family home video, audio letters and other forms of historical documentation and film footage, the narrative represents Elena initially migrating to New York alone in pursuit of an acting career in the US film industry. The move is unsuccessful and Elena returns home, but Elena's mother Li An as well as Petra later return with her to New York in a second attempt at launching her career. Throughout her travels, the film represents Elena's feelings of saudade for family and home in Brazil as a counterpoint to her feelings of alienation and depression in the country of migration. However, it is evident in this film that saudade continues, beyond its 1960s representation in *Macunaíma*, to evolve as an emotion and particularly in its expression in art. Saudade is no longer so strongly linked to Brazil, nor even Lusophone culture in general, as the emotion is directed back and forth across the space between São Paulo and New York. The city of New York, too, becomes a saudado in this transnational, bilingual film, not only the city in which Elena first established her home in the late 1980s, but also the New York that would later attract her younger sister Petra as an undergraduate student at the turn of the century, and as a director in the current decade. Petra Costa herself is an example of a second generation of Brazilian directors who have pursued international careers, with personal and artistic ties to the US and other transnational film industries, following in the footsteps of directors like Walter Salles, Fernando Meirelles and Sandra Kogut.

In her autobiographical films, which include *Elena* as well as the short film *Olhos de ressaca* (*Undertow Eyes*) (2009), Costa still reveals the affective relevance of saudade in a number of significant ways. Firstly, she often evokes emotional memories through multiple sensorial associations beyond the visual including touch and sound, narratively highlighting and cinematographically exploring the surfaces of treasured items such as a floral-print dress or a souvenir conch given to her by her sister. The latter object is explicitly connected to saudade in the narrative of the film, through Petra Costa's voice-over that recounts how her sister gave her the conch on her seventh birthday in São Paulo. According to Petra, Elena told her that she could listen to the conch's oceanic echoes whenever she needed to assuage her saudade for her sister overseas in New York. A second manner in which Costa evokes saudade is in her revelation of the deterioration of the filmic image over time as a metaphor for memory itself, evident in the contrast between Super 8 and aging video sequences on the one hand, with crisp digital footage on the other. Even the texture of digital footage is varied through the exploration of surfaces of various textures and water-filled scenes associated with an Ophelia theme in *Elena*. The Ophelia theme itself connects to the story of her sister's suicide, but also resonates more broadly with what Deleuze ([1983] 2013) would call the film's 'liquid perception', involving sequences depicting bodies (including those of the director and her mother) and objects floating underwater and on its surface. This imagery suggests through its fluidity the possibility of transformation, and is confirmed by the director's voice-over which eventually states that 'little by little the pain becomes water, becomes memory'. The aestheticization of a personal saudade, unmoored from much of the traditional, nationalist and patriarchal framing of the emotion, is represented as a therapeutic process for the artist, her mother and by extension audience members of any nationality having to deal with similar traumatic memories.

Conclusion

In this introductory chapter, we have seen a variety of appropriations of saudade from more hegemonic to more differential perspectives. We have also seen the valences of the emotion revealed in various ways from a number of disciplines, mostly under the aegis of emotion studies and the history of thought on emotion or affect and subjectivity. Over the course of the following chapters, I will apply this revealing theoretical background to analyse in detail representations of saudade in twentieth- and twenty-first-century Brazilian cinema. The topic of saudade bears much further study within this new theoretical context, however, and saudade studies – as outlined in this chapter – could be expanded to analyse not only past centuries in Brazil and Portugal, but also contemporary and historical Lusophone Africa as well. There is also promising work to be done in comparative studies between saudade and existing analyses of nostalgia (e.g. Boym 2001; Davis 1979; Hutcheon [1997] 2000; Jameson 1989; Starobinski 1966), in particular with respect to the relative significance of spatial or temporal understandings and expressions of these two sister emotions across diverse historical periods. Broadly speaking, prior to this study the field of film studies has lacked any sustained analysis of saudade, an emotion so prevalent in Lusophone cinema as in other art forms. I close this chapter, then, with a feeling of saudade for a future in which this emotion will find its proper place in film studies, cultural studies and other related fields. May the analyses in the remaining chapters of this study provide examples of a path forward.[7]

Notes

1 Translations from the Portuguese by the author here and below, unless otherwise indicated.
2 Following Pinharanda Gomes (Costa and Gomes 1976), I will refer to the subject of saudade as the saudoso and its object as the saudado.
3 For instance, Marina Martinez's *Por uma questão de saudade* (*Due to a Question of Saudade*) (1984) features a queen who tries to outlaw feelings of saudade among her subjects. The story ends with the moral 'it was possible to imprison people, but impossible to imprison saudade (era possível prender as pessoas, mas impossível prender a saudade)'.
4 It is only since the late twentieth century that psychology has showed signs of reconsidering this post-Freudian paradigm of mourning. See, for instance, Eng and Kazanjian (2003) and Klass et al. (1996). An earlier theory of emotion moving in this direction can be found in the work of Tomkins (1995), who rejected Freud's theory of developmental stages corresponding with detachment from the mother.
5 In terms of theories of affect, the importance of the face in this regard can be traced back to at least the work of Charles Darwin's (1872) interpretations of emotion in facial expressions.
6 A theory of the fetish as one way of understanding the saudado is developed in Chapter 4.
7 As this book goes to press, a work examining saudade in photography recently published in Brazil has come to my attention. Samuel de Jesus's *Saudade: Da poesia medieval à fotografia contemporânea, o percurso de um sentimento ambíguo* (*Saudade: From Medieval Poetry to Contemporary Photography, The Way of an Ambiguous Sentiment*) (2015) retraces the canonical history of saudade back to medieval Portuguese thinkers and artists, as a background to an analysis focusing on twentieth-century Portuguese and Brazilian photography, which the author interprets as a saudoso art form par excellence. Jesus's brief but insightful analysis of a sequence from one of Manoel de Oliveira's films demonstrates the potential and need for further studies of saudade in Portuguese cinema, not to mention Lusophone African film.

Chapter 2

Traditional Agrarian Saudade and the Rancho Alegre and Vera Cruz Studios

In the decade of the 1950s, considerations of national progress and tradition alike were very important in filmic narratives, film production and the burgeoning field of film criticism. The culmination of several decades of critical demand for an advance in technical progress in Brazilian cinema could be seen in the launching of the Vera Cruz film studios in São Paulo in 1950. At the same time, filmmakers such as Humberto Mauro who had been working in the medium for decades already saw their work as part of an established tradition rooted in national culture. This historical juncture created the conditions for the development of a problematics of change in Brazilian cinema, both within film narratives and even in the very production process. This problematics was worked out in diverse ways by filmmakers of the era, depending upon which side of the cosmopolitan/nationalist divide they leaned towards, and led towards differing representations of saudade, both diegetic and metanarrative. In this chapter, I will focus my analysis first on the work of Humberto Mauro, particularly his feature film *O canto da saudade: Lenda do carreiro* (*Song of Saudade: Legend of the Ox Cart Driver*) (1952), as a representative of the ruralism (and saudade for rural Brazil in general) typical of more nationalist narratives in cinema at the time. Secondly, I will turn to the work of Vera Cruz director Tom Payne, specifically *Sinhá moça* (*The Landowner's Daughter*) ([1953] 2005), as an example of a more cosmopolitan narrative approach to a Brazilian story, which develops its own form of saudade centred around the historical moment of abolition in 1888. Taken individually, either film features distinct forms of nostalgic sentiment on the level of the plot as well as on a metanarrative level, representing the saudade of the filmmakers for rural space on the one hand, and for a certain idealized historical moment on the other. Ultimately, we can see that these two films produced out of differing conceptions of Brazilian national culture both demonstrate the strong association between saudade and a state of liminality. In the case of Mauro's *O canto da saudade*, liminal spaces in the Brazilian rural landscape (such as hilltops, ridges and riverbanks) are highlighted in the narrative and framed with the varying saudoso feelings of characters from upper and lower social classes. On the other hand, *Sinhá moça* produces both diegetic and metanarrative saudades primarily out of the temporal liminality of a historical moment bridging two regimes, the old regime of the Brazilian Empire and the new regime of the first Republic. In either case, spatial or temporal liminality characterizes the condition of unstable zones in history and personal experience, which tend to produce saudade on various levels of the filmic narrative as well as metanarratively. Mauro's film, in general more reticent about the benefits of politico-economic progress for traditional Brazilian culture, tends to celebrate or frame positively all forms of saudade in the Brazilian rural landscape, while Payne's more progress-oriented film is critical of nostalgic longing associated with the ancien regime.

O canto da saudade: A Nostalgic Elegy to Rural Brazil

Maria Rita Galvão and Jean-Claude Bernardet, in a survey of critical commentaries of the first half of the twentieth century on Brazilian film, state that a common nationalist vein of Brazilian cinema had been established prior to 1950 in which

> progress [up-to-date (typically European or Hollywood) cinematographic language and technique] is used to represent and advertise precisely that which is not progress and even opposes it [e.g. the interior, the history of Brazil, and related Brazilian literature] (o progresso é usado para representar e divulgar justamente o que não é o progresso e até se opõe a ele).
>
> (1983: 38)

Progress in the latter part of this quotation is understood to mean 'the current phase of capitalism', which one form of cinematic nationalism rejects by 'taking refuge in a previous phase, where it will seek authenticity in ways that are being lost' ('refugia-se numa fase anterior, onde vai procurar a autenticidade em vias de se perder') (Galvão and Bernardet 1983: 39). Related to this quest to rescue tradition from the ravages of uneven capitalist development, it has been a prominent tendency amongst filmmakers and critics since at least the 1920s to privilege Brazilian nature and the customs of the interior as characterizing national cinema (1983: 25). A contemporary *Cinearte* review describes Humberto Mauro's second feature film, *Thesouro perdido* (*Lost Treasure*) (1926), in this light (1983: 27). Yet, Andries (2001) emphasizes that this 'characteristically rural universe' excludes regional aspects, in accordance with the influence of producer Adhemar Gonzaga on Mauro at the time (28). Galvão and Bernardet further state that at least since the 1920s, it had been the common sense among Brazilian filmmakers and critics that portraying regional culture was synonymous with portraying national culture; that is, there was no intent to differentiate rural regions from one another (1983: 28).

In Mauro's case, we see in his films of the 1920s a tendency that would continue to characterize his work through the subsequent three decades – the belief that the rural must be framed above all as a national rather than a regional space. Consequently, in affective terms the stage is set for Brazilian viewers of all regions to experience a saudade for rural life on a broad, national scale, independent of the specifics of actually existing rural-regional cultures. One symptom of this national-ruralist perspective is that although the protagonist of *O canto da saudade* is an accordion player, there are neither regional musicians, nor specific genres of regional music or dance, nor any regional festivities referenced in the film. Reminiscent of the musicians represented in Luiz Gonzaga's famous song released the year before the filming of *O canto da saudade*, 'Respeita Januário' ('Respect Januário') (1950), the musician Galdino, who owns a simple 8-button accordion, dreams of acquiring a more modern, 120-button accordion that he sees a professional musician playing in a theatrical production. Yet, unlike Gonzaga, a northeastern musician who stylized music from his region into the *baião* and *forró* genres (cf. Draper 2010, 2011a, 2014), Galdino is not shown to have any cultural ties to regional traditions or even other, more experienced musicians. The actor who plays Galdino, Mário Mascarenhas, fit this national cultural framework perfectly since he was from the region featured in the film, but was also an accordion virtuoso who played a variety of foreign and Brazilian genres from tango to *maxixe* to baião, never having his name associated with a particular region in the manner of Luiz Gonzaga's own firm cultural grounding in the northeast. Similarly, the film's soundtrack also features the music of a variety of composers having no regional associations with the setting in Minas Gerais, and also taken from both classical and popular Brazilian musical traditions, including Heitor Villa-Lobos, Carlos Gomes, Ernesto Nazareth, Noel Rosa and others.

The focus through the 1950s in the nationalist tendency of Brazilian cinema on the authenticity of rural landscapes and peoples, and their culture and folklore, hearkens back to the ruralism of the Romantic era in the nineteenth century. Romanticism treated Brazil's interior as a repository of authentic national folklore and pure, traditional values. Inspired by this earlier artistic tradition, but going beyond it to promote nationalist propaganda for the masses, since at least the 1920s Brazilian film critics determined a patriotic, disciplinary and educational role for cinema (Galvão and Bernardet 1983: 56). This viewpoint was taken up wholeheartedly as part of the propaganda efforts of the Getúlio Vargas administration in the 1930s, which would itself employ Humberto Mauro at the National Institute of Educational Cinema (Instituto Nacional de Cinema Educativo, INCE) beginning in 1936. By the 1940s, some critics were proposing that educating the people (*o povo*) about their culture, history and proper civic virtues and values should be the 'principal goal' of Brazilian cinema (1983: 35). Later in the 1950s, writers for the *Fundamentos* film magazine, from a primarily leftist perspective, would add the educational function of teaching citizens to struggle against US and European cultural imperialism (1983: 71).

Since his earliest films, Mauro tended to agree with this nationalist perspective and it would guide his filmmaking more and more as he approached the latter part of his career in the 1950s. Already in *Favela dos meus amores* (*Favela of My Loves*) (1935), Mauro demonstrates his interest in folkloric, lyrical depictions of the common people (in this case in an urban setting) (Andries 2001). The film is groundbreaking in terms of representing favela residents, including non-professional actors from the Providência favela (then called Favela Hill). As in *O canto da saudade*, the teacher in the story of *Favela dos meus amores* is placed in a privileged position, respected by the whole community who seek to prevent her departure due to marriage. The narrative of Carmen Santos's character in *Argila* (*Clay*) (1942), Mauro's last feature film prior to *O canto da saudade*, resonates with Mauro's personal biography in the early 1950s. It centres around a woman who escapes decadent city life by moving to her castle in the countryside. (It also involves the theft and recovery of a magical maraca, which ties it more to Mauro's earlier adventure films while also introducing a reference to indigenous folklore.) As a wealthy widow, the lady of her manor, the protagonist has more autonomy than the female lead of *O canto da saudade* and she is thus in a similar social position to that of Humberto Mauro a few years later on his ranch in Minas Gerais, head of his own independent film studio.

In his contemporary comments on *O canto da saudade*, Mauro emphasized the authentic Brazilianness of the film's location setting, referring to the 'rural environment' of Volta Grande, Minas Gerais as representing 'the customs of old Brazil' that he characterized as 'less internationalized' (Viany 1978: 157). He emphasized further the documentarian side of this fictional film, that it depicts 'the natural' – the actors are non-professionals 'without make-up' who are authentic 'people of the place, of the ranch' ('pessoas do lugar, da roça') and whose habits Mauro portrays 'in their spontaneity' (158). Following the common nationalist cinematic trend of using modernity and international filmic language to represent the non-modern (as described by Galvão and Bernardet above), Mauro stated that the idea that 'the best actors are those from the anonymous masses' is one that he shares with the great Russian director Sergei Eisenstein (158). Mauro also commented in the year of the film's release that 'a good film of national character should compete to tie man to the land' ('Um bom filme de caráter nacional deve concorrer para fixar o homem à terra') (Viany 1978: 159). This language echoes a ruralist anti-migration project that has roots going back to the nineteenth century, but runs very much counter to the general tendency of urban development in the 1950s in metropolises like Rio de Janeiro, São Paulo and eventually Brasília. Portraying the land, its history and the memories of those who live there as thoroughly under the mastery of the patriarchal gaze of the local cacique (the Colonel Januário character played by Mauro himself in the film) could certainly serve to soothe anxieties about modernization and rural exodus.

The narrative framing of *O canto da saudade* is provided by the teacher (Landa Góry) at a Volta Grande schoolhouse who is telling a local folk tale, 'The Story of the Accordionist in Love' ('A história do sanfoneiro apaixonado'), to her elementary-school-aged students. Even before the teacher's tale begins, Humberto Mauro himself as director appears on screen to detail his own family's ties to the region. The film thus establishes a documentarian and pedagogical framework within which the main diegetic action takes place. Regarding the emotion of saudade specifically in this narrative, Maria Fausta (Cláudia Montenegro) mentions saudade early on, telling her love interest João do Carmo (Alfredo Souto de Almeida) she felt the sentiment for him while he was away. In this way, Maria Fausta's saudade is clearly, and early on in the plot, marked as not reciprocating the love and saudade that the main character, ox cart driver and accordionist Galdino, feels for her. Later, when Maria Fausta disappears for unknown reasons, Galdino is shown playing his accordion mournfully under a tree, and the camera then shows us a series of landscape shots including the chapel, river and other rural scenes. Thus, before the final sequence in which Galdino (and his love, as well as his absence and the saudoso desire for his presence) is associated with the local rural-natural landscape, Maria Fausta has already disappeared into it and similar associations have been made with her character. In terms of class relations, Galdino is placed in a similar position of subalternity to Maria Fausta, who herself ultimately has the good luck of getting the approval of Colonel Januário for her marriage to João Carmo (and of not being sexually assaulted by the white landowner or his overseer like the enslaved women on the plantation in *Sinhá moça*); otherwise she would have found herself in an emotionally and psychologically abject state similar to Galdino's. The tradition going back to Romanticism is to associate the female body and its beauty with that of the natural landscape (cf. Draper 2011b; Ginway 2004); in this sense, Galdino's unrequited love and his class position combine to feminize his character's social role. Accordingly, his saudade takes on feminine connotations, in that traditionally it was the male migrant worker who would leave the woman he loved. This female subject would be left longing, from a static position of waiting, for her lover's return. Here it is Galdino who is left behind, wondering if Maria Fausta will ever return when she secretly elopes.

Continuing the social relations inherited from the time of slavery, it is up to the local land boss (the Colonel) to forgive Maria Fausta's precipitous elopement and to approve or disapprove of her marriage, thereby either allowing her back into the fold of the ranch's community or socially exiling her. In this commanding role, the Colonel thus has the power to enfranchise or disenfranchise his subalterns' saudade, love and other social emotions. He holds this authority over even Maria Fausta's own father, who wishes to shoot and kill João do Carmo. The film culminates with a happy ending in marriage for the couple whom Colonel Januário approves of, and a tragic ending of lonely, melancholy exile from the community for Galdino, whose saudade for Maria Fausta is disenfranchised. Paradoxically, this latter saudade becomes the emotional heart of the folk tale, since it is prolonged and intensified by absence and unrequited love, and then becomes apotheosized at the film's end through a synthesis with the natural landscape of the region. Out of this synthesis is born a folk myth, which the film is seeking to shape and disseminate, that the saudoso spirit of Galdino still haunts the hills of the region with the notes of his accordion. Connecting the spatial liminality of saudade to a kind of cyclical (as opposed to progressive) temporal liminality, Galdino's ghostly accordion is said to be heard in particular at the twilight times of dawn or dusk. There is an appropriate, if unintended, symbolism here of a socially and economically marginalized rural worker haunting the Brazilian rural landscape in the 1950s, since it was an era of development very much focused on metropolises like Rio de Janeiro and São Paulo, to the exclusion of many rural areas.

Mauro's nationalist, Romantic perspective on rural Brazil merges seamlessly with his representations of a voyeuristic male gaze from both elite and popular socio-economic positions. His 1954 description of plans for a film (much later realized as *A noiva da cidade* (*The Town's Fiancée*) (1980) by director Alex Viany) is indicative of his traditionalist, Romantic association of woman and landscape (Viany 1978: 162). The protagonist of this film was to be an 'enchanting' woman visiting a little town of the interior (presumably Volta Grande) with whom the entire population would fall in love. She would be by turns seductive and innocent, thus representing desire for the beauty of woman and rural landscape at the same time that their purity relative to urban Brazil is celebrated. The filmmaker himself thus would channel the desires of the 'anonymous masses' of the area in this rural fantasy, encouraging identification with this desire among urban middle-class audiences. He would presumably direct the gaze of the camera towards this desired woman as his films of the era often featured the landscape or even some of the female characters like Maria Fausta in *O canto da saudade*. In the latter film, this gaze often focalizes the perspective of the Colonel who is the major landowner in the region, played by none other than Mauro himself, but his gaze is also alternated with the working-class perspective of Galdino, the ranch hand.

Spatially we can note a clear class difference in these two forms of voyeurism featured in the film, both of which often target the female lead Maria Fausta as the object of their gaze. Early in the film, Galdino (Mário Mascarenhas) and his acquaintance Vicente (Alcir Damata) are by the riverside observing Maria Fausta washing clothes, just out of earshot, while later in the narrative Colonel Januário spies on Maria Fausta from a commanding position high on the hilltop. In each of these scenes, the camera establishes the position of the man watching and then gives a point-of-view shot of Maria Fausta, but the position of the Colonel is clearly much higher and more distant from the object of his gaze, his goddaughter. Vicente catches Galdino unawares as he gazes at Maria Fausta from the riverbank, and he assumes an air of complicity in appreciating Maria Fausta's beautiful figure, which makes Galdino uncomfortable and seemingly jealous. His fellow ranch hand does not demonstrate any respect for Galdino's special attraction to Maria Fausta, simply wishing to appreciate her body together as an object of mutual male desire. There is no indication that Vicente has a sense of any claim to a special relationship with Maria Fausta on Galdino's part, nor does Galdino himself speak up to suggest that he is more than a friend to her, or wishes to be so. In this sense, Vicente and Galdino's gazes are established as interchangeable, representing men of the same class as Maria Fausta appreciating her beauty in their daily interactions with her on the same social level. Alternatively, when the Colonel later observes in solitude Maria Fausta's romantic moment by the river with João do Carmo, he sits on horseback on a hilltop, far above all the residents of the locality. He is undisturbed by other voyeurs and leisurely waits for an appropriate moment to gleefully break up their intimate moment with a shout. Another distinction from Galdino is that the Colonel openly speaks about Maria Fausta's voluptuous curves within her hearing at a party thrown at his house. His commanding gaze of the landscape and the woman on it is associated with a cavalier attitude that it is his right to speak openly about her sexual attractiveness to his male friends, just as if he were speaking proudly of his ranch property. Regarding the relatively low height, near the riverside, from which Galdino observes Maria Fausta, there is really only one exception that takes place in Galdino's dream sequence, discussed further below, in which he achieves a hilltop position from which to gaze down on the surrounding lands and perform a song on his accordion. Yet, the Colonel's felt presence at the end of this dream sequence, and simultaneously his entrance outside of the dream into Galdino's house, wake Galdino up, thus disrupting the musician's own fantasy of performing for a rapt audience on the commanding heights of the ridge. This is a clear example of the more dominant gaze of the cacique disrupting the gaze of his subaltern, who as a result retreats into an even more passive, saudoso state, transitioning closer to his final status as a ghostly, haunting presence at the end of the folk tale.

The voyeuristic scene of the Colonel spying on Maria Fausta with her lover João do Carmo by the riverside could be read as a criticism of the character's perversity and childish pleasure taken in yelling at the two lovers to interrupt their private moment, while the Colonel might well claim that he is protecting Maria Fausta's honour. However, the scene is acted more for comedic effect than anything else. In any case, the Colonel's commanding hilltop perspective of the landscape and of Maria Fausta in this scene mirrors director Mauro's own preferred camera location for a longing (saudoso) gaze at rural Brazil, once again associating woman and land in the Romantic tradition (this aspect of Mauro's work in the 1950s is explored further in Chapter 7). Related to the desire that multiple men express for Maria Fausta, there is an intertext in the film's plot of a comedic play, which several of the characters go to see, called 'Da necessidade de ser polígamo' ('On the Necessity of Being a Polygamist') ([1949] 1961) by José Silveira Sampaio. Sampaio was a Rio de Janeiro playwright and actor who appears as himself in the film, touring in Minas Gerais with the company performing his play. The incorporation of theatrical intertexts as well as musical celebrations in the plot is reminiscent of the chanchada musical comedy genre, still quite popular at the time. The joke regarding the play broaching the issue of polygamy is that the Colonel's wife Garrincha (Zizinha Macedo) thinks he enjoys this topic too much. The plot of the play itself, not discussed in the film, actually raises the issue of polyandry just as much as more patriarchal polygamous marriages centred around one man. But in Mauro's film there never seems to be any question of Maria Fausta (let alone the Colonel's wife) being involved in a polyandric relationship, despite the fact that she clearly has two ardent suitors and also is an object of the Colonel's desire. The jokes throughout the film about the Colonel's sexual desires or interests, including for Maria Fausta herself, underline the patriarchal sexual politics (which also border on the incestual since the Colonel is Maria's godfather). Mauro does feature a scene in which Maria expresses some discomfort about the way the Colonel describes her body to other men in public; however, this discomfort is dispelled by one of her friends who says she thinks she should consider it a compliment.

The oneiric sequences in *O canto da saudade* reveal vivid representations of the fantasy life, desires and fears of the protagonist with recourse on the part of the filmmaker to haptic visuality, liminal spaces and liquid perception. These oneiric moments happen to be the scenes where Mauro is most earnestly attempting to portray the subjective perspective of his main character, a subaltern worker on the plantation who is not in a position of mastery of either his land or his love interest, and thus is a relatively abject protagonist. As such, he inhabits and/or imagines liminal spaces in which to stage his desires, which are themselves often frustrated or unfilled and thus transform into the longing of saudade. Galdino's fantasy life, as represented in two distinct dream sequences, becomes the best representation of the association between liminal space and saudade/desire in the film.

As part of the performance of the play 'On the Necessity of Being a Polygamist' in the film's plot, a professional musician plays a beautiful 120-button accordion that becomes an object of envy for Galdino, who himself performs only with a simpler, rural accordion typically called a *sanfona*. The subsequent dream sequence allows us to see that Galdino loves not only Maria Fausta but accordion music as well. His longing to play the beautiful, 120-button instrument and his envy of the musician who can play it professionally lead to a wish-fulfilment dream in which Galdino is able to play the instrument in the area of his home on Colonel Januário's ranch. When Galdino falls asleep thinking about the impressive modern instrument, his dream assumes a gaze from a dominant position overseeing the landscape, but in this fantasy position Galdino conceives of the height of the hilltop more as a stage where he is applauded for performing (influenced by his awe of the professional musician) than as a place to observe and control the inhabitants of the ranch as the Colonel does in reality. In this sense, the saudade in the dream is about not only a longing for a better instrument but a desire on the part of a humble ox-cart driver to gain a moment of being the centre of attention and respect, in a community and society where he plays a supporting role to a rural elite itself in decline.

But beyond taking centre stage to play an impressive new accordion, Galdino also directs the movements, through the rhythms he plays, of the farmers and laundresses in the choreography of everyday work that Mauro develops in this dream sequence. Initially in the dream, Galdino plays the accordion in a meadow near a ridge, performing to a rural landscape seemingly devoid of other people. As Galdino plays some impressive trills and flourishes on the instrument, though, we begin to hear cheering on the soundtrack and a voice, probably the Colonel's, exclaiming 'very good, Galdino!'. He also plays the opening notes from Carlos Gomes's 1870 opera, *Il guarany* (*The Guaraní Indian*) here, evoking the indigenous side of Brazilian culture and, in the same vein as Brazilian Romantic art, associating Brazilian Indians with a celebration of the country's natural landscape. The evocation of Gomes's opera also suggests, on Mauro's part, a saudade for Brazil's indigenous past, and also for the related early colonial, untamed wildernesses in which Romantic Indianist stories are usually set. This Indianist saudade will be emphasized all the more by the next song performed in the dream, discussed below. After his initial solo performance on the accordion, Galdino climbs onto an ox cart positioned on a ridge high above the surrounding countryside. He stands upright and continues to perform, assuming a commanding view high above the ranch lands, as we see Colonel Januário do in the voyeuristic scene in waking life discussed above. I emphasize here that Galdino has assumed a liminal position in his dream, on the edge of the ranch lands and looking out over them. This is a position of social power, but affectively it is also a place generative of a saudoso gaze in Mauro's films – a gaze that looks out over the landscape from a distance while it longs for closeness and intimacy with it (this saudoso gaze from the hilltop is discussed further in a different context in Chapter 7).

The sentimental, saudoso viewpoint, rather than the surveillance of the landscape, is more acute and relevant for Galdino in this hilltop position than for the Colonel, as any social power Galdino achieves in this position in the dream is very transient. In addition, the emotion of saudade is more characteristic of Galdino's everyday life, in which he longs for both a beautiful woman and a musical instrument that he cannot have. Rather than placing him centre stage as an object of desire as in this dream sequence, in his real life Galdino's role as musician places him on the edge of the dance floor, on the sidelines merely observing Maria Fausta dance with the man she loves, João do Carmo. Nevertheless, for a few moments in the dream, Galdino does seem to wield a certain power through his instrument as a large group of men raise and lower their hoes to the rhythm of his music, and many women also raise and lower their arms or march up the surrounding hillsides carrying laundry in step with the rhythms of Galdino's accordion.

At the same time, the entire group (which features several hundred extras from the local community of Volta Grande) sings in unison to the tune of the accordionist's interpretation of Heitor Villa-Lobos's 'The Chant of the Medicine Man' ('O Canto do Pajé'). The lyrics of the song performed in this scene again reference indigenous culture (this time of Tupi Indians), in tandem with a broad celebration of the natural world in Brazil, overseen by 'Tupã, the God of Brazil / who fills the sky with sun'. This song also prominently features the sentiment of saudade, which is said to have been brought about by the animal spirit 'Anhangá' who makes the medicine man 'dream about the land he lost'. In Villa-Lobos's work we hear not only a saudade for indigenous culture, but a representation of that sentiment as felt by Brazilian Indians themselves, previous residents of the ranch lands in which Galdino's story takes place. Even as it nostalgically evokes a bygone (at least in Volta Grande) indigenous civilization, the dream sequence becomes a kind of idyllic rural scene, which in its collective depiction of rural workers moving in unison resembles a socialist utopian ideal (here we can recall Mauro's reference to Eisenstein when commenting on the film). Yet, close-ups capturing Galdino's reaction to the many workers moved by his music suggest that he is somewhat bewildered by his own power, and does not quite understand or feel comfortable with the magical effect of his accordion on the local community of his fellow labourers.

Clearly he is not used to wielding this amount of influence in his social environment, but his astonished facial reactions also serve to draw the viewer's attention all the more to the surreal quality of the images in this dream montage. Workers and everyday tools and objects associated with farm labour are presented as a kaleidoscope of different textures and colours moving in several distinct trajectories, including moments where several shots are superimposed in a spatial montage, thus making visible spatial liminality (Figure 1). Further, these images and Galdino's reaction have a synesthetic effect, leading the viewer into the realm of what Laura Marks has termed *haptic visuality*, in which 'the eyes themselves function like organs of touch' (2000: 162). Regarding the impact of haptic imagery in film, Marks writes that '[t]he haptic image forces the viewer to contemplate the image itself instead of being pulled into narrative' (2000: 163). Pulled out of the film's narrative, appreciated for their textures and collective movements across the screen, these images achieve a (passing) timelessness that resonates with the imagining of return or redemption inherent in the more joyful manifestations of saudade. And yet, even in this dream Galdino is subject to the Colonel's interference, who appears in dark silhouette on the hilltop at the end of the sequence, shocking Galdino and consequently bringing the dream to an end as he wakes up,

Figure 1: The haptic visuality of Humberto Mauro's spatial montage represents Galdino's liminal, saudoso perspective in the first dream sequence of *O canto da saudade* (Courtesy Museu de Imagem e Som – Rio de Janeiro), 1952.

only to see in waking life the Colonel darkening the doorstep of the small house Galdino lives in, ominously wielding a cane.

Later in the film, Maria Fausta disappears without telling anyone where she is going, and as a result, a search party is sent to look for her all throughout the Colonel's lands. Galdino, in love with the missing woman, is one of the most active searchers and, knowing her to be a laundress who does much of her work at the riverside, he takes a small boat along the shore and marshes to see if he can find any trace of her. This liminal space of the river at the edge of the ranch sets the stage for Galdino's second dream sequence in the film. The dream Galdino has, after a long day of searching along the river for Maria Fausta, takes place at the riverside as well. Paralleling the dream state itself, liquid water (in this case a river) marks a border between distinct bodily sensations, forms of movement and perceptions of reality. Here we can recall Gilles Deleuze's ([1983] 2013) theory of liquid perception, a metaphor for a fluid, flexible perspective that lies somewhere between more quotidian solid and more ephemeral/fantastic gaseous perceptions. In addition, Gaston Bachelard ([1942] 2006) has identified an 'Ophelia complex' in western art associating femininity and mortality with water, which is relevant to an understanding of the images of Maria Fausta and the other young women surrounding her on the riverbank. In the context of the narrative at this point, in which Maria Fausta may be in mortal danger, her association with water takes on Ophelian connotations. Here the water becomes liminal in yet another sense, as a transitional space between life and death as imagined by Galdino, who has entered a dream state tinged by his anxiety over the possibility of harm or death coming to his beloved. For this reason it is to be expected that the saudade arising out of this situation would have a more melancholy note, and as we shall see, this note is indeed struck by the particular song played during the dream sequence.

At the beginning of his dream, Galdino appears in a dark and misty space akin to a riverbank at night and begins to play a tune on his accordion. As soon as he begins to play, he notices before him a group of more than twenty women, called forth as if magically by his music. The women are seated in ascending rows holding accordions, with Maria Fausta herself in a central position at the front of the group. They are all clad in white blouses and dresses, contrasting sharply with their dark, nocturnal surroundings and thus in their innocence and youth, echoing somewhat the unnatural, watery death of Shakespeare's Ophelia. The eeriness of their location is emphasized by the voice-over of the schoolteacher (Landa Góry) telling the story, who says that Galdino hears 'strange melodies which emerge *from within* the water' (emphasis added). When Galdino observes the women from a distance and recognizes Maria Fausta among them, a smile spreads across his face and both he and the women continue to play the song together on their accordions while the women sing the lyrics, now recognizable as those of the folk song 'Peixe vivo' ('Live Fish'). The lyrics not only match the watery theme of the dream, evoking ocean imagery, but also tell a melancholy tale of saudade for a distant lover without whom the singer is utterly lost, like a 'live fish' trying to survive 'out of the cold water' of the ocean. Maria Fausta in particular sings as a solo in close-up the lines 'It's the wind that delays us / It's the sea that hinders us / from arriving in port' ('É o vento que nos atrasa / É o mar que nos atrapalha / Para no porto chegar'). These lines are delivered in a slow, melodious and heartfelt manner, seemingly directed at Galdino across the river.

Through image and sound, then, the emotion of saudade is represented as the affective register of the margins, a sentiment evoked and strengthened at the borders between land and sea/river, life and death, romance and rejection. Like the music itself floating across this misty space (evoking the river where Maria Fausta washes clothes), saudade temporarily bridges the gap of desire, creating a transitory moment of emotional togetherness filled with the hope for a future reunion or redemption that would forever close the temporal and spatial gulf that keeps the beloved at a distance. The bittersweetness of the moment is emphasized in this sequence, as Galdino's face is filled with joy while he sings and plays along with Maria Fausta; however, he also seems to be under some considerable strain since his face is covered with a heavy sheen of perspiration. Though generally a certain distance is kept between Galdino and the women in this scene, with the use of shots and countershots as if they were singing to each other across the waters, the distance from Maria Fausta is not entirely maintained. At one point we see Galdino walk directly in front of her as he continues to play his accordion. Thus, the dream scenario allows for a limited (though not complete) transcendence of the gulf, emotionally and physically, that separates Maria Fausta from Galdino in reality. Tragically for the latter, this is a gulf that will never be crossed once he wakes up.

There is also an implied temporal liminality for rural Brazil in Mauro's work, in the context of the rapid urbanization and industrialization of the 1950s. This involves progress being associated with uneven development favouring urban areas over the rural, and is reflected in Mauro's commentary on *O canto* at the time (quoted above), such as his assertion that a film of national character should attempt to tie man to the land. Rural-urban migration was helping to destabilize traditional rural society and Mauro saw this film as a way of 'competing' (*concorrer*) with the economic pressures driving migrant workers out of rural Minas Gerais and other agricultural areas to the cities. In this context, the idea of Galdino's spirit fusing with the landscape and eternally haunting it (as revealed at the close of the film) takes on a larger symbolism of refusing the seeming inevitability of out-migration from rural Brazil. At the same time, in the pedagogical context of the film discussed further in Chapter 7, the folk tale serves to inculcate respect in urban Brazilians for cultural traditions and a way of life that should not be abandoned. Yet, the emphasis in the narrative on the rehearsal for musical performances and dances on the ranch, and the explicit involvement of the Colonel and his overseer in managing the music of these local events, along with Mauro's on-screen introduction to the region at the film's start, and indeed also the schoolteacher's narration of the story of Galdino, all serve to give the impression of the rural being a thoroughly mediated space in the present day. Indeed, Mauro himself liked to emphasize that the region should be exploited more by filmmakers and he offered his own Rancho Alegre Studios to assist any interested directors.

Sinhá moça: Saudade and Liminal Historical Time

As a counterpoint to the spatial liminality that frames saudade in Mauro's work, we can consider the more specific, historical era between Brazilian Empire and Republic that allows for a temporal liminality highlighting several distinct forms of saudade in Tom Payne's *Sinhá moça* (*The Landowner's Daughter*) (1953). This film's approach to Brazilian history is best understood within the context of its production by the Vera Cruz studios. In the 1950s, there was a debate between those including Nelson Pereira dos Santos who criticized the 'cosmopolitanism' at the service of US cultural imperialism of those studios in the vein of Vera Cruz or even Atlântida on the one hand, versus those who criticized the 'nationalist idiocy' of Santos and the *Fundamentos* film review writers who were defending putatively bad cinema and related legislation as part of their efforts to recreate the Brazilian film industry and authentically represent the common Brazilian people on film (Galvão and Bernadet 1983: 63). For the former group, the national bourgeoisie in general were considered to be overly cosmopolitan and thus alienated from Brazilian reality. Both groups were more or less guided by an import substitution model, with more capital available (and thus less return on investment due to the limited number of theatres) to the big studio Vera Cruz. The big difference is that Vera Cruz placed an emphasis on importing foreign technical expertise (including film directors) in order to jump-start a Hollywood-inspired model of big budget studio production (funded by São Paulo industrialists), a move that contributed to its critics' perception that the studio could not possibly understand Brazilian people nor reliably tell their stories. More recent assessments by both a film scholar as well as an actor/director who worked for Vera Cruz (Lopez 1998; Merten 2004) have tended to downplay this polarized view and emphasized the important technical knowledge and filmmaking experience gained by everyone involved in Vera Cruz's films, which they passed along in their collaboration with other Brazilian filmmakers in subsequent decades on a variety of projects from Mazzaropi's many popular country-bumpkin (*caipira*) comedies to Anselmo Duarte's Cannes Golden Palm-winning *O pagador de promessas* (*The Given Word*) (1962).

With regard to the ideological framework of *Sinhá moça*'s narrative and the related structures of feeling operative in the film, they largely match up with the liberal, cosmopolitan and elitist perspective one might expect to find amongst the big bourgeoisie of São Paulo who were Vera Cruz's owners and proponents. While critical of any saudade for the old regime of the Brazilian Empire with its slavery-based economy, the film evokes and amplifies the same nostalgic sentiment when directed at those who helped to overthrow the old regime, and is particularly saudoso in its representation of the (white) members of the elite and middle classes, as well as more progressive priests in the Catholic Church, who sided with the abolitionist cause and aided those Africans and Afro-Brazilians escaping slavery in the lead-up to abolition in 1888. In the discussion that follows I will consider this period of abolition and the end of the Brazilian Empire as a liminal historical period on to which the filmmakers project these various forms of saudade, which, like the more spatially oriented saudade of Mauro's film, are born out of the contemporary historical conjuncture of rapid industrialization and urbanization in the Brazil of the 1950s.

The romantic narrative, rural/plantation *mise-en-scène* and costume design of *Sinhá moça* clearly reveal some international, Hollywood cinematic influences – in particular *Gone with the Wind* (Fleming, [1939] 2009), but also *The Mark of Zorro* (Mamoulian, [1940] 2005). References to slavery and abolition in the United States begin early in the film when the title character Sinhá or Sinhazinha (Eliane Lage) reads Harriet Beecher Stowe's *Uncle Tom's Cabin* ([1852] 2007) on the train back to her plantation home. Since abolition has already occurred in the United States by this point (the story takes place in the 1880s), the presence of the book foreshadows a similar historical transition in Brazil while also marking out Sinhazinha as a kind of class traitor who, despite being the heir of a slave-owning wealthy family, sympathizes with the increasingly powerful abolitionist cause in Brazil. In this sense she becomes a character that elites of the 1950s can easily identify with, an object of saudade as a white, upper-class woman who stands for the noble cause of liberty and thus, by the 1950s, can clearly be understood as having taken a stand on the right side of history. Sinhazinha unexpectedly meets an ally in her cause on the train, Rodolfo Fontes (Anselmo Duarte), a young, charming middle-class man who is returning from São Paulo after graduating law school and flirts with Sinhazinha under the less-than-watchful eye of her sleepy chaperone. Though Rodolfo will soon hide his support for the abolitionist cause to become an undercover activist, his physician father Dr Fontes is shown early in the film to be a leader in the movement, and thus both men become symbols of middle-class support for abolition.

The elder Fontes also directly references the American civil war in his first scene in the film, continuing to uphold the United States as a model for abolition. This kind of international perspective was criticized by Vera Cruz's critics, to whom cosmopolitanism was often equated with a surrender to cultural imperialism (cf. Galvão and Bernardet 1983: 67–68). It is fair to say that the international influence notable in the film's plot reflects the general position of Vera Cruz filmmakers that Brazilian film needed to imitate and then remake foreign models in order to advance as an industry. Yet, such opinions had already existed for decades in Brazilian cinema, as detailed above, and even Humberto Mauro was sometimes influenced by them (such as the Eisensteinian influence on some scenes in *O canto da saudade*). Further, there is clearly a common Afro-diasporic history shared by the enslaved Africans and their descendants in Brazil and North America, providing ample justification for the establishment of a transnational, hemispheric background to the story of *Sinhá moça*. While some anachronistic saudade from the film's era of production is directed towards the heroes of abolition whose stories it tells, the opening scene on the train also begins to suggest that the saudade existent during the period itself was politically regressive and thus worthy of opprobrium. Sinhazinha's elderly cousin and chaperone on the train complains about this 'new form of traveling' and is lightly mocked and disregarded by Sinhazinha herself as well as Rodolfo. The ideology of technological, technocratic progress so prevalent in the 1950s reveals itself here, putting a penchant for horse-and-buggy travel on the same level with the slave-based economy as anachronisms already consigned to the dustbin of history by the mid-1880s.

However, a clear conflict arises in the film when Sinhazinha interacts with her father, Colonel Ferreira, who is still a wealthy slaveowner and plantation master in this last decade of Brazilian slavery. As she returns home, Sinhazinha is very conflicted about her family's involvement in slavery, for though she is an admirer of Harriet Beecher Stowe, she also mentions she has 'so much saudade' for the plantation. The expression is echoed by her childhood nanny, an elderly black woman and house slave who says she felt the same saudade for Sinhazinha while she was away. The nanny character also quickly establishes the patriarchal order on the plantation by reminding Sinhazinha to obey her father and not to 'make her mother cry' by being rebellious. Thus, the contemporary saudade felt by elites and their subalterns in the old regime is portrayed as pathological, a structure of feeling that threatens progress. These sentiments of longing for the old plantation are revealed as all the more dangerous, in that they are so deeply engrained and experienced in personal relationships that cross over racial, class and gender boundaries.

Colonel Ferreira in particular is portrayed at first in a paternalist light, but he grows crueller to his enslaved plantation workers and harsher in response to his daughter's criticism as the resistance to slavery increases. It is clear that there is no apologia for slavery in the film, which emphasizes the various kinds of violence enslaved African and Afro-Brazilian men and women were subjected to at the time. One leader amongst those in captivity is mercilessly whipped to death, and women are raped by the overseer, all explicitly shown or made obvious in the film's narrative and approved of explicitly or implicitly by Ferreira. Paradoxically, though, Ferreira's perspective has much in common with the white abolitionists of the elite and middle classes in the film. Rodolfo especially is operating according to a similar logic to Ferreira, since he tries to convince the landowner's enslaved workers to escape little by little. From Rodolfo's perspective, this low-level resistance through slow flight is less dangerous and more feasible because it will not arouse as much repression from Ferreira as a 'general rebellion' would. Rodolfo is also desperate to stop slave violence when the plantation workers finally do attempt a mass escape, even as those running to freedom are themselves being brutally hunted down. In one climactic scene near the film's end, Rodolfo rides in front of Ferreira in order to prevent him being shot by the escaping slave Justino, who has acquired a gun and wishes to kill his former master rather than to be recaptured. Rodolfo ends up taking the bullet meant for Ferreira, and after being shot gasps to Justino, 'This was not the way … you could lose everything … this was not the way' ('Não era assim … você poderá tudo perder … não era assim'). After being shot, Rodolfo is aided by Ferreira himself and Justino slowly walks away, dazed, but no longer resisting and thus easily recaptured by Ferreira's henchmen. The implication is that the guilt and shock of having shot his ally in the white elite hold him back from any further violent resistance, and he is taken away to be put on trial for attempted murder. This scene, in combination with the subsequent scene in which Rodrigo serves as defence counsel for Justino in his attempted murder trial, paints a portrait of the ideal relationship between white elite and black subaltern being one of patronage and dependency, as opposed to a new, autonomous social position for Afro-Brazilians after escaping slavery.

Thus, there are some significant ties between liberal and conservative paternalism, even as the film's main narrative thrust directs saudade towards the former while criticizing the latter. When Rodolfo tells Ferreira's enslaved workers to escape in an orderly, one by one fashion, a white liberal saudade of the 1950s is revealed, its object being the members of the Brazilian elite who sought to live in harmony with freed blacks, but still very much within a racial hierarchy. Rodolfo, though concealing his abolitionist intentions to Colonel Ferreira and his family, is portrayed as on the right side of history; he is the main hero of the film's action (a kind of Brazilian Zorro), with his own father as well as the black workers escaping slavery portraying supporting roles. In the scene where Rodolfo appears wearing a black mask over his eyes, there is very likely an influence from the several Hollywood Zorro films that had been produced prior to *Sinhá moça*'s release. The Zorro character, too, was a member of the elite who fought for justice (in his case in Spanish California).

In Rodolfo's final court scene, in which he defends Justino, he speaks not only for the man who accidentally shot him but by extension for all those of 'humble colour' (as he puts it). His defence of Justino, along with his other interactions with Afro-Brazilians in the film, is thus a sign of the *new paternalism*. The fact that Rodolfo also took a bullet for the Colonel further emphasizes his serious effort to mediate on behalf of the old regime and bring its members along into the new one. In his closing argument defending Justino in court, Rodolfo also praises Princess Isabel and suggests her as a kind of model woman of the time, further revealing a continued attachment to the old regime and its elite. His praise for Isabel serves as a foreshadowing of her 'Golden Law', which when announced becomes a *deus ex machina* at the close of the film, allowing for a generally happy ending for liberal elites and newly liberated lower classes alike. Isabel is the regent who ruled over the legal system in which Rodolfo argues his case, and whose criminal code the slaveholder Ferreira cites directly to justify 'moderate' punishment of slaves in an earlier scene. Since 1830, imperial law allowed for such punishment (see *Código Criminal do Império do Brasil*), and Ferreira emphasizes this law not only to justify violence towards resistant enslaved workers, but also to rein in his own overseer and affect a paternalist air of forbearance from excessively harsh punishments.

The representative of the Catholic Church in the film, Friar José, also contributes to the establishment of the new paternalist order. Friar José, like Rodolfo a latent abolitionist, presides over an integrated congregation including black and white children and during mass he openly prays for the Afro-Brazilian leader Fulgêncio while he is being brutally whipped on the *pelourinho* (whipping post). Friar José's claim that 'before God, all are equal' could be seen as a precursor to liberation theology, and yet like Rodolfo, through much of the film's narrative the priest does little to directly challenge the authority of the slave-owning landholders. As Fulgêncio is beaten to death for insubordination, Friar José prays for him, but only intervenes in the punishment after the fatal blow has already been struck.

In the wake of this brutal and fatal punishment, the general slave rebellion that Rodolfo had worked so hard to stave off finally occurs, much to his consternation. The escaping men, women and children are put on an equal footing with those that pursue them in the cinematography of the chase sequence, with many low-angle shots utilized to frame both sides in a final epic struggle before the arrival of abolition. Upper-class women, as well as army officers, are portrayed as helping those escaping their slavemasters, primarily through passive resistance or refusal to aid in recapturing them. One soldier says to a woman who protests their chasing after Afro-Brazilians on behalf of their former masters, 'you're right, ma'am, the army is not a slave catcher' ('tem razão, senhora, exército não é capitão do mato'). A scene in which soldiers nominally defend a bridge from former slaves, while really allowing them to escape across the river underneath the bridge, is based on a real historical event (*Memória Vera Cruz*). In this way the film gives a good sense of the expanding public resistance to slavery, which helped pressure the imperial government finally to sign the Golden Law outlawing the treatment of human beings as property in 1888.

A consideration of the interactions between the male and female leads in the latter half of the film, in contrast to the novel on which it is based, will prove revealing of the specific manner in which saudade retroactively frames race relations to create a more or less inclusive notion of the Brazilian national 'family'. To her dismay, because she still thinks he is pro-slavery, Rodolfo buys a dance with Sinhazinha in a charity auction but she emphasizes that 'no one can command' her feelings and thoughts. In both the auction and the two characters' dialogue, there is some suggestion of the parallel oppression and resistance of women and slaves, but of course the primary (and only relatively) empowered female character is an upper-class woman. In the final scene after abolition is announced, when Rodolfo has been revealed as a protector of the enslaved and a supporter of the abolitionist cause, Rodolfo and Sinhazinha arrive at a central platform where the *pelourinho* post used to stand, and the camera shows newly freed women, men and children discarding their chains on the platform and looking happily upwards at the couple who have found each other amidst the crowd. A shot-reverse shot jumps from Sinhazinha to one freed Afro-Brazilian man below her, giving the appearance that his discarding of his chains is also an offering of thanks to the elite woman sympathetic to his people's plight. The next shot-reverse shot repeats the same gesture with Rodolfo and a woman and her son discarding their chains as they smile adoringly up at the lawyer who has just defended Justino despite having been shot by him in his attempted escape. A final shot-reverse shot between Rodolfo and Sinhazinha as they raise their gazes up to look into each other's eyes leads to a kiss and a climax of saudade in this liminal moment between old regime and new (Figures 2 and 3). Newly freed (but destitute) black Brazilians enjoy a moment of celebration with white elites even as those elites, positioned high above them through *mise-en-scène* and camera angles, resolve

Figure 2: Sinhazinha gazes intently at Rodrigo, with Afro-Brazilians and Africans in the background celebrating the announcement of abolition in *Sinhá moça* (Courtesy Cinemateca, São Paulo).

Figure 3: Sinhazinha and Rodrigo prepare to kiss as church bells ring celebrating abolition and foreshadowing their marriage, the marriage of the old and new white elites in *Sinhá moça* (Courtesy Cinemateca, São Paulo).

Figure 4: A production still from the abolition celebration scene of *Sinhá moça*, illustrating the *mise-en-scène* and extras, some of whom receive close-ups as they gaze upward adoringly at Rodrigo and Sinhazinha (Courtesy Cinemateca, São Paulo).

their own differences through the intermarriage of Rodolfo, the urbane professional, and Sinhazinha, the liberal-minded scion of the region's most powerful landholder (Figure 4). Will she now, married to Rodolfo, become a compliant supporter of the new paternalism of the bourgeoisie and reformed landed aristocracy? The arc of the narrative suggests this to be the case. As the only child of Colonel Ferreira, Sinhazinha stands to inherit all of his land and Rodrigo will thus, through his marriage, become a new and powerful representative of the landed elite in the region. In this way the church bells announcing the end of slavery are transformed into wedding bells with Rodolfo and Sinhazinha's kiss, linking their impending marriage to abolition and to a new era led by a reform-minded elite. The liberal elite of São Paulo behind Vera Cruz Studios could find no better lineage in Brazilian history to which they might lay claim.

The symbolism of the film's ending diverges significantly from the novel upon which it is based, in such a way as to emphasize the future survival of a hierarchical and cordial relationship between white elites and black subalterns. In Maria de Zonne Pacheco

Fernandes's eponymous novel (1950), the final scene takes place also at the moment of abolition; however, Rodrigo and Sinhazinha have already been married for years at this point and have a daughter named Regina. Regina is speaking to Justino at the moment when the news of abolition is received, and wishes to celebrate with him. She believes him to be sleeping and attempts to wake him, but unbeknownst to her the elderly Afro-Brazilian man, who had spent most of his life in captivity, has just died. Understanding what has occurred, Rodrigo says quietly to Sinhazinha, 'Look… the Spring, the Future, caressing the old slave who was chained, repudiated, martyred, and died free, in the memorable moment of his emancipation' ('Veja… A Primavera, o Porvir, acariciando o velho escravo que foi algemado [*sic*] repudiado, martirizado, e morreu livre, no momento memorável de sua emancipação') (Fernandes 1950: 223). Thus, the symbolism of the novel's ending very clearly associates the white child of the landowners (with her 'golden hair' ['cabelos dourados']) as the future of Brazil, while the deceased Justino represents the end of slavery – but his old age and death, contrasted with Regina's youth, also associate Afro-Brazilians themselves with the country's past rather than its future. In this sense the novel's closing symbolic move is more reflective of the ideology of whitening of the early twentieth century, which imagined a gradual reduction and ultimate dying out of the black population of Brazil through intermarriage and European immigration (cf. Skidmore 1992). In contrast, following more closely the later ideology of racial democracy developed from the thought of sociologist-anthropologist Gilberto Freyre ([1933] 1986), the resolution of the filmic narrative poses a national 'family' that includes Afro-Brazilians of several generations displaying deferential, cordial attitudes towards the descendants and inheritors of their former masters. Indeed, since Rodrigo and Sinhazinha do not yet have any offspring at the end of the film, the Afro-Brazilian man, woman and child who stand beneath them (in the *mise-en-scène* described above) take the position of grateful, admiring children in the emergent family suggested by the couple's kiss (accompanied by the sound and then image of church bells).

Ultimately, *Sinhá moça* paints a picture of a moral continuum amongst the imperial elite with regard to slavery at this liminal moment for this ignominious institution and for Brazilian society itself. Even the slaveowners and their families are deemed to be compassionate towards the suffering of their enslaved workers, albeit to varying degrees and in the case of Colonel Ferreira, allowing for much violence and cruelty on the part of his overseer and hired guns (*capitães de mato*). The abolitionist elites, including the members of the upper-middle class and some members of the landholding class depicted in the film, are framed in the light of a 1950s saudade for a moment of solidarity between the oppressed and the upper classes. The *noblesse oblige* of Rodrigo, Sinhazinha and Friar José becomes an object of saudade and identification for the industrial elites of the mid-twentieth century. The alliance between white elites and poor blacks culminating in the celebration and kiss at film's end come to frame the 1880s as a 'simpler time' when the struggle for justice seemed clear. We can imagine this liminal period to be an all-the-more attractive target for saudade in contrast with the more ambiguous era for race relations in the 1950s. By that time, a liberal, tolerant ideology of racial harmony or 'democracy' had been established, yet the stark inequality between the races had survived the era of slavery in many areas of social life. When *Sinhá moça* was released in 1953, this continuing inequality and related prejudice against non-whites had already begun to be revealed in shocking detail by Brazilian social scientists such as Luiz de Aguiar Costa Pinto (in his *O negro no Rio de Janeiro* (*Blacks in Rio de Janeiro*) [(1953) 1998]). Discrimination against Brazilian blacks and their subaltern political and socio-economic status in the society would be further demonstrated over the subsequent decade by national and international scholars, including Florestan Fernandes and Roger Bastide at the University of São Paulo amongst others. The saudoso structure of feeling in *Sinhá moça* should be interpreted as an alternative emotional discourse, or narrative framing, which seeks to consolidate the social position of a modern white elite at the pinnacle of a racialized class hierarchy, even as it criticizes the sins of the Brazilian Empire's slaveholders and the historical injustices suffered at their hands by enslaved Afro-Brazilians.

Chapter 3

1960s Brazilian Cinema and Narratives of Rural-Urban Migration

We are the peasants of cinema.

(Glauber Rocha 1970)

The solution of sentimental problems depends in part on the solution of economic problems.

(Joaquim Pedro de Andrade 1973)

One of the great narratives of Latin America in the twentieth century is the story of rural-urban migration, and this massive populational movement continued to be a significant historical phenomenon among the popular classes through the 1960s and 1970s. However, as Latin American countries like Brazil became more and more urbanized, the urban surplus labour pool also grew, leading to a certain disillusionment for migrants who had once seen the city as a place of easy employment if not limitless opportunity. This transformation of the internal migration narrative was reflected to some degree in Brazilian cinema by a shift in migrant narratives from the early 1960s to the latter part of the decade. *O pagador de promessas* (*The Given Word*) (Duarte, [1962] 2005) and *Macunaíma* (de Andrade, [1969] 2006) are two seminal films in this respect, which also represent the first, *sertão* (northeastern backlands) era and the third, Tropicalist era of Cinema Novo. The aesthetic influences of this movement in tandem with changing attitudes about migration to the cities helped to transform and disperse the sentiment of nostalgic longing, better known as saudade in Brazil. The object of saudade was traditionally the whole rural way of life, symbolized in the simplicity and folkloric authenticity of the common man from the countryside. Even as the *cabras* (cowherds or peasants) from the countryside were shown to be victimized by Brazilian society, they were still often held up as symbols of the common man, his plight and his potential. *O pagador de promessas* attempts to maintain this nostalgic symbolism in a modern, urban context with results that are by turns tragic and hopeful. *Macunaíma*'s parody allows for no central locus of nostalgia, yet at the heart of its narrative lies a *saudade do futuro*, or longing for some future idealized subject that could fill the void left behind by the peasant class, now incapable of revolution in the dictatorship years (and thus 'a hero without any character' like Macunaíma himself).

The relationship to the rural interior and to the popular classes and their cultures, both urban and rural, is informed by various forms and degrees of saudade that play out on screen in various aspects of these filmic texts such as artistic influence, popular-cultural background and icons, genre, *mise-en-scène*, character development and score/soundtrack. The representations of saudade in the respective filmic narratives, in turn, develop largely out of the distinct personal background and career paths of the two directors, Anselmo Duarte and Joaquim Pedro de Andrade. Duarte, director of *O pagador*, began his film career as an actor in the *chanchadas* (musical comedies) of the Atlântida Studios in the 1940s and would later star in some dramatic roles with São Paulo's Vera Cruz Studios, including the part of Rodrigo in *Sinhá moça*, discussed in the previous chapter. His directorial debut came with a successful chanchada called *Absolutamente certo!* (*Absolutely Correct!*) in 1957. Below I demonstrate how this background influenced Duarte's depiction of the rural migrant/peasant, ultimately leading to a fatalist nostalgia for the common man of the rural interior combined with a more hopeful saudade for the authenticity and agency of the urban popular classes. On the other hand, Joaquim Pedro de Andrade was very much a member of the young Cinema Novo generation, just getting its start in filmmaking in the early 1960s. These young directors like Andrade, Glauber Rocha and Cacá Diegues had ideas of revolution in their heads from the moment they arrived on the scene, very much in tune with the dynamic cultural and political atmosphere of the 1960s in Latin America. Andrade developed as a filmmaker entirely within that context, experiencing the same great hope and then great disappointment as the military regime took hold in Brazil after 1964. In comparison with Duarte, Andrade's relationship to pre-Cinema Novo popular cinema was less direct and was itself, as I explain below, mediated through a certain form of saudade. This saudade should be called a *reflective* saudade in the sense that Boym (2001) uses the term in her analyses of nostalgia. Andrade did not wish to bring back popular cinema like the chanchada, but he respected it enough as part of Brazil's cinematic past to make frequent citations and references to it in *Macunaíma* – indeed, the relative box-office success of this film compared to earlier Cinema Novo films was in large part due to the stylistic influence of chanchada and the entertainment value this brought for a larger group of spectators. But the ironic, Tropicalist style of *Macunaíma*, along with the director's lack of any direct personal connection to earlier popular cinema, does not allow the film to maintain the same level of earnestness about the popular classes themselves that we find in *O pagador*. Ultimately, the longing of Andrade's film delves into the past in order to celebrate, critique, then transcend it. Neither peasantry nor urban working class are martyred or made sacred by Andrade, as they are shown to be stuck in a historical impasse. Both films analysed here link the sentiment of saudade to a utopian, liberatory impulse, but while Duarte represents this impulse within the structure of his filmic narrative by focusing on the urban working class as agents of liberation, Andrade's narrative ultimately directs its more reflective saudade beyond rural and working classes and popular culture, to the popular heroes of an unknown future beyond the scope of the film.

Popular Cinema and the Return of Anselmo Duarte's Repressed: *O pagador de promessas* After *Absolutamente certo!*

To contextualize Anselmo Duarte's second film, *O pagador de promessas*, one should consider his first film *Absolutamente certo!* as an example of his formative years in the popular cinema of the 1950s. The earlier film is an indicator of the artistic influences Duarte would later incorporate or reject in *O pagador* from the cultural education he had received during this era. In both the production of his first film and the career path he set upon shortly after seeing the national box-office success of this film in 1957, we can already find the seeds of the film he would produce in 1962. This latter work would far surpass Duarte's first film in terms of international recognition, since *O pagador* was then, and remains today, the only Brazilian film ever to win the Palme d'Or for best film at Cannes. Nevertheless, Duarte's earlier career in popular cinema, including writing the screenplay for, playing the lead role in and directing *Absolutamente certo!*, informed his approach to filming *O pagador*, especially the emotional framing of the protagonists' storylines and the genre and stylistic approach to the subject matter of the film.

Absolutamente certo! was produced by Cinedistri Studios and shot at their facilities in Rio de Janeiro. In terms of genre, the film qualifies as a romantic comedy with significant musical interludes, thus fitting easily within the category of chanchada. The film's plot centres around a character named Zé do Lino (played by Anselmo Duarte himself), a man who works for the telephone-book department of a printer. Zé is portrayed as a working-class everyman with one remarkable ability – he has memorized the entire phonebook for Rio de Janeiro. This ability, when it catches the attention of his boss's enterprising son, leads to an offer to show off his memorization skills on 'Absolutamente certo!', a fictional television game show that gives the film its title. According to Dennison and Shaw, this programme was based on a real-life game show on TV Tupi called *O céu é o limite* ('The Sky's the Limit') (2004: 117).

Duarte himself said of the film that he wished to portray modernization in Brazil by demonstrating how the telephone and television had become a part of everyday life in Rio de Janeiro, and also to criticize the 'pre-tape' era of Brazilian television (Merten 2004: 95). Thus, the director establishes a concern with the mass media and the possible alienation of the people via that media in this first film. The lead character is caught up in the celebrity culture and exploitativeness of the media to some degree, but he ultimately insists that he cannot cheat as a contestant on 'Absolutamente certo!' because, in his words, 'The people believe in me' ('O povo acredita em mim'). Thus, concerns about the media's influence on society are combined with a populist message – and this message is all the more tied to Anselmo Duarte personally, since in addition to directing and writing the screenplay, he cast himself to play the everyman character of Zé do Lino. This casting suggests an interest in working-class, common-man types and even an identification with them on the part of the director.

Yet, as far as the stylistic approach to the film, Duarte also was interested in bringing some innovations to the chanchada genre and considered the final result to be somewhere 'in the middle of the road between two tendencies, the art film and the popular film' ('no meio do caminho entre duas tendências, o filme de arte e o popular') (Merten 2004: 96). As an example of an element that pushed the boundaries of the genre, Duarte noted the rather abstract, modernist theatrical performance inserted in the film when Zé do Lino goes out to a night club with Odete (Odete Lara), a singer/dancer who represents the female chanchada star in the film (as emphasized by the fact that she is played by Odete Lara and has the same name as this famous chanchada actress). The fact that Zé do Lino is out on the town with Odete reflects his alienation from his previous, working-class life in which he had vowed to marry the girl next door, Gina. This latter character, played by Maria Dilnah, is a young woman who literally lives next door to Zé in a working-class neighbourhood where residents gather at Gina's house because her family owns the only television on the block. At the night club, Zé and Odete watch a cameo performance by popular singer Almir Ribeiro of an orchestral samba (samba canção) entitled 'Where am I?' ('Onde estou?'), written by Hervé Cordovil and Vicente Leporace. Duarte later described Almir Ribeiro's performance as 'existentialist' – a description meant to capture the haunting melody and the *mise-en-scène*, a mysterious landscape of denuded trees and volcanic shapes, shrouded in mist and filled with dancers providing a further stark visual contrast with their black and white, stylized ballet costumes (2004: 99).

The lyrics of Ribeiro's song invoke mortality and a questioning of existence, but more directly relevant to the film's plot are the following lines: 'And the crystalline laughter that I don't hear where is it? / And the whispering of one thousand simultaneous kisses where has it gone?' ('E os risos cristalinos que eu não ouço onde estão? / E o rumor de mil beijos simultâneos prá onde foi?'), The laughter and kisses referred to here clearly reflect the new-found fame of Zé do Lino as a television star, and suggest the ephemeral nature of the admiration he is receiving in his new mass-media status. Through this relatively avant-garde stage performance in a dystopian space outside the film's main narrative, Duarte seeks to give a larger existential resonance to the loss of authentic self experienced by the protagonist. We see stylistic elements of modernist theatre combined with the popular-cultural element of samba, all framed in a larger context of concern with media exploitation of the common man. The resolution of this comedic film involves a victory over these mediatic and other corrupting, criminal forces, but the dystopia represented in the 'Where am I?' performance plants a seed for Duarte's next film, the drama *O pagador de promessas*.

Based on his actions shortly after the successful release of *Absolutamente certo!*, one gets the sense that Duarte was asking himself the question 'Where am I?' with regard to his artistic career. Rejecting offers to make another chanchada in the same vein as his box-office hit, Duarte subsequently took his earnings from this film and moved to Europe, where he steeped himself in the cinematic environment of the nouvelle vague while contemplating his next directorial project (Merten 2004: 103–16). *O pagador* would become Duarte's attempt to make international cinema that could be appreciated by critics in Brazil and abroad, and thus demonstrates a clear move beyond his past in popular cinema. The genre, stylistic approach, casting and narrative structure of the film can all be revealingly understood in this light as an attempt to depart from Duarte's chanchada past while still maintaining some of the thematic and political concerns he had already raised in *Absolutamente certo!*. The action of *O pagador* takes place in a Brazilian city, but the location has moved outside of Rio de Janeiro, the typical setting of chanchadas, and the protagonist now represents the peasant of the rural northeastern interior rather than the urban popular classes. However, his name is Zé do Burro, a similar name to that of the protagonist of the earlier film and reflecting the same everyman status (this time with a rural twist to his nickname indicated by the 'Burro', a farm labour animal, rather than the 'Lino' or linograph machine that Zé do Lino works with in *Absolutamente certo!*).

In addition to the focus on the oppression of the rural working class in the figure of Zé do Burro, the film also shares the use of location shooting in a northeastern Brazilian setting with other Cinema Novo films of the early- to mid-1960s. This approach was certainly not thanks to the producer Osvaldo Massaini of Cinedistri Studios, who suggested casting Mazzaropi, the quintessential chanchada country bumpkin, in the lead role of Zé do Burro (Merten 2004: 124). Massaini was no doubt thinking of the proven box-office draw of Mazzaropi's comedic persona, which had been established already in the early 1950s in the films he starred in for Vera Cruz (at the same time that Anselmo Duarte was working there as an actor). In Duarte's effort to leave behind his past in popular cinema, the rejection of Mazzaropi for the lead role was a key symbolic gesture, while casting newcomer Leonardo Villar would have a considerable impact on the dramatic nature of the role – ultimately depicting Zé do Burro as martyr rather than clown. Here we can consider the divergent form of saudade Duarte represents in his film, distinct from the more folkloric-popular saudade of Mazzaropi's films. Dennison and Shaw explain that Mazzaropi's films represented a 'sense of collective experience' for rural migrants to São Paulo (2007: 150). One key result of the films being produced and consumed as organic to the community of internal migrants is that the emotional orientation towards the rural in Mazzaropi's *oeuvre* was not heterogeneous with respect to the emotion experienced by rural-urban migrants themselves (especially *caipira* migrants from the Central South of Brazil). The nostalgia for the peasant migrant developed in Duarte's *O pagador*, on the other hand, is better categorized as a middle-class saudade for the rural. This more mediated nostalgic discourse can still be found in the late twentieth and early twenty-first centuries in films like Walter Salles's *Central do Brasil* (*Central Station*) ([1998] 1999) and in the 'university' or middle-class versions of Brazilian country music like *forró* and *música sertaneja*. It is not so much a saudade for a rural lifestyle of which the director or actor has any personal experience (which would make for an emotionally homogeneous discourse like that of Mazzaropi's films), but rather the saudade for *an idea* of the rural peasantry and the sense of loss and dissatisfaction that that idea crystallizes in modern-day Brazil. This middle-class saudade places Duarte closer to the primarily middle-class directors of Cinema Novo; however, there are important distinctions between the object of Duarte's saudade and that of *cinemanovistas* like Joaquim Pedro de Andrade, which I will detail further below.

The prominence given to a Brazilian Catholic ethos and narrative tends to distinguish Duarte's film from other Cinema Novo productions as well. When represented in the films of Nelson Pereira dos Santos, Glauber Rocha, Joaquim Pedro de Andrade and others in the 1960s, the Catholic Church and its doctrine are either largely excluded from the narrative or are portrayed unambiguously as a source of alienation or oppression of Brazil's people. Duarte does not go this far, but his representation of popular Catholicism is significantly critical of the Church itself, and also shares a certain anti-Hollywood inspiration with other Cinema Novo works. The director explained that when he visited the Cannes film festival in 1961, there was a lot of advertising for the upcoming Hollywood release of Jesus Christ's story, *King of Kings* (Ray [1961] 2009). His personal reaction to these advertisements was the following: 'Forget this *greatest story of all time*. I wanted a simple and human story [...] I wanted to make my Christ against that of Hollywood' ('Nada de *a maior história de todos os tempos*. Queria uma história simples e humana [...] Queria fazer o meu Cristo contra o de Hollywood') (Merten 2004: 115–16, original emphasis). So in a sense, Duarte, too, was positioning himself as one of the 'peasants of cinema' as Glauber Rocha termed the cinemanovistas. Duarte saw his film as representing a humbler, authentic martyr without the same Hollywood emphasis on big budgets and artificial spectacle. Thus, Duarte's identification with the figure of the common (Catholic) man character, already present in his own role of Zé do Lino in his first film, is reflected this time in his approach to directing.

Nevertheless, the film does not question the very idea of fetishizing a martyr to the same degree that Glauber Rocha does in his various films of the 1960s – rather, Duarte brings along from his Vera Cruz Studios years in the 1950s the (economically impossible) desire to best Hollywood at its own game. Rather than challenging the Christian framework of martyrdom, Duarte wanted to portray a Brazilianized version of the martyred popular saint with his *O pagador de promessas*. It is in the Catholic saudade for such a figure, his own version of a simple carpenter from Nazareth who saves the world, that we find the biggest divide between Duarte and the 1960s generation of Cinema Novo directors. Probably for this reason, Glauber Rocha describes *Absolutamente certo!* as a better film than *O pagador* (2003: 165). Duarte later remarked, with good reason, that Rocha's criticism was intended to distance Duarte himself from the Cinema Novo movement, suggesting he had reached his peak with his directorial debut in the 1950s and thus belonged to a previous era (Merten 2004: 149). As I have outlined here, there are various aspects of *O pagador* that align the work with the Cinema Novo movement, so it is unfair to pretend that it was not connected to that movement stylistically in many ways. On the other hand, Duarte's popular cinema past certainly inflects his approach to portraying the rural and urban poor and working classes, as already seen in my discussion here with the examples of middle-class and Catholic saudades for the rural and the humble, popular martyr. As we shall see, these nostalgic orientations combine to form a fatalist perspective on the destiny of the rural poor, but leave out hope for the future of the urban popular classes.

The film begins with Zé appearing to be praying at a Candomblé (Afro-Brazilian religious) shrine during a traditional rite of divine possession somewhere in the countryside. In the next scene, we see Zé and his wife Rosa (Glória Menezes) begin a journey through the varied rural landscapes of the Recôncavo region surrounding the city of Salvador, Bahia, across the more arid, interior and more tropical, coastal ecosystems. It is immediately clear that there is some kind of religious significance to Zé's journey as he bears an enormous wooden cross on his shoulder, and the viewer will learn that this cross relates to the religious vow or 'promessa' referenced in the film's title. It should be noted that Zé's wife's name, Rosa, suggests that she is meant to represent the common woman of the northeastern interior – indeed, 'Rosa' or the diminutive 'Rosinha' are the names of countless northeastern female characters in Brazilian films and popular songs. In this opening sequence, then, the idea of religious penance or sacrifice is combined with the story of rural-urban migration typical of so many peasants' lives during the twentieth century in Latin America. The female migrant is included in the story, but primarily as a dependent of the male migrant whose desire to go to the city is what drives the migration. The divergent motivations of Zé and Rosa cause strife in their relationship that increases as the film progresses.

The journey to the city passes relatively quickly in terms of screen time, comprised of a montage of different landscapes Zé and Rosa cross as the credits roll for about four minutes. As they enter Salvador and begin to walk down the streets of the old section of the city late at night, other characters associated with the night life of the city begin to be introduced. The couple, with Zé still dragging the cross, walk past Bonitão (Geraldo Del Rey), a man who shortly thereafter is revealed to be the pimp of another character, Marly (Norma Bengell). Bonitão immediately shows a malevolent interest in Zé and Rosa, and proceeds to follow them. Meanwhile, Zé and Rosa arrive at what we now understand to be their destination, the Church of Saint Barbara. The church is closed at this late hour so Zé puts down his cross and decides to wait for the church to open on the enormous staircase leading up to its front doors. This sloped staircase area in front of St. Barbara's Church becomes the primary setting for the film, a transient space in between church and street that also suggests a hierarchy with the church at the pinnacle, due to the fairly steep slope of the staircase. Duarte commented that the space for him was reminiscent of the Odessa steps in Sergei Eisenstein's *Battleship Potemkin* (1925) (Merten 2004: 129). There are editing techniques and plot elements that recall this sequence from Eisenstein's classic as well, such as the police violence against the working class and the montages of close-ups of a diverse array of characters on the staircase in various emotional states. The homage to Eisenstein is another example of Duarte's desire to make international, art cinema with this film.

Returning to the plot, Bonitão soon arrives on the staircase with Zé and Rosa and offers to take Rosa, who is exhausted, to go find a room at the nearest hotel. Zé insists on staying on the staircase, but allows Rosa to go find a room with Bonitão. Zé seems far more interested in his mission to deliver the cross to St. Barbara's Church than in the welfare of his wife, who does not want to sleep outside in the rain. Bonitão then proceeds to make sexual advances on Rosa when he is alone with her on the street, and enters her room at the hotel with her. Rosa's response is somewhat ambiguous; whether she feels more fear or more desire for Bonitão is unclear, though it seems she has betrayed her marital vows. The film suggests that the city's corrupting influence acts immediately upon immigrants, and that only a man of extraordinary faith like Zé, stubbornly committed to his vow, is able to withstand this corruption. As in *Absolutamente certo!*, the protagonist is a common man who stands out because of one extraordinary quality. Zé's extraordinary sacrifice is emphasized here by a close-up on his shoulder, severely bruised and lacerated where he had rested the cross in his pilgrimage. Of course, the imagery of a man carrying a cross over many miles also establishes Zé as a Christ-like figure.

Come morning, Zé meets Olavo (Dionísio Azevedo), the priest of the cathedral, who is interested to see what brings this stranger with his giant wooden cross to the church doors. At this point the hierarchy suggested by the very wide shots of the steep staircase begins to be reflected in the religious differences between Zé (as representative of the Brazilian popular classes) and Olavo (representing the official Catholic Church). Zé explains to Olavo that he prayed to Iansã to heal his sick donkey (*burro*), promising to make a pilgrimage with the giant cross to her church and give his land away to the poor should she grant him his request. In the Afro-Brazilian religion of Candomblé, native to Salvador, the Yoruban *orixá* (goddess or spirit) named Iansã is traditionally identified with the Roman Catholic Saint Barbara; however, official Catholic doctrine does not recognize this association. Thus, Olavo quickly becomes suspicious of what he deems to be Zé's pagan vow (not to mention the rather humble motivation for his prayer), and for this reason the priest does not wish Zé to enter the church with his wooden cross to fulfil his promise. Zé, on the other hand, throughout the film is shown to be such a humble and simple man that he is genuinely perplexed (and gradually becomes frustrated and angry) that Olavo or the Church would question his religious devotion.

This basic difference in religious belief, articulated in a conversation between Zé do Burro and Father Olavo on the steps of the cathedral, establishes the central conflict in the film around which everything else revolves. Duarte, following the script he adapted from a play by Dias Gomes, proceeds to utilize this central conflict as a focal point for analysing the influence of diverse sectors of modern, urban society. The placement of Zé's humble, simple and popular-rural faith at the centre of this urban *mise-en-scène* is the key to understanding the specific manner in which saudade frames Duarte's narrative. The authenticity of the protagonist is established not just by Zé do Burro's simplicity and sincerity, but by the saudade for the rural of the urban population (a saudade, I will argue further below, that is shared by the film's director). The rural protagonist's authenticity, framed by saudade, trumps politics in the film's narrative and posits him as a uniquely ethical subject in this politicized urban environment. By 'politicized' here I do not mean just the presence of electoral/party politics but the fact that everyone else in the film is shown to have ulterior motives, some kind of implicit politics or 'angle' governing their actions. Yet, the purity associated with Zé's uniquely ethical nature does not translate into the power to fulfil his own desires; instead, it rather ironically serves as a blank screen on which the media and others can project their own fantasies and agendas. The fact that this film makes explicit how much is projected onto the rural worker/migrant by other sectors of society singles it out from other Cinema Novo films of the period. For instance, Glauber Rocha's *Deus e o diabo na terra do sol* (*Black God, White Devil*) ([1964] 2010) makes it clear that the cattleherd Manoel (Geraldo Del Rey) has mistakenly projected his fantasies of liberation on various religious and outlaw figures, yet the film does not thematize the manner in which the urban population (certainly including filmmakers) projects its own fantasies of tradition and/or revolution on to the rural worker (more on these projections below). Thus, considered outside the contemporary polemics of what constituted 'New Cinema' at the time, we can see some innovative approaches in *O pagador de promessas* – even as the film also maintains some typically melancholy emotional dynamics vis-à-vis the common rural man and woman (dynamics that no Cinema Novo film of this first phase escapes).

To clarify the point of how Zé do Burro serves as blank screen for the fantasies of the urban populace, let us consider the manner in which he is seen and represented by the various sectors of society or 'interest groups' characterized in the film. One such group mentioned briefly above is the media, which initially shows up on the scene with print journalists but later television reporters as well. The latter are less prominent in the film, but recall the *Absolutamente certo!* theme of television's exploitation of the common man and also serve to mirror the work of the filmmaker. Yet, the contrast between the TV journalists' inability to get any comment from Zé do Burro and the ability of cinema to capture his entire story arc is telling, suggesting a clear limitation to the amount of self-reflection about cinema in the narrative. Nevertheless, as noted above there is so much thematization of fantasies projected onto the peasant in this film that, intentionally or not, the filmic text begs the question of how the filmmaker might be doing so as well (more on this later).

The print journalists are given the most screen time in the film, particularly one reporter played by Othon Bastos. This journalist sets out to interview Zé do Burro with the understanding that his editor wants 'sensationalist journalism' – thus, in his interview on the church steps with Zé he translates everything the pilgrim says into the political polemics of the day with respect to the rural worker. The resulting headline in the *Jornal da Ba…* (probably *Bahia*, the title is truncated by someone's head in the shot of someone reading it) shouts 'NEW "CHRIST" PREACHES THE REVOLUTION: Saint or Demon?' ('NOVO "CRISTO" PREGA A REVOLUÇÃO: Santo ou Demônio?'). The article goes on to detail how Zé do Burro supposedly walked 'seven leagues carrying the cross for agrarian reform' and 'is against the exploitation of man by man'. By contrast with Zé's actual confessed motivation of fulfilling a promise to St. Barbara for curing his donkey, the media manipulation of the rural worker's perspective is highlighted. The reporter additionally suggests to Zé do Burro that he enter into politics and that he will help him do so, doubly emphasizing the politicized, tendential nature of the media's perspective – but the end result of this manipulation does not succeed in bringing Zé himself into electoral politics; instead, it makes him feel all the more alienated.

The impact of the newspaper headlines regarding Zé do Burro draws the attention of several other groups and moves them to action. The second group I will consider represents the urban, primarily Afro-Brazilian popular classes of Salvador. The man that is first shown reading the newspaper article about Zé do Burro is Coca (Antônio Pitanga), the leader of a group of *capoeiristas* or Brazilian martial art/dance practitioners. Coca seems attracted to the revolutionary rhetoric and exhorts his fellow capoeiristas to go meet Zé at the Church of Saint Barbara. Thus, we see that the media representation of Zé serves to gain him allies amongst the urban popular classes, despite the fact that he does nothing himself to encourage such an alliance. Beyond the media representation, though, there is real common ground for class solidarity here in the sense that both the capoeiristas and Zé, like the urban and rural popular classes as a whole, are largely excluded from the structures of power in the city. A group of females representing the popular classes are the *baianas* or *mães-de-santo* who have already met Zé by this point of the film since they sell food in the area. They also perform religious rites in the environs of the cathedral like washing the cathedral staircase, a very traditional ritual akin to that performed annually at the Church of Nosso Senhor do Bonfim in the same city. These *mães* and *filhas-de-santo* are Afro-Brazilian women who are practitioners of Candomblé and thus share the belief with Zé do Burro's popular Catholicism that St. Barbara is identical with the orixá called Iansã. They are also shown very clearly to be excluded from the church by the priest because of their pagan religious beliefs, just like Zé do Burro. Tia (Maria Conceição), a leader of the local Candomblé *terreiro* or religious centre, repeatedly suggests to Zé that he bring his cross to her terreiro and thus fulfil his vow to St. Barbara at an alternative shrine. Zé, however, stubbornly insists that it is 'not the same' and that he must enter the church with the cross exactly as he had vowed to do. Despite the fact that Zé tends to solipsistically isolate himself in the particularity of his vow (part and parcel of the film's portrayal of his authentically ethical, apolitical stance), the urban working class of Salvador recognizes a commonality with him through the help of the media framing of his story and the church's exclusion of him as an apostate. Zé becomes a catalyst for this sector of society to fight against the discrimination of the powers that be, especially the Catholic Church but also the Brazilian state as represented by the police (though the latter are relatively slow to involve themselves in the conflict between Zé and Olavo the priest).

The third and final group I will consider that projects their own narrative onto Zé do Burro is the institution of the Catholic Church. Olavo, the priest of the St. Barbara cathedral, fairly quickly draws the conclusion that Zé do Burro's religious beliefs and vow to St. Barbara are heretical. But the Church hierarchy responds not to Olavo's immediate religious condemnation, but to the media coverage and resultant publicity that Zé do Burro receives. The Church's measured political response to Zé's demand to enter the church can best be understood in the context of the Second Vatican Council, which began in the same year that this film was released. As epitomized by Vatican II, in the early- to mid-1960s the Church was involved in a reformation of its relationship to modern society and to the laity and thus understandably would not want to be viewed as martyring a religious pilgrim due to rigid insistence on its own doctrine. Thus, the Church hierarchy projects its anxieties about distancing itself from the laity onto Zé and his grassroots spirituality. The Monsignor (Carlos Torres) holds a meeting with the church leadership and decides that he must intervene in the situation personally because it must be handled very delicately. After meeting with Olavo in the church in order to explain the 'political aspect of the case' to him, he goes outside to publicly offer reconciliation to Zé, should he choose to renounce his pagan vow and replace it with a vow deemed orthodox by the Church. However, Zé insists that only St. Barbara herself can release him from his vow and so he refuses the offer of reconciliation. This rejection confirms Zé's apostate status in the eyes of the church and the Monsignor feels that he is now politically safe, since he has made a public effort to accommodate the laity yet has stood firm on church doctrine regarding the incompatibility of Catholicism and Candomblé.

In the end, despite Duarte's efforts to distance himself from his past in popular cinema, the core of *O pagador*'s story is very similar to *Absolutamente certo!* – the common man with the heart of gold tries to resist the forces of corruption in modern Brazilian society. This popular hero is the major focus of Duarte's saudade, a sort of humble exception that proves the rule and thereby serves to criticize the status quo. The key distinction is of course that Duarte introduces the rural worker in his second film, whom he makes the object of a far more melancholy saudade. The overall temporal structure of saudade in the narrative of this later film, incorporating various levels of urban fantasy and desire projected onto the peasant protagonist, corresponds to the form of nostalgia Hutcheon describes as a 'complex projection' in which 'the invocation of a partial, idealized history merges with a dissatisfaction with the present' (2000: 195). Hutcheon explains further, citing Mikhail Bakhtin's notion of 'historical inversion', that this complex nostalgic projection involves a specific set of attitudes towards past and present:

> The simple, pure, ordered, easy, beautiful or harmonious past is constructed (and then experienced emotionally) in conjunction with the present – which, in turn, is constructed as complicated, contaminated, anarchic, difficult, ugly, and confrontational.
>
> (2000: 195)

In light of the discussion of the film up to this point, it should not be difficult to see how Zé do Burro can be seen as representing a simple, pure past thrown into the midst of a complicated, contaminated, confrontational present in the form of the modern city of Salvador. In this sense, *O pagador* shares a certain romanticism regarding the rural with Rocha's *Deus e diabo na terra do sol*. In a discussion of Rocha's film, Tolentino (2001) describes Rocha's 'romantic view of the Brazilian peasant' as stemming from an appreciation of

> his values, loyalties, respect for hierarchy and disposition to face a challenge, unquestioning, unto death. (It was not very different from that which the parties of the left expected from their militants.) [...] [Tolentino continues, arguing more broadly that Rocha's film] takes the northeastern sertão as a metaphor for the authentically Brazilian, resituating the rural as the root of genuinely national culture in opposition to the urban and modern, tarnished by imported elements.
>
> (2000: 198)

The character of Zé do Burro encapsulates a similar respect on Anselmo Duarte's part for the fortitude, faith and authentic, folkloric Brazilianness of the rural worker. However, Duarte is both more pessimistic about the rural worker and more optimistic about the urban popular classes than Rocha. To some degree, Duarte's film shares with earlier 'nordestern' (Brazilian Western) films like *O cangaceiro* (*The Bandit*) (Barreto, [1953] 2011) an emphasis on the backwards nature of the northeastern interior, a region that despite its folkloric authenticity is portrayed in these films as uncivilized and thus belonging far more to Brazil's past than its future. On the other hand, Rocha portrays the rural worker as a proto-revolutionary subject and does not feature the urban working class as protagonists of his films of the 1960s.

Therein lies a key distinction between the two filmmakers, as Duarte portrays the urban proletariat with far more agency than the peasantry in his film – and an immediate agency rather than a potential one as suggested in Rocha's work regarding the peasantry. In fact, in both of Duarte's films discussed here, the urban everyman is successful in his resistance to the powers that be, be it Zé do Lino with the help of colleagues and friends, defeating those who wish to exploit his celebrity status, or be it the urban-popular masses who bear the martyred Zé do Burro into the church after he fails to breach this barrier on his own. On the other hand, the actions of the two women in the two Zé's lives at the end of both films underline not only the change in genre but the fatalism regarding the rural popular classes. Gina, a working-class woman, participates in Zé do Lino's final triumph and clearly will marry him – indeed Gina's mother Bela (Dercy Gonçalves) hams for the cameras of the game show and says it is 'Absolutely Correct!' that they are getting married. Yet, Rosa stands tragically alone outside the cathedral after her husband's death, leaving the *capoeiristas* and other members of the urban popular classes to carry Zé do Burro on his cross over the threshold of the church entrance, to the slow, insistent rhythm of a berimbau.

Prefiguring Postmodern Emotion in Film: *Macunaíma* and Reflective, Ironic Saudade

Joaquim Pedro de Andrade's *Macunaíma* is in its very origins a different kind of film than Anselmo Duarte's *O pagador*, since the former is based on a rather fantastical modernist novel written by Mário de Andrade in 1928. Various critics have noted that the 1968 film is actually more realist than the novel, in the sense that the protagonist himself does not have magical powers and is not immortal. Yet, the film's plot is far from realist and includes many representations of supernatural myths, folklore and religious rites like the original text. In this sardonic film, one searches in vain for any saudade like that seen in Duarte's and others' films for the peasant, the rural migrant or the urban popular classes. The saudade in Andrade's film, I will argue, works on a different level than that of the diegesis. It should be understood as a reflective saudade in the sense that it works on two levels, allowing for an acerbic look at Brazilian society on the level of the basic diegesis, while demonstrating a nostalgic longing for Brazilian art and cultural production of the past that Andrade believes is necessary to construct Brazil's future, or at least the future of Brazilian cinema.

The notion of reflective saudade can be best understood with reference to Boym's theory of restorative and reflective nostalgias. For Boym (2001), restorative nostalgia is associated with ethno-nationalist and/or exclusive, traditionalist imaginaries of the lost home or homeland.

On the other hand, reflective nostalgia is characterized by a more ambivalent longing for the lost home/era that can be critical of its flaws and focuses more on the potentialities of what this home 'could have been' rather than imagining it as an actual ideal place that one must return to or reconstruct, as restorative nostalgia does. Boym tends to associate reflective nostalgia with political exiles and their conflicted relationship with their native country. The state of exile certainly reflects the experience of many Cinema Novo directors, who were at various times imprisoned or exiled from Brazil and whose films were heavily censored by the military regime, especially after 1968. Andrade himself was imprisoned for several days shortly before he started filming *Macunaíma*, and along with other dissident artists could be described as experiencing a state of internal exile, so it is not surprising that we should see a form of reflective nostalgia in his work.

In addition to this reflective nostalgia, *Macunaíma* incorporates a certain level of irony that is inherent to the Tropicalist aesthetic of the late 1960s. Tropicalist artists in cinema, popular music and the visual arts often were motivated by an ironic nostalgia, a nostalgia in quotation marks, such as the reappropriation of Carmen Miranda as a representative of Brazilian popular culture. This ironic nostalgia for kitschy or outmoded art and popular culture anticipates a common affective blend in the postmodern era, as described by Hutcheon. She notes that '[i]n the postmodern [...] nostalgia itself gets both called up, exploited, and ironized', and this irony serves to make nostalgia 'palatable' (2000: 205, 207). The main point to be grasped from these various theories of nostalgia when one considers *Macunaíma* is that neither self-reflection nor irony signals the absence of saudade, nor do they really oppose it; indeed, the two work hand-in-hand with this emotion in Joaquim Pedro de Andrade's seminal film.

Macunaíma begins in an impoverished rural setting described by Xavier as 'a symbolically "rural Brazil" living in a time after that of the autochthonous tribe, despite keeping some traces of its material culture, its relation with nature, and its mythology' (1997: 134). This symbolic rurality with tribal vestiges manifests itself in the first image of the protagonist Macunaíma, when he is born on the dirt floor of a longhouse made of leaves. His family seems to live a subsistence lifestyle somewhere in the rainforest. The absurdist and often fantastical tone of the film, influenced by the even more fantastical novel it is based on, reveals itself here at the start in the fact that the baby Macunaíma is played by the fully grown, famous chanchada actor Grande Otelo. Otelo plays the part of man-child to great comic effect, always exaggerating his immaturity with awkward movements and making good use of his decades of training as a star in the chanchada heyday of the 1940s and 1950s.

Indeed, as Dennison and Shaw note, Macunaíma as a character is similar to the anti-heroes of the chanchada, precisely the kind of slapstick characters Grande Otelo himself would often play (2004: 138). The same authors also point out that Otelo and Oscarito (for whom Otelo often served as sidekick in a famous black-white comedic duo) were the 'embodiment of the pervasive ethos of *malandragem* on screen, an unofficial tenet of Brazilian popular identity' (Dennison and Shaw 2007: 139). 'Malandragem' refers to behaviour associated with a *malandro* or hustler/trickster. I am in agreement with Xavier (1997: 150) that

Macunaíma as a whole is critical of malandragem, since Macunaíma's selfishness and laziness are shown to be primarily damaging to himself and his family over the long term. The fact that Andrade's film attacks the ethos of the malandro is actually one of its biggest critiques of popular cinema in Brazil of the previous three decades. This critique stands the test of time, and was applicable to Brazilian cinema in both democratic and authoritarian eras. If Brazil was consuming itself as Andrade's film suggests, the individualist malandro was not a hero who could help the Brazilian people escape a vicious cycle of exploitation. Thus, the casting of Grande Otelo and the call-backs to chanchada are a form of saudade, but very much a reflective, critical saudade.

Various critics have analysed the scene in which Macunaíma and his family approach a fountain and discover that the water has magical properties that change Macunaíma's race from black to white. This scene occurs after they have already become rural migrants, driven out of their isolated rural home by starvation to look for work elsewhere. The scene's origins go back to the source novel and the author Mário de Andrade's rendition of an indigenous folk tale explaining how human beings ended up with different skin colours. Critics such as Stam (1997) have tended to focus on the racial implications of the scene, which make explicit a prejudice against black/dark skin colour in Brazilian society. Yet, the connection between the racial transformation in the image and the music the audience hears on the soundtrack has yet to be analysed as a commentary on the dependency of the Brazilian film industry. As Macunaíma approaches the magical fountain in the middle of a dry plain, a song called 'Sob uma cascata' ('Under a Waterfall') sung by Francisco Alves begins to play on the soundtrack. Alves was a famous singer who was prominently featured in early chanchadas; thus, his voice nostalgically evokes that era of Brazilian cinema. Johnson (1984a: 32) notes that Alves's song is actually the Brazilian version of a North American song called 'By a Waterfall' (Irving Kahal and Sammy Fain) featured in Lloyd Bacon's famous musical *Footlight Parade* ([1933] 2006).

The saudade here for the chanchada, emphasized all the more by the presence of the famous chanchada star Grande Otelo in the scene, is ironic due to the racial overtones supplied by the magical fountain. The reference to chanchadas and their often extremely close relationship with Hollywood films, tied to a message about latent popular belief in white superiority, serves to criticize a propensity of Brazilian cinema to want to be something it is not, to copy supposedly superior foreign models (from 'white' North Atlantic nations – especially the United States in the case of popular cinema). The subtext of the music in this scene can be further teased out in a larger historical context. From the perspective of Brazil as a dependent nation in the world economy, chanchadas were part of the national film industry's imperfect attempt to copy the European and then North American, First-World aesthetic models, with roots as far back as the whitening ideologies under slavery (nineteenth century) and the First Republic (1889–1930). The Tropicalist aesthetic guiding the film leads the director to *highlight* the absurdity of the Third-World copy and use its difference as a fulcrum for creativity and aesthetic transformation, rather than shamefully rejecting it as a cultural-nationalist approach would.

Therein lies the Tropicalist version of saudade, more in line with the combination of irony and nostalgia that we see in the postmodern as described by Hutcheon. Grande Otelo and the chanchada genre are not simply rejected by the film; there is a certain level of bemused attachment and affection for this history. When Macunaíma becomes a white, non-chanchada actor he is not shown to be an improved person in any way. There is a message here that goes something like this: for all its attempts to be like the Hollywood musical, to 'whiten' itself, the Brazilian musical comedy had some uniquely popular-national elements that really are the only thing worth being nostalgic for in the genre. This message originates in a reflective saudade that teases out the important lessons of what is very much Brazilian in past national popular cinema, but could also be a cultural and/or political dead end if not renovated.

After this scene with the magical fountain, the white actor Paulo José plays Macunaíma for the rest of the film, but he continues very much in the same grand comic vein as Otelo in terms of his acting style. The scene immediately following the fountain scene begins the reference to specific, historical populations of migrant workers. Macunaíma, his brothers and friend Iriqui (Maria do Rosário) are shown being dropped off on the furthest outskirts of Brasília by a *pau-de-arara* (migrant worker truck, literally 'macaw branch' after the rows of benches crammed into the truck beds for migrants to sit on). Thus, the characters are placed in the same position as the largely northeastern migrant construction workers who built the city of Brasília, called *candangos*. It should be recalled that this film was released only nine years after the foundation of Brasília as a city and as the nation's capital, so candangos were continuing to pour in to work on the many construction projects still ongoing. The reference to real, historical migration here recalls Joaquim Pedro de Andrade's previous film, a documentary about the city called *Brasília: Contradições de uma cidade nova* (*Brasília: Contradictions of a New City*) ([1967] 2006). This film was deemed too critical of the social and political situation in the city and was banned from being released by the military regime, which ultimately would also imprison Andrade for several days immediately prior to beginning the production of *Macunaíma*. *Brasília* films the central part of the city, designed as a utopian community (by architect Oscar Niemeyer) that provides a pleasing built space for the government bureaucrats and other generally middle-class residents. But shortly thereafter the film covers a strike at the university to protest government intervention in education and hiring, and then travels out to the previously invisible satellite communities of candangos, many of whom are forced to live in *favelas* (slums) on the outskirts while they work to build up the centre of the city. The transition from rural to urban lifestyle appears quite easy for the lucky Macunaíma, who seems to survive fairly well in the city for a time with the help of his wife, Cy. But Macunaíma's brothers Maanape (Rodolfo Arena) and Jiguê (Milton Gonçalves) end up in a favela, like many if not most poor migrants represented in *Brasília*.

The female member of the group, Iriqui, follows a different path, ending up in a brothel in Brasília's red-light district. Along with the previous, somewhat documentarian scene of migrants being dropped off at the edge of the city, we get a hint here of what might be a typical prospect of a young, poor woman arriving in the city with nothing but the clothes on her back (and no help from the men in Macunaíma's family). Iriqui's involvement in prostitution is subtly tied to commodification and consumerism in general in the city during her final scene in the film, when she is walking towards the centre of Brasília, across the street from some large billboards. She is captured in a medium close-up with the camera tilted upwards, revealing the billboards behind her advertising a variety of things including Ypiranga-brand house paint, toothpaste and a sale at a men's clothing store called 'Sua Majestade' ('Your Majesty'). One additional billboard is plastered with what seems to be a public service announcement regarding the dangers of driving while colour blind.

A closer analysis of these ads in relation to each other, to Iriqui and the voice-over about her, and to the scene with the magical fountain a few minutes before, can provide us with some revelations about the connections between the humble rural origins of Macunaíma and the seemingly urbane, more civilized environs of the capital city. These hidden connections between diverse regions of the country tie in to a larger narrative arc about national cultural characteristics (such as malandragem mentioned above) that Andrade suggests should be left behind with the death of Macunaíma at the film's close. The director drives home the point that saudade for certain aspects of Brazilian popular culture or cinema does not imply an acceptance of all the sexist, racist, classist and other prejudicial baggage to be found in Brazil's social history. Firstly, the hypersexualized nature of Macunaíma and the dominance of male desire in a patriarchal society are given further resonance by these billboard ads. As the narrator tells us that Iriqui finds work in a brothel, we see the words 'Everything for men, boys' ('Tudo por homens, rapazes') in the clothing ad and the following suggestive tagline in the toothpaste ad: 'Crazy flavor – a brilliant explosion in your mouth' ('Sabor de loucura – uma explosão brilhante em tua boca'). Male dominance, the objectification of the female body and the obsession with sex already suggested before the family has fully arrived in the city are now taken to even greater heights through the power of the mass consumer media. We can recognize that, on closer inspection, these cultural factors differ between rural and urban spaces only by degree, not quality. Iriqui herself, a new arrival to the city, already seems successfully interpellated by the call of commodified and normatively gendered sexuality in the ads, since she stares directly into the faces of the toothpaste models and smiles back at them. There have indeed already been some suggestions in the film that the border between rural and urban is fairly porous, since Iriqui is already wearing a modern-looking, red cocktail dress while living in Macunaíma's rural home.

A closer analysis of the colour-coded message of the toothpaste ad along with the colour blindness public service announcement reveals the urban amplification and commodification of racial prejudice that we have already witnessed in rural culture/folklore. The text of the PSA reads like a concretist poem, in that the graphic depiction of the text is part of the message (Figure 5). In the text from the billboard, everything appears as black and white except for two inverted colour words – the word 'green' is in red font, and the word 'red' in green.

I I	se você	[if you
I O I	confunde	confuse
I O I	verde com	green with
I I	vermelho	red
	seu futuro	your future
	é	is
	negro	black]

Figure 5: Schematic depiction of billboard with public service announcement in *Macunaíma*.

The image on the far left is a simplification of the somewhat stylized, black-and-white images of traffic lights on the same side of the billboard. The announcement clearly demands that its audience focus on the differentiation of colours in a more literal, visual sense. The theme of switching or confusing colours easily brings to mind the recent scene where one character's skin colour has switched from black to white. But the final word 'black' in this ad-poem also has a clearly figurative connotation that is very negative. Blackness is associated here with ill fortune, danger and even death (presumably in a traffic accident). Just as in the magical fountain scene all of the characters wanted to avoid blackness in terms of their skin colour, here blackness is held out as an ill fate if one does not take precautions regarding a visual deficiency. What had been associated with traditional, rural culture or an older era of popular cinema in the previous scene is now fully embedded in the modern, urban milieu – to such an extent that it is featured not only in a glossy ad but in the 'erudite' format of avant-garde poetry.

Turning back to the neighbouring billboards with toothpaste ads, it should be clarified that there are two of them, one with a man and one with the woman. The entire space from top to bottom of the billboards is filled with the man' and woman's head, respectively, and both are smiling widely to reveal their brilliant, white teeth. Both are also racially very white, that is, Euro-Brazilians with no apparent hint of admixture from Brazil's large populations of indigenous or African descent (the woman is blond). If we recall that the tagline repeated on both these billboards references a 'brilliant explosion in your mouth', it is quite clear that the ads are selling whiteness and that the colour is associated with cleanliness, beauty, happiness and even sexual fulfilment. The contrast with the connotations of blackness is plain to see in the neighbouring billboard warning of a black future, but again these associations should be placed in dialogue with the very recent racial transformation of Macunaíma. Clearly the same extremely positive associations with whiteness and extremely negative ones with blackness are operative in both the most rural of popular culture and the most urbane, middle-class settings. Racial prejudice, and the whitening aesthetic, cannot be placed purely in the cinematic past or in a rural space marked as backward – they remain very much as a subtext of everyday life in Brazil's most modern city.

Saudade is next referenced in the film when Macunaíma suffers the death of his wife Cy, who accidentally explodes herself and Macunaíma Jr. (Grande Otelo again) with a bomb she had planned on using in a terrorist attack. Macunaíma, who has drunk himself into a stupor and somehow ended up alone on a deserted beach, pathetically sings to himself the Mário de Andrade song 'Mundu sarará', taken directly from a song Macunaíma sings to himself in the novel. The song combines an ambiguous saudade for childhood memories mixed with adult melancholy. The saudade is again ironized by the image – a large amount of bird guano drops on Macunaíma's face and he becomes absurdly pathetic, looking up to find that a vulture in the palm tree above is defecating on him, but he is too drunk to move away. Shortly thereafter Macunaíma is abducted from this beach by three beautiful, young women led by an older woman who decides that he must be a wealthy castaway. The forró classic 'Respeita Januário' ('Respect Januário') by Luiz Gonzaga and Humberto Teixeira enters the soundtrack at this point, which references the travels of the migrant to find success in the big city and then to return to his home. In the song, the singer Luiz returns to discover that in his native region they think he is now too big for his britches and needs to remember where he came from, respecting his father Januário and the rural tradition/popular culture associated with him. With Macunaíma's story there is a suggestion that perhaps he too, has received his comeuppance, but even before returning home. Though he is a migrant with some similarities in his story of migration to those of musician Luiz Gonzaga and other northeasterners, the irony of the song is that the idea of 'respect' (and some notion of the appreciation of one's forebears and their traditions) is completely foreign to Macunaíma. While Gonzaga by writing the song and performing it with his own father belies the suggestion that he has lost his respect for the past, Macunaíma perfectly fits the stereotype of an arrogant man who has left his humble place of birth and family and no longer gives them a moment of thought. The real popular culture of migrant workers, and their saudade for their home region, is inserted into the narrative in order to criticize Macunaíma, more malandro than migrant worker himself.

Providing further evidence of saudade for the chanchada in Andrade's film, Johnson (1984a: 32–33) notes that the director recreates a shot from the film *Carnaval Atlântida* (Burle, [1952] 2007) when Macunaíma is captured with a net by Wenceslau's wife (the original shot is of Oscarito, playing Professor Xenofontes, who throws a net over a thug chasing him). *Carnaval Atlântida* is a chanchada about the making of a film and the conflict that arises over the plot composition between erudite, classical Greek culture (as represented by Professor Xenofontes) and popular Brazilian culture (carnival/chanchada) as supported by Grande Otelo, who plays an unnamed assistant in the Atlântida Studios. This chanchada evokes a battle between elite and popular but purely on the level of cultural production in the 'film within the film' – and ultimately Brazilian popular culture wins the day with a very carnivalesque musical number for the grand finale. In Joaquim Pedro de Andrade's scene from *Macunaíma* at the house of the industrialist Wenceslau Pietro Pietra, that battle is being carried out to a grotesque extreme between a cannibalist elite devouring their own country and Macunaíma, who resists them and kills Pietra in his own cannibalist stew.

The concept of a pre-existing social conflict that remains unresolved and has become more aggressive and violent can also be found in the disjunction between the love song 'Arranha-céu' ('Skyscraper') and the sequence in which Macunaíma and Cy first meet. After Macunaíma first makes advances on her in a parking garage, Cy, a female urban guerrilla, violently beats him into submission. However Jiguê then knocks her unconscious with a block of concrete, and Macunaíma is able to subdue her. Cy is protected by a magical amulet called a *muiraquitã* that allows her to recover quickly from her injury and so she starts to run away, but suddenly decides to kiss Macunaíma after calling him a 'pervert' ('seu safado'), thereafter having sex with him (or 'playing' ['brincando'] as Macunaíma always calls sexual relations). When they begin to kiss, Sílvio Caldas's melancholy old love song 'Arranha-céu' ('Skyscraper') plays on the soundtrack, performed in the same sentimental vein as 'Sob uma cascata' (from the magical fountain scene) and likewise an oldie from the 1930s.

This violent and erotic scene between Cy and Macunaíma, along with the larger narrative context of the film, serves to dramatically reinterpret the lyrics to Caldas's classic in four major ways. Firstly, the original song focuses on unrequited love in a more traditional sense of passive rejection, but in the film Cy rejects Macunaíma by beating him senseless and he and his brother respond with brutal violence in order to subdue her. Secondly, 'Arranha-céu' makes reference to an urban context and the hoped-for chance of laying eyes on the singer's beloved in a certain elevator. In the sequence of scenes where the song appears on the film's soundtrack, Macunaíma and Cy have a fight scene followed by a love scene that takes place on a car elevator, beautifully choreographed utilizing various camera positions on and off of the rising and falling elevator platform. Thirdly, the song also notes the combined visual impact and duplicity of advertising in the city, which, as discussed above, was highlighted in the initial Brasília *mise-en-scène* focused on Iriqui (the previous girlfriend of Macunaíma) and the billboards behind her signifying the commodification of sexual desire and racial/colour stereotypes in the modern city. Fourthly and finally, the final verse of 'Arranha-céu' foreshadows the fact that eventually Macunaíma will wake up alone without Cy, sorely missing her till the last moments of the film. Thus the original song from 1937 was a fairly modern look at saudade for a lost love in a big city, while the connotations added to it as part of *Macunaíma*'s soundtrack tend to heighten and exaggerate what was initially either implicit or far more subtly framed regarding the conflict between one man and one woman's desires. A nostalgic song choice thereby serves to emphasize both historically enduring problems in sexual relationships and some seemingly anarchic changes that are taking place in the context of increasing involvement of women in public life under a repressive dictatorship.

Like the singer of 'A volta da asa branca' ('Return of the White Wing') (Luiz Gonzaga and Zé Dantas), Macunaíma ultimately returns to his home in the country *as if* he were a nostalgic migrant worker. The irony is that, unlike in 'A volta da asa branca', there is nothing in particular to be nostalgic for, and the modern, urban accoutrements that he has acquired as trophies have little or no use value in his place of birth. This rural space is perhaps even more uninviting than before, and to drive this point home the region literally eats him alive in the final scene of the film. However, Andrade does utilize popular music again to set a nostalgic tone when Macunaíma and family first arrive back at the 'old farmland' ('roçado velho'). The song 'Paisagens da minha terra' ('Landscapes of My Country') by Lamartine Babo is heard when the brothers and new friend Princesa approach the ruins of the old longhouse. This song is from the same era of the early chanchadas when 'Sob uma cascata' (discussed above) was recorded and is performed by the same artist, Francisco Alves. It again nostalgically evokes the cinematic and popular-musical history of the earliest years of the sound era of Brazilian film, but this time the lyrics of the song itself are quite saudoso (filled with saudade). They connect a melancholy feeling of solitude with nature, and suggest that the singer sees echoes of his own lost love in the natural environment.

The theme of solitude is correspondingly driven home in the diegesis first by the fact that the family is completely alone again at their old longhouse in the jungle, and then by Macunaíma's self-isolating behaviour of extreme laziness, which causes his brothers and last girlfriend Princesa to desert him. But Macunaíma's own saudade for Cy is also emphasized at this point in the film – in fact, he talks so much about his longing for the deceased Cy that he ignores Princesa's sexual advances and this helps to push her away. Macunaíma speaks fondly of Cy and explains that she now lives up in a constellation in the sky, a reference to Cy's magical end in the original novel and one that, like the song 'Paisagens da minha terra', reflects man's frustrated desire in the natural environment. It could be said that the only thing that really defines Macunaíma's character at this point in the film besides utter laziness is his saudade – but this nostalgic longing is of a kind that is inverted from the usual rural-urban migrant narrative. Instead of longing to return to the beautiful countryside and marry the woman waiting for him there (as does the singer of 'A volta da asa branca' and the earlier song 'Asa branca'), Macunaíma has returned to the country and longs for the woman who represents, like the city of Brasília itself, the most modern, urban face of Brazil. This lack of rootedness in his place of origin is foreshadowed early in the film when Macunaíma sings 'For a father I had exile' ('Tive por pai o desterro'), a line from the song 'Mandu sarará' featured in the original novel (M. de Andrade [1928] 1988: 68). Macunaíma's exilic state of being forecloses any possibility of homecoming on an emotional level, reflecting Joaquim Pedro de Andrade's belief that Brazil's economic dependency (and lack of democracy) would make difficult the resolution of 'sentimental problems' derived from uneven development (Johnson 1984a: 17–18). The massive displacement of subsistence farmers and rural workers encapsulated in the figure of Macunaíma created many sentimental problems, one of the most prominent among them being saudade for the home region and those left behind there; on the other hand this populational shift also left isolated rural workers pining for the perceived opportunities in the metropolises of Brasília, São Paulo and Rio de Janeiro. At various points and from various voices in the filmic text of *Macunaíma*, Andrade is able to represent these popular sentiments as pointing to structural economic and political problems that the country was far from resolving.

Conclusion: Two Popular/Avant-Garde Dialectics at a Standstill

At the close of the 1960s, Glauber Rocha and fellow Cinema Novo directors were beginning to think about the end of the movement they had started, or at least to consider another way forward. In 'From the Sequoias to the Palm Trees' ('Das sequóias às palmeiras') (1970), Rocha chose to think the way forward in the language developed by the film *Macunaíma*:

> It is necessary that the fire devour Cinema Novo like Iara devours Macunaíma. Yet, before being devoured Cinema Novo should devour the Brazilian market [...], should devour the foolishness and snobbery of our intellectuals [...] (É necessário que o fogo devore o *cinema novo* como a Yara devora Macunaíma. Porém, antes de ser devorado o *cinema novo* deve devorar o mercado brasileiro [...], deve devorar a tolice e o *snobismo* de nossos intelectuais [...]).
>
> (2004: 235, original emphasis)

Iara (or Yara) is the mythical water creature that eats Macunaíma alive in the final scene of the film. Here she is portrayed as a force of renewal and Macunaíma is an icon of the Cinema Novo movement, which will itself be consumed only 'to be reborn from its ashes' in some new form (2004: 235). Rocha's concerns about snobbery and capturing the Brazilian market in 1970 echo the more crowd-pleasing impulse behind *Macunaíma* released the previous year, but they are also a photographic negative of Anselmo Duarte's ideological and aesthetic path as a filmmaker a decade earlier. *Absolutamente certo!* was an innovative chanchada designed for success at the box office while, stylistically speaking, *O pagador de promessas* was much more concerned with what the 'snobs' of cinema would think, and would receive their applause in the form of a Palme d'Or. Yet, the film was undeniably still marked by Duarte's roots in popular cinema as explained above. Thus, we can consider *O pagador* and *Macunaíma* as something like snapshots of inverted historical trajectories, or what Walter Benjamin (1999) would have called 'dialectics at a standstill'. The earlier film is evidence of the transition from popular cinema and the chanchada into the era of Cinema Novo's avant-garde, guerrilla cinema. The later one is evidence of the *cinemanovistas*' realization that perhaps the baby (or Macunaimic man-child?) had been thrown out with the bathwater. That is, a reflective saudade for popular cinema in *Macunaíma* revealed that its entertainment value and roots in the real popular culture of Brazil were something that, if skilfully retrieved from the dustbin of cinematic history, could again enliven and enrich Brazilian film. The result over the following decade or so would be some great works by Cinema Novo directors and the next generation of filmmakers that were also huge box-office successes, such as Carlos Diegues's *Xica da Silva* ([1976] 2014) and *Bye Bye Brasil* ([1978] 2007) as well as Bruno Barreto's *Dona Flor e seus dois maridos* (*Dona Flor and her Two Husbands*) ([1976] 2008).

Chapter 4

Cinematic Visions of Brazilian TV on the Road and in the Clouds

Film scholars have noted the increasing importance of the road movie in Brazilian and Argentine cinema since the 1990s (Bayman and Pinazza 2013; Brandellero 2013; Pinazza 2015) and the continuing relevance of the genre internationally (Orgeron 2008). This chapter analyses a classic Brazilian road movie, *Bye Bye Brasil* (Diegues [1978] 2007), along with an early twenty-first-century example of the genre, *O caminho das nuvens* (*The Middle of the World*) (Amorim [2003] 2004) in order to trace representations of saudade and the related mediatization of popular culture over the time period that separates the two films. According to Orgeron, important road movie directors like Wim Wenders make use of the road as setting to take characters out of their everyday lives and thus to provide a slower, more careful focus on their psychology and emotions, their relationships with others, their personal pasts and their potential futures. In broader terms, the same author also describes the road film as 'a genre that appears to move forward, though always longs for some mythic past' and which comprises part of 'a longstanding tradition that posits a hopeless and lamentable mobility in an effort to eulogize or find stability' (Orgeron 2008: 2, 5). In this light, we can see that, as a genre, there are elements of the road movie (and to some extent even of the cinematic form itself) regarding a longing for homecoming, stability and a mythic past that resonate deeply with the emotion of saudade. Amorim's film chooses the bicycle as means of transportation and thus clearly follows in the vein of Wenders to slow down the lives of his characters, in this case focusing on a story of rural-urban migration in the early 2000s that has roots going well back into the previous century. In its fetishism of an imagined *Brasil arcaico* (or 'archaic' Brazil, in director Carlos 'Cacá' Diegues's words), *Bye Bye Brasil* very much paints a picture of a mythic past in the road movie tradition, one fast disappearing in the rear-view mirror. Amorim's work tends to question romanticizing such a past even as it is evoked, subtly demythologizing the working-class father's patriarchal dream of supporting his large family on one income. Both films feature characters who are nomadic but also those who eventually find some kind of home, if only temporary. For these Brazilian film directors of the television era, stability in the sense of tradition, and a home with deep roots spanning generations, seems to be more associated with the past, or at least an idea inherited from the past and something saudade is directed towards. Unlike the films of Walter Salles and Daniela Thomas analysed in the next chapter (not to mention those of Wim Wenders), Diegues and Amorim do not focus greatly on the personal pasts and childhoods of their characters, rather the past is a collective one based in popular culture including religion, folklore, festivities and music. Diegues's more marked fetishism of an imagined past highlights what he deems most stable in Brazilian culture, but also that which he sees as disappearing. The possibility of stability in the future, that seminal road movie concern, in these films is very much framed by the relatively new mass culture, and thus dependent on the successful updating of the national popular in the televisual medium.

Bye Bye Brasil: Saudade as Fetishization in Response to the Transculturation of the Traditional and the Modern

The perspective of Diegues's film can be situated in the conservationist vein (Draper 2008) of Brazilian art. It relies very much on a fetishistic notion of an archaic Brazil that is 'beginning to disappear', as Diegues puts it, a Brazil of the past replete with traditional regional cultures (Diegues 2014: 442). Saudade arises from the perception of a liminal moment for that past Brazil, but it is not a melancholy saudade, as reflected in Chico Buarque's love song mentioning saudade during the open credits. There is a certain degree of acceptance of change along with a celebration of Brazil's past that allows for the portrayal of renovation in Brazilian culture, what is often referred to as *antropofagia* in the words of Oswald de Andrade, who theorized a process of cultural cannibalism in Brazilian art. Thus, *Bye Bye Brasil*'s narrative, following the fluctuating emotional valences of saudade, reveals that these conservationist and renovationist tendencies often operate in tandem in Brazilian art and culture. My analysis here departs from some earlier analyses of the relationship of the impresario character of Lorde Cigano (José Wilker), and the forró musician Ciço (Fábio Jr.), to modernity in Brazil. Randal Johnson (1984b: 130–31) develops a more dualistic understanding that associates Ciço with rurality and tradition and Lorde with urbanity and modernity. Ana Maria Mauad's analysis of the film similarly associates Lorde Cigano with the modern and Ciço with the archaic, but goes further to trace a dialectic between the two that leads to Ciço's transformation into a 'new image' by the end of the narrative (2001: 81). Ciço's updating of his own image into a televisual one by film's end is an important aspect of his character development, but it actually distinguishes him from Lorde rather than making the characters more similar, and neither character should be defined as cultural cannibals, as Mauad suggests. Nor should Ciço be associated primarily with the rural and Lorde with the urban, as Johnson argues. Both Lorde and Ciço are best described as cultural conservationists, since they remain true to the regional culture of the popular circus and forró music to the very end of the film, even as they seek to update it by linking it to the modern media of television and visual spectacle to some degree. These attempts at updating or 'modernizing' tradition vary between the two men, though. The younger Ciço fully embraces the medium of television by broadcasting his musical performance in the film's final sequence, while the older Lorde simply adds some TVs as accoutrements to his circus caravan. To a certain extent Lorde might be able to extend the reach of television and the mediatic spectacle into far-flung regions of Brazil's interior with these television screens on his caravan, but the medium itself was already doing this by 1979 when the film was released. Ciço is the one who fully enters the medium, thus transforming his cultural production into the most modern form of audio-visual mass culture. To some extent, then, Lorde Cigano keeps alive the hope for an in-person and interactive, dialogic form of cultural performance with roots in traditional popular culture. There is a recognition that mediatization of culture leads to an increasingly virtual world of art and performance, yet the film's narrative still relies on a fetishization of a cultural 'real' that remains outside the virtual realm of the televisual medium.

Lorde Cigano specifically mentions saudade in one of his circus acts, suggesting with the emotion a longing for colder climes when he does a magic trick by making snowfall in the dry northeastern backlands (*sertão*) before an amazed audience of locals. He explicitly associates snow with 'civilized' countries, thus recalling a centuries-old form of Brazilian saudade which early twentieth-century author and statesman Joaquim Nabuco referred to as his 'saudade for the world', a desire to return to seemingly more cosmopolitan, 'advanced' countries in Europe (Santiago 2001: 154). Lorde thus suggests he is bringing civilization or worldliness to the sertão with his performance, bringing its residents out of their isolation from the wider world. Lorde's romantic and business partner Salomé (Betty Faria), for her part, brings another kind of international flavour to the circus with her sensual, pan-Latin rumba, intended to evoke 'el amor como solamente se faz en el Caribe' (her phrase mixing Spanish and Portuguese translates roughly as 'love the Caribbean way'). Salomé's dance is a cosmopolitan performance, certainly far more so than performing a local northeastern dance like forró or xaxado would be. Mauad (2001) associates Lorde with television and suggests that he and his travelling show, like the burgeoning medium, perform a civilizing function in far-flung rural regions such as the sertão. Yet, as noted, Lorde's references to civilization are best understood as part of a longer tradition of cosmopolitan saudade that predates the existence of mass media in Brazil. Lorde's character is not an agent of transformation like television any more than Ciço or the backlanders for whom he performs – he is affected by it just as they are by the end of the film, updating his caravan with television screens, but still maintaining his more traditional touring cabaret/variety act. Lorde is a circus barker, magician, master of ceremonies and some-time pimp throughout the film, all centuries-old professions.

Of course, a touring show like the Caravana Rolidei can perform a certain civilizing function by bringing influences from other parts of Brazil and the world to tiny villages in rural Brazil – but it is an influence of a different order than television as represented by Diegues in the film. For instance, Lorde, in an act of revolt that recalls the etymology of the word sabotage, feels he must explode a public television everyone is watching in the town square to bring the attention of the residents of Maceió back to a live performance like his. Displayed on that television (before its explosion) to the townspeople is *Dancin' Days*, a prime-time soap opera (*novela*) aired in 1978–79 (Brazil: Rede Globo de Televisão) that featured the influence of US pop culture and European high fashion on Brazilian elites. Modern mass media in the form of 'fish bone' antennas and televisions are portrayed as an entrancing and unidirectional form of communication, apparently more of a threat than cinema due to their increasing omnipresence and affordability, and more than radio due to the mesmerizing visual spectacle.

In the context of a road movie where television is associated with modernity, one might expect it also to be associated with movement in the genre's common dichotomy of mobility and stasis. If TV represents the future, should it not be thematically linked to progressive movement? Yet, here Diegues defies such expectations and inverts the typical association of technology with acceleration and forward motion (progress). The Brazilian people before Globo's television transmission appear as if in a catatonic state – they are static, passive spectators/consumers of canned cosmopolitan culture. The protagonists of the film and their performances tied to traditional, regional (and some pan-Latin American) culture are much more associated with mobility, always on the road. The film thus implodes the dominant association of tradition with unchanging, static and localized cultures. The connotations of the sea in Brazilian cinema, too, are upended. Since Glauber Rocha's *Black God, White Devil* (*Deus e o diabo na terra do sol*) ([1964] 2010), the ocean had become a symbol of upheaval and change – yet, in Diegues's narrative, it is merely a dead end for the Caravana Rolidei, from which the travelling performers quickly take a U-turn in order to return to Brazil's northeastern and northern interior. In Diegues's post-cinemanovista perspective, there is no longer redemption to be found by breaking free of the chains of tradition.

Dasdô (Zaira Zambelli) and Ciço, a young couple of humble rural origins who join Lorde Cigano's circus, are ironically the characters who become most associated with television. Rather than fighting the medium they ultimately become a part of it, utilizing television cameras to broadcast their forró performance near the film's end. While still representing the popular culture of the region, in the film's final sequence they have become regional 'content' for the TV network. Only in this way can they effectively challenge international culture like disco, which had already become popular on Brazilian television as revealed earlier in the film by the discotheque scenes from *Dancin' Days*. As João Luiz Vieira (2003: 166) has noted, the spectators of television in the film are subject to a 'double mode of cultural colonialism' of US pop culture disseminated via the dominant Rio de Janeiro network of TV Globo. Since, instead of the passive, frozen spectators of TV focused on before, during Ciço's broadcast we only see the televisual image of the protagonists making music and dancing, the medium is put in motion and associated more with mobility and a living community. In this sense, the scene can be considered a form of resistance to cultural colonialism, offering up an alternative vision for the future of Brazilian media. This interpretation of the scene is in keeping with Johnson's assertion that the film as a whole 'does not so much critique television as it implicitly calls for its democratization and its integration with other national forms of expression' (1984b: 127). However, the director does not go so far as to visualize an audience for this intervention of cultural conservationists into the televisual medium. Competition with Globo's telenovelas is an uphill battle for popular artists from Brazil's subaltern regions, much like the struggles of musicians from outside of Rio de Janeiro in the halcyon days of radio (cf. Draper 2011a on Luiz Gonzaga's 'war of maneuver' to challenge the omnipresence of samba music on Rio's radio stations).

As Ciço and Dasdô perform on television, Lorde and Salomé show up outside their Brasília dance hall cum studio to show off the new, more electrified neon look for their truck, part of their attempt to update the Caravana Rolidey (even changing the spelling in an attempt at a more 'correct' spelling of the English word 'holiday'). But the televisions installed in the truck's sides are blank screens, mere ornamentation rather than communications media like the cameras and screens in Ciço and Dasdô's dance hall. Ciço and Dasdô politely turn down the invitation to travel again with the updated Carivana Rolidey in their final scene in the film. Thus, rather than the older cosmopolitan/regional, international/national or urban/rural cultural divides that predate television, Diegues's concern seems to be a fetishized, unmediated archaic Brazil that is being replaced by the modern Brazil of the Globo TV network and its fare of *novelas* and US pop-cultural influences. Television for Diegues introduces the problematic of the society of the spectacle as defined by Guy Debord ([1967] 1994), wherein social relationships are now largely mediated through televisual images rather than face-to-face interaction. Some version of regional, popular culture in Brazil may survive but only by becoming part of the spectacle.

Within this context, the film's primary object of saudade is a fetish, as characterized by Pietz (1985, 1987, 1988). As Pietz suggests in the African colonial context, the fetish is produced out of a liminal moment of contact and mutual influence between distinct cultures – essentially it is a side-effect of transculturation that signals heterogeneous elements. As Brazilian media become increasingly internationalized, the introduction of television on a national level presumes a universal mediation of Brazilian culture and thus the destruction of a 'pure' cultural fetish object, the lost Brazil posited by Diegues as a previously unmediated culture in Brazil's underdeveloped northeast and north. We could also label the fetish-images of peoples and cultural production from these regions as 'imagined communities' and 'inventions of tradition' in the vein of Anderson (1983) and Hobsbawm and Ranger (1983), to indicate that they only exist as the product of a particular cultural context and sociohistorical process in the present. In this liminal historical juncture, the emotion of saudade becomes the affective valence of the fetishization narrative. The subjective yearning of saudade, projecting all manner of associations onto its object, conforms to the nature of the fetish as a product of desire for the (imagined) other. Diegues's wide-ranging, transregional vision of the rural and small-town landscape recalls Humberto Mauro's saudade for a generic rural Brazil, but with more anthropological details indicating regional variations between northeast and north. The additional regional diversity results from the location shooting, which is both characteristic of the modern road movie and a trend that had been pioneered by Mauro at his Rancho Alegre studio and greatly expanded by Diegues's generation, the cinemanovistas of the 1960s, utilizing increasingly mobile sound and camera technology.

Nevertheless, Diegues clearly did not intend to present a regionalist narrative – he stated that 'the idea of the film is to deculturalize, to remove the regionalist cultural character' ('a idéia do filme é de desculturalizar, de tirar o caráter cultural regionalista') (Diegues and Oroz 1984: 162). His fetish is not of a particular region of Brazil but of a generalized, national popular culture and traditional way of life. Diegues claimed the name Caravana Rolidei was taken from a real travelling circus, that it was 'one of the last' because they were being eliminated by television, and that he had seen it 'numa cidadezinha do interior' ('in a little town in the interior') – again a generic designation for a small town in the rural Brazilian landscape (1984: 151). In this light, the minor characters encountered along the road should also be interpreted first and foremost as fetish objects symbolic of the common Brazilian people (*o povo*) rather than any particular regional group or ethnicity. These people, ranging from residents of the city of Maceió to northeastern backlanders to Amazonian Indians, are portrayed mostly as immobilized or stationary spectators of either television, the Caravana Rolidei performers or both. Sara Brandellero (2013: 54–55) notes that Diegues often utilizes a stationary camera on the roadside to capture the Caravana Rolidei in motion, rather than a camera emphasizing movement positioned on the truck itself. In this context the stationary camera can be understood as the (at least initially) passive, static perspective of many of the common people encountered on the road.

As of 1978 when the film was shot, television had not yet become a common household item even in the capital city of Alagoas (Maceió), and so in one scene we see the city's residents gathered together in a square to watch a 'public television' as it is labelled. These particular representatives of the common folk in Brazil are the most seemingly catatonic group in the film, so transfixed by the television screen they hardly make a sound. Rather than being a realist depiction of an audience in a public square, this group of couch potatoes symbolize the impact of technology and the culture industry on the common folk, who have become passive consumers rather than responsive, engaged observers, let alone politically active citizens (a convenient state of affairs for the military regime still in power at the time). As noted above, they are watching a Globo network novela instead of attending the show of the visiting Caravana Rolidei, and so Lorde Cigano and Salomé feel compelled to destroy their competition, the television set. Even after this act of sabotage, the circus's audience is pitiful, and so Lorde and his troupe retreat to the interior in hopes of finding some people who have not yet come under television's sway.

The northeastern backlands that they visit at this point in the film do offer them better audiences – television seems to be less of a threat, and consequently archaic Brazil has not yet disappeared here. The minor characters in this largely rural region include the audience who watch Lorde Cigano's magic trick of making snowfall in this semi-arid, subtropical region, in addition to his paranormal performance of communicating with the dead and telepathy. With regard to the latter parts of Lorde's show, this audience seems much more engaged than the television audience in Maceió, actively participating with questions and requests for the performer. As fetish objects of Diegues's narrative, and as saudados, they represent the traditional Brazilian people – credulous, suffering from poverty and drought, full of saudade for loved ones who migrated or passed away, but less passive and inert. Ciço and Dasdô, too, come from the same population, and demonstrate the creativity inherent in that group as folk musicians and performers who travel with the Caravana Rolidei for a time.

Another minor character met in this region, also with a connection to creativity and art, is the old film projectionist, Zé da Luz ('Joe Light', played by Jofre Soares), who represents not only another fetish of archaic Brazil, but also Diegues's perspective on cinema in an emergent era of television. Like the director of *Bye Bye Brasil* himself, Zé da Luz is a man representing the film industry who travels around the rural interior, but screening Brazilian films instead of making them. Zé arrives in a small rural town where the Caravana has stopped in order to give a screening of *O ébrio* (*The Drunkard*) (Abreu, [1946] 2006), a Brazilian drama whose main character migrates from the country to the city, tying it to the larger theme of modernization and the rural-urban divide in *Bye Bye Brasil*. In a conversation with Lorde, Zé advises him when to perform his show to avoid conflicting with the religious activities in the small, devout town, and tells him 'I have a business similar to yours' ('Tenho um negócio parecido com o seu'). The fact that the projectionist is in a similar situation to Lorde Cigano's troupe, in terms of the rural-popular audience he seeks out, associates national cinema – in the only explicit reference to it in the film – more with the archaic Brazil than the modern one. Diegues even explicitly acknowledged his folkloric perspective on cinema in the region, stating that he had originally intended to have Zé da Luz arrive in town in an ox cart, but something he saw on location in the interior of Alagoas made him understand 'the ingenuity and ruralism' ('a ingenuidade e ruralismo') of his perspective, which he had based on memories from his childhood when he lived in the same state (Diegues and Oroz 1984: 160). The sight that revealed to him his own folkloric, ruralist perspective was a real projectionist driving a Rural Willys (an SUV-style truck), which as a result is the more modern form of transportation that Diegues then decided to provide for the projectionist in his film. Along with the film's focus on the traditional performers of the Caravana Rolidei itself, the Zé da Luz character functions to differentiate film from television in an era just before the distinction between the two media would be greatly diminished. Indeed, even the casting of novela stars Betty Faria and José Wilker, and rising novela star Fábio Jr. (whose career would soon however, like his character's, go in a more musical direction), as the leads in the film reveals the already existent influence of television upon cinema. By the late 1970s cinema had an established history of telling national/regional stories, giving images of the common Brazilian people back to themselves, while television did not, and thus Zé da Luz shares a far greater kinship with traditional circus performers than with the producers of television. He also represents the precarious nature of national film distribution in Brazil, a distribution system that would be very quickly and vastly outperformed by the accessibility of television. Decades after making *Bye Bye Brasil*, in an address given to the Cinema Sub-committee of the Brazilian Senate, Diegues was still criticizing the distribution and theatrical system of Brazilian cinema, which by then he suggested could be ameliorated by increasing the percentage of national films aired on domestic television networks and cable (Diegues [2000] 2003).

After visiting the northeastern interior, the Caravana Rolidei performers drive their truck to northern Brazil and they meet some minor characters from the Amazonian region on the roadside. Again, we are introduced to a group of locals who provide, on first glance, more fetish-images of immobility or stasis, this time a displaced Brazilian Indian tribe. They are literally immobilized by the side of the road, looking for a ride to the town of Altamira. The first shot pans across the members of the small tribe, who face the camera in a line, standing mostly silent and motionless, wearing a mixture of modern clothing such as colourful polyester shirts, suit jackets and aviator sunglasses, along with indigenous necklaces of beads and teeth, also carrying with them a pet monkey and tortoise. The references to modern Brazil in their costuming hint that Diegues does not wish to present the viewer with stereotypical images of tribal Indians. Brandellero argues that Lorde's initial magic trick for the tribe when he meets them 'establishes [their] reduction to exploited consumers within a market economy', adding that they are situated as 'spectators rather than agents in a place they can no longer call their own' (2013: 57). In a realist vein, the film here begins to dispel a utopian, Edenic picture of the Amazon that Lorde Cigano had suggested during an earlier performance in his description to his audience of the paradisiacal 'land so green, Altamira' (later the dictatorship's myth of the Amazonian region as a land of economic opportunity is dispelled as well, since the Caravana Rolidei troupe find little success here and resort to prostitution to gain an income). The young cacique of the tribe (Rinaldo Genes) explains that 'my village ended when the white man arrived' ('minha aldeia acabou quando o branco chegou'), and jokes that he is now travelling to the city 'to pacify the whites' ('pacificar os brancos'). The 'archaic Brazil' of this tribe has apparently already disappeared.

For the most part, the cacique and his tribe appear bemused rather than melancholy, curious about the various amenities of modern life they find in urban Altamira when they arrive, including frozen popsicles, Coca Cola and jet airplanes. They still maintain various signifiers connecting them to Amazonian tribal life that mark them as heterogeneous from the other residents of Altamira, and the manner in which they speak of 'Brazilians' clearly does not include themselves within that national identity, yet now they are what Darcy Ribeiro ([1995] 2000) would call generic Indians, detribalizing and in the process of incorporation into modern, urban society. Nevertheless, this is not a saudoso group themselves, and unlike the backlanders of the northeast shown earlier in the film (who are referred to by Zé da Luz as still living 'at the end of the world' ['no fim do mundo']), these are Indians who have been forced out of village life and directly into modern Brazil (to the extent that it exists in Brazil's poorest region). In comparison with the main characters, they are most like Ciço and Dasdô, who also left behind their small-town life to explore the wider country and ultimately transform their musical performance into a televisual one.

Perhaps this should be no surprise, since of the populations met by the Caravana Rolidei along the road, this tribe are the only ones to actually mobilize themselves, to travel with the performers on the truck itself. As a historical fetish-image of the Brazilian people, these Indians are the most hybrid, approaching something like Oswald de Andrade's culture hero, the *bárbaro tecnicizado* (technicized barbarian), whom Andrade imagined as a synthesis of the communitarian indigenous lifestyle with modern technological knowledge. The social and political implications of the hybridity of Diegues's detribalizing Indians, closely related to the destruction of the Amazonian rainforest, are not explored nearly as deeply as they had been in Jorge Bodanzky and Orlando Senna's *Iracema* ([1974] 2015), a film shot in the same region a few years earlier but banned from release in Brazil by the military regime due to its political and social critique of rampant environmental and economic exploitation. Diegues's Indians are posited as a kind of happy (though impoverished) medium between the archaic and the modern, not entirely catatonic like Maceió's television viewers, but not desperate and isolated like the residents of the sertão. They are interested in television as an emblem of modernity, but are not yet shown to be under its spell. In this sense they have moved somewhat beyond the status of mere spectators, and at the very least have achieved the agency of movement and migration by catching a ride with the circus. Nevertheless, once in Altamira, the cacique of the tribe signs up to take a job that may well bring him into debt slavery, making uncertain the survival of the tribe as a kinship network in the city.

Overall, the minor characters as fetish-images are an important component of the message being sent to 'the Brazilian people of the twenty-first century' to whom the film is dedicated. The archaic Brazil presented is not yet a fossil but the film itself is fossilizing it, producing characters who are 'radioactive fossils' in the Deleuzian sense (this concept is explored further in Chapter 7) that will be able to revivify this particular historical constellation in a future that is now our present. Indeed, the film's dedication itself was inspired by a memorial in Piranhas, Alagoas commemorating the beginning of the new century in 1900 and dedicated to the future Brazilian people of the twentieth century (Diegues 2014: 457). The fetish-images of Brazilian popular 'types' serve as memorials to the Brazilian people's relationship to modernity qua television and mass consumer culture in the historical period of the film.

With regard to sexuality, the changing role of woman as fetish is also explored in the film. In the traditional patriarchal social paradigm, a woman on the road or street (*rua*) is associated with prostitution. Dasdô, on television with Ciço, demonstrates a different way for both women and men to sell their own images, virtually. Prostitution, the business of selling bodies for sex, shares with the traditional notion of cultural production a fetishistic, materialist relationship to desire, while television serves in this context to mediate and thus distance the object of desire, creating a virtual, immaterial relationship. Lorde might still be Salomé's pimp if the opportunity and necessity arise in the future, but Dasdô and Ciço's 'pimps', those who sell their images, will only be a television network and its executives. Yet, updating and mediatizing do not necessarily mean a destruction of tradition – both the circus performers and the forró musicians at the film's end conserve certain forms of traditional popular culture, despite doing so in distinct real (the mobile stage/tent on tour) and virtual (the television set) performance contexts. There is also a connection to giving birth to a child on the one hand, as Dasdô does while still with the Caravana Rolidei, and giving birth to a televisual image on the other, as she does with Ciço; sexual desire is transformed in either case into a derivative version of the self, a legacy. In one case, the legacy is bodily and material, in the other it is immaterial and networked – and therefore has the potential of infinite reproducibility. As a fetish-image of modern Brazil, the baby Mirinha is tied to both these material and immaterial legacies, having been born in the Caravana Rolidei, but ending the film a few years later in an appearance with her parents on television.

This televisual performance of Mirinha's family is part of the film's final sequence. Ciço, Dasdô and Mirinha perform a televised university forró, on stage with a band of young musicians playing electric guitars, along with other traditional forró instruments. Ciço is now 'The Famous Ciço – Accordionist of the Planalto (Brasília area)' according to the sign outside. With regard to whether the country's future is deemed to be hopeful or tragic at this point in the film, Diegues noted a divide in opinion between North American and European critics after the international release:

> In Europe, it is seen as a very sad, melancholy film, about a paradise that is being destroyed, that ended. While in the United States it is seen as a very happy film, euphoric, full of hope, about a civilization that is beginning. [...] I prefer the vision of the Americans (Na Europa, é visto como um filme muito triste, melancólico, sobre um paraíso que está sendo destruído, que se acabou. Enquanto que nos Estados Unidos é visto como um filme muito feliz, eufórico, cheio de esperança, sobre uma civilização que está começando. [...] Prefiro a visão dos americanos).
>
> (Diegues and Oroz 1984: 160)

The emotional dichotomy presented here is very close to the distinction Orico (1940) makes between European Portuguese saudade and Brazilian saudade, with the former described as more melancholy and the latter as more joyful. Diegues's agreement with North American critics signals a Brazilian saudade with a greater emphasis on love for the country in its transitional moment rather than grief over the loss of archaic Brazil. Ciço's fame and the next generation as represented by his daughter Mirinha should be understood as a happy ending from the director's point of view – Diegues even says the moment he likes best in the film is Mirinha's birth, 'the birth of something new' (1984: 160). The child's full name, Altamira, was given by Lorde Cigano and is a reference to the utopian Brazilian paradise on earth he had envisioned in his clairvoyant performance on stage. It is fitting, then, that Ciço and Dasdô have settled their young family in Brasília, a national capital produced out of a utopian modernist vision less than two decades before the shooting of *Bye Bye Brasil*, and representative of the nation's hopes for rapid modernization and further integration of its diverse regions.

The Brazilian People of the Twenty-First Century in *O caminho das nuvens*: Brazil's Evolution Has Been Televised

In *O caminho das nuvens*, a nuclear family travels together by bicycle from the sertão of Ceará to Rio de Janeiro. Like *Bye Bye Brasil*, it is a road movie, and even shares a producer with the film made 25 years earlier, Lucy Barreto. Barreto has remarked on the new vision of the northeastern people in this more recent film (Webcine n.d.), but in some ways, the central family appears more traditional than the rather hodgepodge group of characters who end up travelling with the Caravana Rolidei. At the turn of the twenty-first century, Romão, Rose and their five children can be considered as part of a long line of rural-urban migrants, and of families from the sertão, featured in Brazilian cinema, including the main characters of the films discussed in Chapter 3 and some of those in Chapter 5, among many others. Nevertheless, in line with the producer's comments, the family's relationship to modernity in the shape of television and mass culture is far less antagonistic or conflicted than that of Lorde Cigano and his troupe. In contrast with the temporal liminality so acutely experienced by the travelling performers of *Bye Bye Brasil*, Romão (Wagner Moura) and Rose's (Cláudia Abreu) family appear thoroughly imbricated in the modern, national, televisual pop culture, despite their status as unskilled (and mostly illiterate) labourers from an economically underdeveloped region. The eldest son of the family, Antônio (Ravi Ramos Lacerda), seems unfamiliar with the sight of a wide-screen television when he happens upon it at a gas station mini-mart, but it quickly becomes clear that TV per se is by no means a novelty to him. The now firmly established medium likely helped to develop his family's love for national rock/pop idol Roberto Carlos, and reminds them of this common cultural touchstone when they are apart. Indeed, the life-like nature of the Spanish-speaking actress from a telenovela whom Antônio sees on the TV screen is emphasized, and seems to fascinate him just as much as the sight, in person, of an attractive young woman in a mermaid costume later in the film. The society of the spectacle is taken for granted; consumption of mediated images is not thematized as essentially distinct from face-to-face interactions with family members and other acquaintances and strangers met on the road. Authentic, heart-felt emotions and desires can be expressed and received through television. The Brazilian people's evolution has been televised.

As an illustrative contrast to the distinctive nature of live performance highlighted through the circus in *Bye Bye Brasil*, we can consider a pivotal scene in *O caminho das nuvens* featuring the family's participation in a dance for a live audience in a Porto Seguro, Bahia tourist resort from which the film takes its title in Portuguese, 'The Road in the Clouds'. The manner in which the characters experience this dance performance stigmatizes it as a kind of cheap trick for tourists, rather than a magical force associated with worldliness and mystical, far-away places like the circus acts of the Caravana Rolidei. Unlike Lorde Cigano, the impresario behind the Road in the Clouds resort is portrayed as entirely cynical and not at all concerned with presenting an accurate image of Brazilian culture, nor entertainment for the Brazilian people themselves. Panamá (Sidney Magal), tellingly named after a Spanish-speaking foreign country, is only interested in providing a performance that will appeal to the highest bidder, foreign tourists. The spectators of the performance in Panamá's beach resort are virtually all international tourists, addressed in English and Spanish. They are presented with the 'archaic Brazil' of indigenous ritual (the *quarup*, an Amazonian funereal dance) as if it is an entirely commodified practice, easily reproducible outside its cultural context in the Xingu river basin (a 'Brazilian Halloween' as Panamá explains it in English for a crowd of tourists). The performers in redface in this scene, including Romão and three of his children, recall the era of silent cinema in Brazil, when film narratives commonly featured

Brazilian Indians, but only as represented by non-Indian actors and with plots set in the distant past. The gaze of Antônio, who is coming of age and increasingly questioning his parents as the film progresses, is very dubious and disappointed as he watches his father Romão perform on stage with siblings Suelena (Cristina de Lima), Clévis (Felipe Newton) and Rodney (Manoel Sebastião). Romão perceives his son's astonished, then piercing and unyielding gaze as one of judgment, and he responds by ending the charade and abruptly departing the stage with his children in tow. Thus in this film a much more reductionist, commodified fetish is directly critiqued – a fetish of international tourists for Brazil as exotic, Amazonian paradise.

While the authenticity of this pure, Amazonian 'archaic Brazil' is thoroughly undermined, the family's various performances of Roberto Carlos's rock music in other scenes are never presented as inauthentic. Even as they use a pre-combustion engine era technology to travel on a quest approximating a pilgrimage, Romão, Rose and their children are shown to be thoroughly conversant in the mass media of the late twentieth/early twenty-first century via their collective love of Roberto Carlos. They consistently perform his music across the varied geography of Brazil, aware of his likely popularity in rural and urban areas from the northeast to the southeast that they have never set foot in before. Indeed, the bicycles used by the family are a curiosity because they are anachronistic – the vast majority of emigrants from northeastern Brazil travel by bus, car or plane to reach their destinations. Their uncommon form of transportation is the oddity, not their prior familiarity with pop music produced in Rio de Janeiro. Emotionally speaking, saudade becomes something that can be transmitted through and by the televisual medium and the national pop culture it broadcasts, rather than a conservationist saudade for a disappearing way of life in the vein of *Bye Bye Brasil* or Humberto Mauro's films discussed in Chapter 2. National popular culture with some international roots, as broadcast via television in one crucial scene towards the end of the film, is presented as having so thoroughly penetrated the regional space of the rural, northeastern interior that this family from the middle of nowhere can fluently perform Roberto Carlos's songs, even identifying with them deeply on an emotional level.

In the name of the heterogeneity of the northeast, some have critiqued the omnipresence in the filmic narrative of national pop culture not native to the region (Câmara et al. 2006). The film's director Vicente Amorim spoke up for its authenticity by pointing out that it successfully suspended the disbelief of perhaps the most famous northeastern migrant, President Luiz Ignácio 'Lula' da Silva. According to Amorim, Lula was visibly moved by the film, identifying strongly with the poor migrant protagonists as he watched at a presidential palace screening in 2003 (Cohen 2003). On the other hand, the film's producers, including the already mentioned Lucy Barreto as well as her husband Luis Carlos Barreto, acknowledge and appreciate the more modern vision of the northeast (Webcine n.d.). Luis Carlos Barreto is not only one of the most preeminent producers in Brazil, but also a well-respected cinematographer most famous for his work on an early Cinema Novo classic shot on location in the sertão, *Vidas secas* (*Barren Lives*) (Santos [1963] 2005). In any case, notwithstanding critiques of the film's anthropological accuracy, my purpose here is not to analyse closely *O caminho das nuvens*'s realism with respect to the people of the sertão, but to note director Amorim's shift beyond the saudade for archaic Brazil – a cinematic transformation of the region, and symbolically of rural Brazil as a whole, made with the imprimatur of some producers seminal to Brazilian cinematic history.

Moving away from the saudoso fetish of the archaic Brazil already marked as disappearing in Diegues's work, Amorim develops a new perspective on the region, and on poor, rural Brazil in general, in relation to the modern culture industry and television. It should be noted that by no means would all northeastern backlanders be equally versed as Romão and Rose's family in the music of Roberto Carlos or other stars of Brazilian rock or MPB (*música popular brasileira* or Brazilian pop music). Other rural residents of the region, or migrants leaving it behind, might find more compelling and directly related to their lived experience the music of sertão native Luiz Gonzaga and that of his artistic descendants in the country genre of *forró* (which I explore in depth in Draper 2010, 2014). In *Bye Bye Brasil*, Ciço represented this regional culture through his accordion performances. Yet in the more recent film, it is made believable, and indeed thanks to the expansion of television deep into the Brazilian interior it is entirely possible, that a family from the rural northeast are devout fans, and form a kind of familial cover band, of a rocker from the more urbanized southeast (Roberto Carlos). Thus, Amorim expands greatly on the impulse towards deregionalization that Diegues pursued through his use of MPB stars Chico Buarque and Roberto Menescal on *Bye Bye Brasil*'s soundtrack. Amorim does this by introducing the non-regional music into the diegesis of the film, making it profoundly important and meaningful to his characters rather than just a directorial commentary as in Diegues's film. It also happens to be the case that Roberto Carlos's sentimental pop rock produces, both diegetically and non-diegetically, an affective context of saudade for the family's story. This saudade remains, like that of Carlos's music, on a personal level, describing the family's emotional state rather than being directed at an idyllic vision of rural, traditional Brazil.

In general, Carlos's songs on the soundtrack of the film, and as performed by the family themselves, serve simultaneously to emphasize the ubiquity of televisual, mass pop culture across the Brazilian landscape and to tell the story of their journey, including experiences of love, loss and religious inspiration among others. For example, we can consider the performance of Roberto Carlos's 'Como é grande o meu amor por você' ('How Great is My Love for You') by Rose and her son Clévis (an electric guitarist and singer, and the most talented performer in the family). This is a straightforward love song which Clévis and Rose clearly enjoy performing, on the patio of a humble restaurant along the highway. Alternating close-ups during the performance demonstrate that the entire family and audience are indistinguishable in their enjoyment of (and familiarity with) this song, and they receive tips from the audience for the performance. It is also clear here and throughout the film that it is far easier for the children of the family to enjoy and identify with the music of Roberto Carlos than with the religiosity of their father and his devotion to northeastern popular saint Padre Cícero. Religiosity is not demonstrated to be under threat, however – it coexists and even blends with popular culture as the ambient presence of Carlos's 'Jesus Cristo' ('Jesus Christ') suggests in an earlier scene. Romão's pious character certainly does not resist or complain about the omnipresence of Roberto Carlos's music in any way, ensuring the absence in the film's narrative of a saudade more resistant to contemporary, urban culture.

The emotion of saudade itself is explicitly mentioned in the lyrics of Carlos's 'Detalhes' ('Details'), heard on the soundtrack early in the film when the family rest from their journey in the town of São Bento, Paraíba. In São Bento, 'Detalhes' plays on a diegetic radio somewhere nearby as 14-year-old Antônio, having walked alone down a dusty road near the Piranhas River, exchanges flirtatious glances with two adolescent girls. Despite the youth of the three adolescents in this scene, the song heard is ironically not so much about young, innocent love but about love lost and feelings of saudade. The lyrics and nostalgic sentimentality anticipate the fact that the family will leave this area soon, but also resonate in a broader sense with the emotional impact of continual uprooting for this family on a journey of thousands of kilometres. In leaving São Bento behind, Rose in particular will be pulled away from a job she enjoys to follow her husband's patriarchal quest for employment to support his entire family. The latter goal represents the main example of fetishism in this film. Romão's search for a 1000 Reais monthly salary (something like three times the minimum wage at the time), despite his lack of job skills and education, is gradually revealed over the course of the film's narrative as outdated in two ways – firstly in its self-centred machismo, and secondly in its incompatibility with the modern economy of Brazil.

Romão's dream job is a fetish symbolizing a stability that may well be out of reach for a family of northeastern backlanders who are better described as members of the 'precariat' than the proletariat, limited primarily to low-paying jobs in the informal economy that require the entire family to work (Standing 2011). As before in *Bye Bye Brasil*, the fetish highlights an aspect of rural Brazilian culture that is heterogeneous to the realities of the more developed, urban areas of the country – in this case, the desire of the rural-urban migrant for social mobility. The major distinction from *Bye Bye Brasil* in Amorim's film is that this fetish and its affective frame of saudade are far more constrained, limited primarily to the perspective of one character and not incorporated into the narrative framework, making conservationist saudade's overall significance to the national image of Brazil much more marginal, a kind of vestigial trace of the past rather than a symbol of rural, traditional Brazil in its entirety. Nevertheless, Romão's fetish does have a significant impact on the lives of his own family members. Rather than wait to see if a possible trucking job arises in São Bento while his wife works in the local hammock industry, Romão insists that the family leave so he can continue his search for a job. This economic quest is simultaneously a spiritual quest, in that Romão guides the family to a large statue in Juazeiro do Norte, Ceará, of his patron saint Padre Cícero (the second-largest statue in Brazil after the Christ the Redeemer in Rio). Romão's identification with an honoured local patriarch (celebrated unofficially as a saint in the region) reemphasizes his saudoso, pious machismo. His personal hero is a masculine, traditional, patriarchal figure who cared for the poor and marginalized of the northeast. Ironically, Romão's personal saudade for the stability of the old order, represented by this traditional patron, displaces his own family and reinforces the saudade of the rest of the family for all the places and people they must leave behind in the present to pursue their husband and father's spiritual-economic fetish.

The tension Romão's fetish creates with his family is made most obvious in his confrontations with his eldest son Antônio. Upon learning that his father has decided they must leave São Bento and continue their journey, Antônio immediately rejects the idea and desperately attempts to escape his father on his bicycle in order to delay their departure. Clearly Antônio has been hoping this town will become their new home, a place where his mother has found a job and where he has begun to pursue friendships and budding adolescent romance. Nevertheless, his father forces the family to depart despite the various connections they have started to form to this locale, producing the saudade in his family anticipated by the song 'Detalhes' earlier. This moment of tension, particularly between Romão and Antônio, introduces the context for Clévis's private, roadside performance to the family of the next Roberto Carlos song on the soundtrack, 'Se você pensa' ('If you think'). The lyrics of 'Se você pensa' emphasize choosing mutual love and respect over personal pride or ego. Clévis joyfully sings the song in an attempt to lift the family's spirits and patch over their differences. In this performance and others along the way, Clévis also demonstrates dance moves that we can only assume were learned from television. Again, the cultural references of the family are situated within the national, audio-visual networks of the Brazilian culture industry. Emotionally speaking, Clévis tries to soothe his parents and siblings with the song, both reaffirming the family's love for each other and encouraging its members to choose to focus on that love rather than a melancholy saudade for a possible home left behind.

Nevertheless, at a certain point on the road, the tension between Antônio and his father becomes so great that the son decides to leave the family and make his own way. His decision is influenced by his observation of his father performing the inauthentic quarup dance as a temporary job, a deviation from Romão's quest for a dream job that causes Antônio to profoundly question his father's spiritual and temporal authority. On his own, Antônio befriends some older men and goes with them to dance in a nightclub, as if living out himself the contemporary equivalent of the disco scene portrayed on television to northeasterners in *Bye Bye Brasil*. Even illiterate, poor backlanders are a mobile population that can now experience some semblance of the consumer pleasures that had only begun to be revealed to the poorer regions of the country on Brazilian television in the 1970s. Earlier in the film, Antônio had been introduced to adult female sensuality and begun exploring his own adolescent sexuality when he stumbled upon an almost life-sized image of a woman in a tight-fitting red dress on a television soap opera, whose dialogue at that moment was coincidentally, 'Antônio'. Thus, from the film's beginning we are given a sense that the televisual image plays a role in the coming of age of one of the characters, and by extension virtually any Brazilian adolescent. At the very end of Antônio's story arc in the film, he again interacts with a television when he watches a performance of Roberto Carlos's 'As curvas da estrada de Santos' ('The Curves of Santos Highway') on TV, which clearly is a saudoso moment that links him to his family who have travelled on, leaving him behind in a town where he found a construction job. Till the end, the film continues to shift unproblematically back and forth between romantic and familial love in its application of Carlos's lyrics to the reality of the protagonists. The effect is to frame Carlos's music in a general logic of love, separation and resulting feelings of saudade for a variety of Brazilians across the national landscape.

The politics of the film are not explicit, but the constant displacement and mobility of Rose and Romão's migrant family can be interpreted, on a sociological level, as the twin curse of historical underdevelopment of the northeast and modern-day neo-liberalism on a national level. The family is much more like economic refugees than canonical road movie heroes. Complicating matters, the father's fetishism of a stable job adds an element of self-displacement, even as his inability to find the job highlights twenty-first-century capitalism's tendency to eliminate such formal employment (particularly in the manufacturing, construction and transportation sectors where a northeastern migrant might typically look for work). There are also references to the interrelated historic problems of drought, hunger, displacement and homelessness afflicting the northeastern rural poor. At one point in the film, André Abujamra's score features a lively, forró-inspired instrumental piece to accompany a sudden downpour of rain. The family of sertanejos from the dry interior, especially the children, have their spirits raised by the rain and several of the children dance for joy. Their celebration resonates with similar scenes in Brazilian cinema, popular music and other art forms when northeasterners have welcomed the return of the rains after punishing droughts that threatened their very survival. At the same time, the abandoned bus that the family are lodged in for the night highlights their homelessness – they do not have a mobile home such as this bus might provide if it were functional. The family is mobile and rootless like the Indian tribe in *Bye Bye Brasil* – the film never shows us a space that could be considered their familial home, even when they may have reached their final destination in Rio de Janeiro.

The family's migrant condition is given a certain saudoso framework, and also tied to the road movie genre, by the final Roberto Carlos song on the soundtrack. The song 'As curvas da estrada de Santos' ('The Curves of Santos Highway') connects Antônio to his family after they have gone their separate ways, via a Roberto Carlos television performance (noted above). Within this narrative context, in which Antônio and his now distant brother Rodney both enjoy Carlos's singing on TV simultaneously, the song recalls the perennial ability of saudade to maintain affective ties to distant loved ones, making their presence felt even in their absence. The specific lyrics of 'As curvas da estrada de Santos' reemphasize the themes of relentless road travel, the shiftlessness caused by lost love and the hope for finding true love again and ending the journey:

> I cannot stop
> I prefer the curves of Santos Highway
> Where I try to forget
> A love that I had and saw in the mirror

Losing itself in the distance
But if love that I lost
I should find again, oh
The curves will end and on Santos Highway
I won't travel again

(Não posso parar
Eu prefiro as curvas da Estrada de Santos
Onde eu tento esquecer
Um amor que eu tive e vi pelo espelho
Na distância se perder
Mas se amor que eu perdi
Eu novamente encontrar, oh
As curvas se acabam e na Estrada de Santos
Não vou mais passar)

(Carlos 1969)

Again, Carlos's song about romantic love is shifted into the sentimental context of the migrant family's emotions. The imagery of a lost love viewed in a rear-view mirror resonates with the two brothers gazing at television screens and fondly remembering their distant sibling and/or parents. The subject of the song who prefers the highway to stopping echoes the desire of Romão to find his fetishized dream job before settling down. Carlos's song ends with a reference to the hope of finding one's love, which applies to the film in a broader sense of reaching one's desired goal or object (saudado). 'As curvas' is featured on the soundtrack in the film's closing sequence, both in the voice of Roberto Carlos and the voices of Clévis and Rose covering the song. Thus, the film ends with the song's ambiguity and shifting valence between melancholy over loss on the one hand, and joy of love and continued hope on the other, confirming on an emotional level an uncertain future for this migrant family.

Chapter 5

The Ghost of Home in Brazilian Cinema of the 1990s

Walter Salles expresses a Brazil desired, yet distant.[1]

(Strecker 2010: 17)

Writing on the road movie, director Walter Salles (2007) has stated that 'films [of the genre] are not about what can be seen or verbalized but about what can be felt'. In the same text, Salles argues that 'a road movie should be transformed by the encounters that occur on the margins of the road'. In this sense the road movie should be at least somewhat improvisational. We can see contextual improvisation at work already in Salles's first road movie, *Terra estrangeira* (*Foreign Land*) (1995, co-directed with Daniela Thomas), in the incorporation of Lusophone African characters as well as the Gal Costa song 'Vapor barato' ('Cheap Steamboat') discussed further below. For *Central do Brasil* (*Central Station*) (Salles [1998] 1999), even the choice of Vinícius de Oliveira to play protagonist Josué has an element of improvisation to it. Salles met the boy, a non-actor, at an airport where he was shining shoes rather than at a planned audition. Consolidating these aspects of the road movie along with a documentarian approach to cinematography that Salles also says is characteristic, one gets an overall sense of many ingredients blending together to produce the emotional realism of Salles's films (and of the Salles/Thomas team in *Terra estrangeira*). 'What can be felt' in these films is grounded in the realities of the people in a particular culture, generally the common people who are often on journeys of their own, independent of the films' protagonists. These common folk are those who Salles (2007) refers to as 'the small communities we came across' in the South America of *Diarios de motocicleta* (*The Motorcycle Diaries*) ([2004] 2005), or the displaced migrants of Lisbon, Rio de Janeiro and other parts of Brazil in his Portuguese-language films including *Terra estrangeira* and *Central do Brasil*.

Rossini (2005) characterizes the latter two films as marked by lack, particularly the lack of a Brazilian identity, which the filmmakers search for in the narrative of the films along with their characters. Clearly such a focus, along with the frequent existential and emotional themes of solitude and loneliness, make for films strongly tinged with saudade. As suggested by the epigraph of this chapter, the object of this saudade is a lost Brazil, distant in time and/or space. Thus, it is not surprising to find that Salles, a world cinephile, has emphasized his interest in the films of Michelangelo Antonioni, in particular *Zabriskie Point* ([1970] 2009), for its representation of 'the implosion of, and subsequent attempt to recuperate, identity' ('a implosão e posterior tentativa de recuperação de identidade') (Almeida 2002: 22). Brazil is depicted first in a process of disintegration and then in one of reintegration over the course of *Terra estrangeira* and *Central do Brasil*. The attempt to recuperate identity, in the specific (trans)national context of these films, can be equated with the search for a Brazil made distant by various larger socio-economic forces, but still longed for by its citizens. In the same interview, Salles further explains that

> [b]eyond the crisis of identity, the question of exile, be it political, economic or affective, and the possibility of people getting a second chance in life, are other themes that can be found in almost everything I do (Além da crise da identidade, a questão do exílio, seja ele político, econômico ou afetivo e a possibilidade das pessoas se outorgarem uma segunda chance na vida são outros temas que podem ser encontrados em quase tudo que faço).
>
> (Almeida 2002: 22)

The idea of *affective exile* here is very important, as it allows for an internal exile within Brazil, which both Dora (Fernanda Montenegro) and Josué (Vinícius de Oliveira) of *Central do Brasil* experience to varying degrees. One might say, too, that an affective exile of Paco Eizaguirre (Fernando Alves Pinto) in *Terra estrangeira* precedes his actual departure from Brazil. Of course, an affective exile is typically associated with a longing for home and thus the emotion of saudade – though home might be conceived in a variety of ways from more idealized to more realist or critical. Affective exile is also a manner in which Salles and Thomas can find common ground between their own somewhat marginal position in an international film industry as Brazilian artists, and that of Brazilians who could be more traditionally defined as exiles from the homeland due to economic need or political oppression. Salles's interest in a 'second chance' can be seen in the redemptive message of *Central do Brasil*, and also in his pivotal role as director and producer in bringing about the *Retomada* (Renaissance) of the latter half of the 1990s, a second chance for Brazilian cinema after its crisis earlier in the decade.

Salles cites João Guimarães Rosa's literature as an influence on his documentarian (or neo-realist) style. He describes Rosa's work thusly: 'His *oeuvre* was not oriented by a catechizing desire. He listened and shared what he heard from others' ('Sua obra não era norteada por um desejo catequizante. Ouvia e dividia aquilo que ouvia com os outros') (Almeida 2002: 24). The director demonstrates a desire to allow for the presence of the other's voice and perspective in his films – he reemphasizes this years later when talking about allowing for improvisation in his journey or road movies like *Terra estrangeira* (*Foreign Land*) or *Diarios de motocicleta* (*The Motorcycle Diaries*) (Strecker 2010). The various representatives of the common folk at the train station and in the sertão in *Central do Brasil* are further evidence of this documentarian urge, which is then synthesized with the larger narrative and character development involving the recuperation of identity. In *Central do Brasil*, interactions with real, authentic Brazilians begin to evoke a saudade in Dora for her own interiority and authentic sentiment from which she has become alienated. Dora can be rescued from alienation because she listens to the people, just as the director is attempting to do in his process of shooting the film itself.

It is no accident that both *Terra estrangeira* and *Central do Brasil*, saturated by saudade on a narrative level, are so characterized by liminarity – both literal and symbolic. Some of the most intense, critical moments for the protagonists take place in and around the space of Portugal's border, in the passage from Brazil to Portugal, or between coastal and interior Brazil. Correspondingly, these are the scenes in which the crises of identity, or resolution thereof, become most evident. Naficy (2001) has characterized liminal subjectivity as one of the fundamental attributes of diasporic and exilic cinema. Yet as indicated by Salles, and fully within what I call the Brazilian Romantic tradition, the liminarity and related saudade bend in a homeward arc, as they are linked to a quest for national self discovery and self-esteem. Salles has emphasized the close relationship between cinema and nation, both 'the projection of an idea greater than reality, in which an entire collectivity rediscovers itself' ('a projeção de uma idéia maior que a realidade, na qual toda uma coletividade se reencontra') (Almeida 2002: 40). Paco's, and even more so his mother's, saudade for the Basque country in Spain (where her family comes from) seem to depart from a Brazilian nationalist saudade. Yet, even this saudade remains in the traditionalist vein, directed at a home identified with an ethnic identity, a Basque nation. Taking into consideration that this Iberian regional nation is never seen or experienced directly, whereas later in *Central do Brasil*, Dora has some deeply emotional interactions with Josué in the Brazilian national heartland, the combined impact of the two films is to restore the privileged position of the Brazilian rural people and their folklore as the ethical ground and the ethno-cultural essence of the nation.

Salles himself and others have noted the clear influence of Wim Wenders's work on his own, such as *Alice in den Städten* (*Alice in the Cities*) ([1974] 2016), which, much like *Central do Brasil*, features a child and adult who form an unexpected bond on the road as they search for the child's home. Orgeron's analyses of Wenders's road movies could very well be descriptions of *Terra estrangeira* or *Central do Brasil*. For instance, 'inarticulateness, [the] inability to maintain communication or community, [...] pushes many of Wenders's protagonists onto the road where, perhaps strangely, sometimes futilely, they begin to rebuild both structures' (2008: 130). Further, Wenders's *Im Lauf der Zeit* (*Kings of the Road*) ([1976] 2016)

> is about slowing down, a process linked in Wenders's understanding to notions of home, both at the micro [character] and macro [national] level. The road's supposed disconnectedness allows these characters to connect with each other, with their past, with what they have left behind, with what lies ahead. Perhaps most critically, the viewer is also connected, also communicated with.
>
> (Orgeron 2008: 133)

In both Wenders and Salles, the viewer is to a large degree an imagined nation with the same, often frustrated desire to find home again out of a condition of existential exile. Yet as we shall see below, Salles and Thomas's specific focus on saudade and Brazil's postcolonial relationships with Portugal and Lusophone Africa, and Salles's exploration of saudade in conjunction with the great internal regional and social-class divides in Brazil, place their films of the 1990s solidly in a Luso-Brazilian tradition that cannot be subsumed within the generic and narrative parallels we can trace to Wenders's road movies.

Terra estrangeira: The Luso-Saudade of Brazilians in Affective and Economic Exile

To shoot *Terra estrangeira*, the directors and cinematographer Walter Carvalho selected a granulated film stock, which Salles stated 'could in some way reflect the social and psychological deconstruction that the film focalized – the ruin of a country' ('pudesse de alguma forma refletir a desconstrução social e psicológica que o filme focalizava – a derrocada de um país') (Almeida 2002: 34). The emphasis on disintegration in the very visual presentation of the film, though subtle, frames the narrative nostalgically under the spectre of imminent loss. At the same time Carvalho, who shot *Central do Brasil* as well, describes his ideal for cinematography as analytical, critical and a departure from the Hollywood norm in the sense that it should be 'a photography that investigates [...] a decolonized photography' (2007: 18). Thus, the sensibility of his cinematographic approach complements Salles and Thomas's desire to study their characters' emotional development in a postcolonial Portugal or a developing country like Brazil. Both cinematographer and directors agreed that they needed to capture the specificity of the unique, transatlantic, postcolonial Luso-Brazilian-African context of *Terra estrangeira* and later, the uneven development of Brazil itself as represented by the contrast between Rio de Janeiro and the northeastern backlands (*sertão*) in *Central do Brasil*.

Regarding the main character of *Terra estrangeira*, Salles states that '[t]he loss of innocence that the character of Paco experiences also is a theme with which I identify in cinema' ('A perda da inocência que o personagem de Paco experimenta também é um tema ao qual eu me identifico no cinema') (Almeida 2002: 36). The idea of a loss of innocence implies a prior Edenic state, which is itself associated with childhood. This framework has a long history in texts emphasizing a saudoso affect – connecting Salles's perspective back to Brazilian Romantic literature and even Portuguese poetry from the Romantic era and before (not to mention the melancholy genre of *fado*, sung in one scene of *Terra estrangeira*). The cinematic tie to Brazilian Romanticism, which as we have seen is one that had already been established by Humberto Mauro in the 1950s, will become all the more evident in *Central do Brasil*.

One thing relatively sparse in *Terra estrangeira*'s narrative that will become much more pivotal in Salles's *Socorro nobre* (1996) and *Central do Brasil* is the structuring element of epistolarity. Naficy has described epistolarity (or letter-writing) in films made from a diasporic or exilic point of view as 'an important instrument of self-exploration and self-narrativization' (2001: 104). Orgeron has demonstrated that in the road movie specifically, and in its precursors such as *The Searchers* (Ford [1956] 2007), the letter is often a missive targeted at the space of home, linking the sender to the space of domesticity while documenting his or her journey (2008: 68). *Terra estrangeira* is notable for its relative lack of epistolarity, as if there is no clear home to send a missive to for the Brazilian characters in affective and economic exile. The condition of existential homelessness and solitude is symbolized best by the film's famous image of an old shipwreck on a beach, and the aimless floating of family photos adrift on the floor of Paco's São Paulo apartment, in the early scene when he allows it to be flooded by the shower while grieving his mother's unexpected death. In keeping with the emphasis on homelessness, the characters never reach the imagined home of San Sebastián, Spain (whence Paco's family emigrated to Brazil) to which they are heading at the film's end. After bonding with him on the road, fellow Brazilian and budding romantic interest Alex (Fernanda Torres) offers maternally comforting words and caresses to Paco along with the hope of finding home – but only as he lies dying (in contrast, earlier she specifically says 'I'm not your mother, buddy!' ['Não sou tua mãe, cara!']).

The final sequence in which the character of Alex is at her most maternal, in fact, presents the closest thing to a letter in the film – Jards Macalé and Waly Salomão's song 'Vapor barato' ('Cheap Steamboat'), whose inclusion on the soundtrack in the pivotal ending sequence occurs first diegetically in Alex's voice, then non-diegetically through the famous recording by Brazilian pop-rock singer Gal Costa. The song was added as an afterthought, when Walter Salles heard lead actress Fernanda Torres singing it on location (Strecker 2010: 109). In this sense it was a kind of improvised missive, a communication of the Brazilian actress with her fellow cast and crew while shooting a film in Portugal. It then serves this function again in the filmic narrative – it is a final missive from Alex to her fellow Brazilian as he crosses the border between life and death, at the same time that Alex drives him in a car across the Portugal/Spain border towards his imagined ancestral home in the Basque region. The missive is not sent home but from one exile to another, promising a return home, as echoed by the lyrics of the love song, 'talvez eu volte' ('perhaps I'll return').

The non-diegetic use of Gal Costa's voice singing 'Vapor barato' after the character Alex sings it could be interpreted as the one epistle sent homeward in the film. Costa's wistful, earnest voice on the soundtrack accompanies an overhead, helicopter shot pursuing the car that Alex frantically drives as Paco lies dying of a gunshot wound in her lap. The song here is at least in part a message sent back home to a Brazilian audience, to whom the music and lyrics will be most meaningful and who may have past memories of their own associated with them. Indeed, Salles himself said he associated the song with home when he heard Torres singing it between takes. The lyrics of the song themselves resonate with the larger theme in the film of displacement and the desire to find home again, and also with the specific imagery of the shipwreck noted above. Generally speaking, the song is about someone saying goodbye to a lover but promising to return after a journey of unknown duration. The singer addresses a loved one ('honey baby' [in English in the original], the epithet sung by Gal Costa with a Janis-Joplinesque bluesy intensity in the chorus) whom she is leaving behind in order to forget her 'grande obsessão' ('great obsession'). She plans to travel to parts unknown by way of 'aquele velho navio' ('that old ship'). The reference to an old ship recalls the imagery of the shipwreck earlier in the film and also Alex and Paco's conversation about Portuguese colonists and their caravels. As we hear the first strains of Gal Costa's version of the song, she performs a kind of duet with Alex, who can still be heard singing to a dying Paco in the car even as the camera has taken a point of view from high above. Alex, inspired by her memory of the lines 'Perhaps I'll return / One day I'll return' ('Talvez eu volte / Um dia eu volto'), tearfully adds her own voice to the song's narrative, telling Paco 'I'm taking you home, my love' ('Eu te levo pra casa, meu amor'). Her missive to an increasingly distant Paco, who is leaving her on his own Stygian ship, becomes entwined with the bluesy, saudoso farewell song of Gal Costa, itself functioning as a letter home to the Brazilian nation/audience from abroad. The message 'One day I'll return' becomes cinematographically prophetic, foreshadowing not only Salles and Thomas's various films shot in Brazil in the latter half of the 1990s, but the return of Brazilian cinema on a significant scale to the screens of Brazil and to the world stage – signalled in part by the critical success *Terra estrangeira* would achieve.

Due to the importance I place on the epistle of 'Vapor barato', I see more continuity between *Terra estrangeira* and Salles's subsequent films of the 1990s than some other scholars who have focused more on the de-centring of Brazilian national identity and the thematization of homelessness in the film (Ferreira 2012; Nagib 2013). With regard to homelessness, Lúcia Nagib argues convincingly that the city of San Sebastián as a destination in the film connotes the cultural movement of Sebastianism, consisting of the nationalist saudade for the lost king Sebastião and the myth that he will one day be resurrected and return Portugal to a state of greatness. Nagib (2013: 174) stresses that the thematic link between the film's narrative and Sebastianism is the association of homelessness and nationhood in the figure of the people without a land, as represented in the narrative by displaced Brazilians like Alex, Paco and Miguel. The recovery of this national home is projected into the future for Alex and Paco, just as it was by the Sebastianists. Yet in Nagib's reading, there is some elision of the important distinction between homelessness, or the perceived absence of home, and the desire to return to an imagined home (saudade) that drives the characters and the structure of the narrative. *Terra estrangeira* does not culminate with the symbolic destruction of the nation (qua home) and the national-popular subject as *Macunaíma* does. The narrative thrust in the final sequences of the film is towards maintaining and retracing affective ties to home, as symbolized best by the song-epistle of 'Vapor barato' and its open-ended line 'perhaps I'll return'. Alex's claim 'I will take you home' in her final scene should be understood in this light, prophetic as to the direction Salles's *oeuvre* was headed in.

As Carolin Overhoff Ferreira (2012) has noted, the film involves a radical de-centring of the nation. Yet within this de-centring narrative lies already the preparatory work for a re-centring of the nation as home, and place of social reconciliation, that would already become obvious in Salles's short film *Socorro nobre*, released within a year of *Terra estrangeira* (and analysed further in the next section). In my emphasis on an affective and thematic progression and continuity across the Salles and Thomas film and then Salles's solo-directed films of the 1990s, my reading is more in keeping with that of Darlene J. Sadlier (2007), who notes a consistent theme of homelessness and displacement (*dépaysement*) in *Terra estrangeira*, *Central do Brasil* and *Diarios de motocicleta*, in tandem with a progressively more utopian viewpoint about the possibility of transcending homelessness. Alberto Elena's interpretation of the film's concluding sequences also supports my own, noting that Salles himself 'insists on an open ending' for *Terra estrangeira* that holds out some hope for the quest for home, and further that the ending in terms of narrative and style is 'beautifully enigmatic', combining a certain level of nihilism with a 'lyrical romanticism' (2003: 218). Such romanticism, I would argue, falls within the cinematic tradition of Brazilian representations of saudade and anticipates the representation of the emotion Salles would later develop in *Central do Brasil*, discussed in detail below.

One aspect of the narrative that is very unique to *Terra estrangeira* among Salles and Thomas's films is the inclusion of a diversity of Lusophone subjects from Portugal and its ex-colonies. Explaining the presence of the Luso-African characters in *Terra estrangeira*, Salles notes that '[i]nstead of being a film about only Brazilians that were in exile, it was supposed to speak of a broader exile, a kind of reverse shot of Portuguese colonization' ('Em vez de ser um filme só de brasileiros que estavam no exílio, devia falar de um exílio mais amplo, uma espécie de contracampo da colonização portuguesa') (Strecker 2010: 106). Thus, there is some attempt to represent the perspective of a variety of postcolonial subjects in Portugal, making for a more complex, varied representation of saudade – however, the film's focus is still the emotional state of two Brazilians. Consequently, the depth to which a wider postcolonial, Lusophone saudade can be explored is limited. Far more so than either postcolonial ties to Africa or epistolarity, in fact, it is the noir genre that structures the narrative, style and emotional tone of the film. In keeping with this tone, the words of Fernando Pessoa regarding the country of Portugal are invoked to describe the existential cynicism, confusion and/or ignorance of the protagonists: 'It is the ideal place to lose someone or to lose oneself' ('É o lugar ideal para perder alguém ou para perder-se de si próprio'). The main Portuguese character in the film, Pedro (João Lagarto), who wears glasses that recall those of Fernando Pessoa, does not himself get lost and in fact helps to orient the displaced Brazilians with a map. The characters who lose themselves are primarily the Brazilians, who also at times intentionally deceive or disorient each other. Alex, in fact, loses more than one person – both the men she loves over the course of the film end up dead. Ígor (Luís Melo) is the prime example of a cynical character, a Brazilian Mephistopheles with whom Paco must make a Faustian pact to pay for his passage to Portugal. Considering all of these characters together, there is certainly no focus on a postcolonial critique of the Portuguese, whom the directors no doubt understand to be occupying a marginal position in modern Europe. The smuggler Ígor himself pointedly works for a German man named Kraft (Tchéky Karyo) rather than a Portuguese. In any case, the noir style – evident both in the black-and-white cinematography and the adventure-suspense story built around the smuggling of diamonds – contributes to a darker, more melancholy valence in the saudade represented in the film. This melancholy saudade is more in the vein of the sentiment as expressed in Portuguese art and philosophy, and not coincidentally corresponds to the writings on the emotion by Saudosista Fernando Pessoa, who posited the Portuguese nation itself as in a state of existential exile from its former greatness as a seafaring colonial power.

More so than the storyline of the major characters, the landscape through which they pass complicates the sentimental and social framework in which the film represents saudade. The directors did a one-day shoot in Cape Verde in order to capture the famous kiss scene in front of a shipwrecked boat on a deserted beach (Strecker 2010: 110). The film thus shares with *Macunaíma*, discussed in Chapter 3, a non-realist topography or subconscious geography of sorts, in this case of the Lusophone Atlantic. The interchangeability of the Portuguese coastline with the African – the characters are supposed to be travelling through northern Portugal in this scene – Africanizes Portugal. To borrow a term Strecker uses to refer to the film's Lusophone African characters, the landscape is shifted from *português* (Portuguese) towards a *pretoguês* (black Portuguese) identity. This hybridization can also be said to work in the other direction, Europeanizing Cape Verde. As it often has in its colonial and postcolonial history, Cape Verde represents an in-between space between Africa and Portugal, but here also one between both those countries and Brazil thanks to the Brazilian protagonists featured in the shipwreck scene.

Since the Cape Verdean location is unacknowledged and the Brazilian characters in the scene are white, in this portion of the narrative the African becomes an unconscious substrate of transatlantic Lusophone travel and affect. In conjunction with the director's comment about a 'wider exile' of Portuguese postcolonial subjects, we can understand the film as clearly positing Luso-Africans and Luso-Brazilians in a similar situation of displacement. One would presume this might place Luso-Africans in a condition of emotional solidarity with Brazilians due to their parallel experiences, but the emotion of saudade is far less emphasized in the primary Lusophone African character, an Angolan migrant to Lisbon named Loli (José Laplaine). A fundamental distinction between Loli and the Brazilians in the film, which arguably explains the lesser degree of saudade he displays, lies in the fact that he has a kind of home within exile in the larger community of Angolans in Lisbon. On the other hand, Paco and Alex are portrayed as isolated, for the most part ignored or discriminated against by the Portuguese and not belonging to the expatriate Brazilian community.

Strecker describes the characters of the film in general as 'seeking out the reconstruction of their affects' ('em busca da reconstrução de seus afetos') (Strecker 2010: 111). This assessment seems to apply primarily to the main characters, Brazilians Paco and Alex, in terms of the fluctuation of their feelings of loneliness, love and fear related to their condition of exile and the relationships they build or lose in that context. However, it should also be emphasized that saudade itself is an emotional constant in the film that accompanies them throughout the narrative. As noted, in keeping with the noir style, saudade tends to be of the more melancholy Portuguese ilk, echoing the sentiment of the *fado* sung in one scene at a Lisbon restaurant. As felt by the characters and expressed in the general atmosphere of São Paulo at the start and later, in the more extensive Portuguese social setting and landscapes, saudade is able to accompany the entire process of the characters' emotional development because of its inherently fluctuating valences of love and grief. The emotion demonstrates its characteristic fluidity, ranging from mournful to hopeful and back again, across diverse transatlantic contexts.

Socorro nobre and *Central do Brasil*: Epistolarity and Saudades in the Brazilian Romantic Tradition

Socorro nobre, a short film released by Salles the year after *Terra estrangeira*, can be seen as a major step beyond the latter film in terms of the incorporation of epistolarity as a significant structuring element of the narrative. As such, it anticipates the many film-letters and epistolary discourses running through the director's next feature, *Central do Brasil*. This documentary centres around the correspondence of a prison inmate in the state of Bahia named Maria de Socorro Nobre with Polish-Brazilian artist Frans Krajcberg. Socorro Nobre writes to a place of freedom, recovery, creativity and rebirth; an imagined future home that she projected onto the figure of Polish-Brazilian artist Frans Krajcberg, whose inspiring story of overcoming the death of his relatives in the Holocaust she had read about in a magazine article. She writes also with a fear of failed communication, stating in her initial letter that she has enough hope to send it, but is unsure it will ever be delivered or received. As Hamid Naficy puts it, epistolary films often feature 'doubt about the epistles' ability to break through the inhibitions and prohibitions against writing and speaking' (2001: 111). Orgeron (2008) also emphasizes that the failure of communication is a common theme of the road movie, so it is not surprising that Salles would later utilize epistles in *Central do Brasil*, a narrative of the road movie genre, to symbolize various inhibitions and prohibitions on communication in Brazil. As we shall see, these obstacles are generally related to poverty, social inequality and illiteracy – some of which Socorro Nobre had to overcome to form a friendship with the artist Krajcberg. Her story is also one of Brazilians from different classes and backgrounds forming a bond of friendship and love, identifying with each other over common struggles, which will be echoed and expanded upon in the fictional story of Dora and Josué in *Central do Brasil*.

While clearly inspired by *Socorro nobre*, the addition of an extensive epistolary element in the narrative of Salles's *Central do Brasil* appears all the more significant when one considers the big shift involved from a relative lack of epistolarity in his previous work on a feature film, *Terra estrangeira*. Displacement is still a major theme in the later film, but the gap between the space of travel/exile and the imagined home is ultimately crossed by several missives; and the two main characters themselves are displaced in order to find a truer home, one less lonesome and alienated. Salles pointedly compares the female lead of *Central do Brasil*, Dora, to the real woman Socorro Nobre, stating that '[l]ike Socorro, Dora too accords herself a second chance, rebaptizes herself' ('Como Socorro, Dora também se outorga uma segunda chance, se rebatiza') (Almeida 2002: 41). Even maternal love, lost to both Dora and Josué by the deaths of their mothers, is reconstituted through their increasingly caring relationship with each other on the road.

As prophesied by Alex's words at the end of *Terra estrangeira*, *Central do Brasil* centres its narrative around homecoming. According to Rossini, this is very much a national homecoming, since in *Central do Brasil*,

> [r]eturning home [...] is to return to the northeastern backlands that are already recognized by the popular imaginary as being *the Brazil*, and their people as being the *face* of the Brazilian (Voltar para casa, portanto, é voltar para o sertão nordestino que já é reconhecido pelo imaginário popular como sendo *o Brasil*, e seu povo como sendo a *cara* do brasileiro).
>
> (2005: 101, original emphasis)

This imaginary is precisely that of the Brazilian Romantic tradition, and long precedes Salles in the work of Humberto Mauro (not to mention nineteenth-century literature). Indeed, cinematically speaking, a strong case can be made that Mauro contributed to consolidating such an imaginary of rural Brazil as the authentic heartland in his short films of the 1950s, many of which were pedagogical films funded by the National Institute of Educational Cinema (INCE) and shown to schoolchildren. No doubt other literature and music from the northeast also played a large role in defining that particular region's national significance, including the social-realist novels of the 1930s and the country music called forró (see Draper 2010, 2011a, 2014 on the latter). Cinematically speaking, the Cinema Novo movement of the 1960s made the northeast and its backlands (*sertão*) in particular a symbol of rural, archaic Brazil and its (hierarchical) social relations.

However, the film certainly does not begin in an idyllic, rural setting. The transition from a very urban, rather dystopian landscape into the sertão is pivotal to the narrative. As Rossini puts it, '[f]rom the gray and cruel city, shown always in enclosed, asphyxiating frames, [the film] transitions to the spaces of open countryside, green and sunny' ('Da cidade cinza e cruel, mostrada sempre em enquadramentos enclausurantes, asfixiantes, passa-se para espaços de campo aberto, verdes e ensolarados') (2005: 102). The big city is represented as the not-home, akin to the 'foreign land' in Salles and Thomas's eponymous film that formerly – as if it were a state of being rather than a nation-state – could not be escaped. In Salles's *Central do Brasil*, however, the 'foreign land' (ironically one of Brazil's largest cities) can be escaped – in other words, returning home and redemption are possible in the rural northeast. Saudade is the affective tie between these disparate parts of the Brazilian landscape and Brazilian national identity alike. Over the course of the filmic narrative, the emotion tends to be directed to the space more associated with home, the heartland of Brazil as represented by the sertão – but the emotion is not entirely unidirectional, since Dora ultimately feels saudade for her own family and childhood (which were in Rio de Janeiro) after leaving the city behind.

One's childhood and parents are very typical saudados in the Luso-Brazilian tradition, and in this film the child Josué serves to activate Dora's latent saudade for her personal past and family: '[...] it is the boy that needs to pull her toward life, to return her to the condition of a supportive human being, full of feelings' ('é o menino que precisa puxá-la para a vida, trazê-la de volta à condição de ser humano solidário, pleno de sentimentos') (Rossini 2005: 102). This function of the young boy Josué in the narrative reflects themes common to the road movie according to Orgeron (2008), including communication and (re)connection to community (and/or lack thereof). Josué serves to make Dora feel again, to open herself up to emotions. It is not surprising that when this middle-aged Brazilian woman finally does so, saudade is very prominent amongst the emotions that emerge – indeed, it is the most privileged sentiment in Salles's epistolary narrative.

Salles states that the proposal of *Central do Brasil* was

> to look, as the name of the film itself indicates, to the heart of Brazil, and to try to perceive that the crisis is, in truth, generated by the elites that control this country – of which, in one way or another, we are members (olhar, como o próprio nome do filme indica, para o coração do Brasil, e tentar perceber que a crise é, na verdade, gerada pelas elites que controlam este país – da qual, de uma forma ou outra, fazemos parte).
>
> (Almeida 2002: 40)

The great emphasis on interiority, indicated by the desire to get to the 'centre' or 'heart' of Brazil, is telling, and works in tandem with the epistolary narrative of the film. The characters reach an idyllic centre that Josué is able to make a home in with his half-brothers, but from which Dora is still displaced – yet the process of healing or recuperation is evident in that Dora has now opened up a line of communication to that centre and is able to address her feelings of saudade for it and 'for everything' in what Naficy would call an 'exilically accented' epistle. The fact that the film ends with the writing of a letter emphasizes all the more the narrative's saudoso affect, as film letters represent 'the desire to be with an other and to reimagine an elsewhere and other times' (2001: 101). Continuing with Naficy, letters also demonstrate the 'intimacy, immediacy and intensity of [the characters'] interiority' (2001: 102). If Dora, associated with the urban elites, must remain essentially distant from the heartland of Brazil, at the very least we know that she has found her own centre, her own heart. The writing of this final letter is an act of 'self-narrativization' that manifests a new interiority and identity – we could even go so far as to say that Dora creates her heart anew in writing this letter (2001: 104). The content of the letter is revealed to the audience primarily through Dora's voice-over, and because 'there exists a unique relationship between voice, interiority, and identity', the soundtrack here, too, helps produce Dora's newly compassionate emotional centre (2001: 121).

Naficy also notes that often 'the epistolary device itself is turned into a fetish' (2001: 133). Again, as in Chapter 4, we can rely upon Pietz's notion of the fetish as produced out of intercultural communication to see the letter in *Central do Brasil* as a treasured, fetishized object highlighting transculturation – more specifically, communication between two subcultures and two classes in one society. The missive sent between heterogeneous parts of Brazil recalls the fetish of 'archaic Brazil' in Carlos Diegues's work, also discussed in Chapter 4. Indeed, Salles claims that in *Central do Brasil* he wished to investigate 'archaic elements' ('elementos arcaicos') in Brazilian culture that had not yet been 'defiled by the means of mass communication' ('conspurcados pelos meios de comunicação de massa') (Almeida 2002: 44). Dora's letter represents the desire not only to imagine this elsewhere/this other but to integrate the sertão and its people emotionally with the urban centres. From this perspective, the feeling of saudade of those in the urban metropolises for Brazilian rural peoples and cultures, and the associated saudade of the elites for popular/folk culture, should be embraced in order to reconstitute a coherent Brazilian national identity. The power gradient of this kind of transculturation is revealed by the ambiguity as to how one-sided the exchange will be – we see Dora writing a letter, but the film ends before any response can be given by Josué. All of the earlier letters in the film were between northeasterners themselves, presumably between two illiterate parties in many cases. The only missive between 'modern Brazil' (Dora) and 'archaic Brazil' (Josúe), as just noted, is the most fetishized in the film. This fetish status is emphasized through various means: the letter's pivotal position at the narrative's emotional climax, along with a close-up of Dora's hand putting pen to page and her voice narration, which, along with facial close-ups, comprise Fernanda Montenegro's profoundly emotional performance of the character. Yet, it is also the only letter in the latter part of the film for which no proof of delivery or response is given. It is as if the very existence of the letter symbolizing Dora's emotional rebirth is enough to guarantee the healing of rifts between social classes and between underdeveloped and more developed regions.

Regarding the character of Josué specifically, Salles asserts that

> in a certain way, […] Josué, the child firm in his convictions, ethical and rigorous, is the projection of a desired country. It is still far from being the country we experience in the present (De uma certa forma, […] Josué, a criança firme em suas convicções, ética e rigorosa, é a projeção de um país desejado. Ainda está longe de ser o país que vivemos no presente).
>
> (Almeida 2002: 46)

Josué, the 'little redemptive angel' ('pequeno anjo redentor') as Salles calls him in the same interview, is an object of saudade, precisely a saudade for the future as Alfredo Antunes (1983) analyses it in Pessoa's prophetic writings. This saudade is a desire for a distant, utopian future (a desired country) heavily shaped by the revival of an Edenic, paradisiacal past – temporally represented for Portugal as the era of colonial greatness, but in Salles's film spatially represented as the 'heart' of Brazil, keeper of authentic national folklore and identity. Thus, *Central do Brasil*, like *Terra estrangeira* before it, not only features saudade, but repeatedly and resoundingly resonates with the Luso-Brazilian philosophical and aesthetic tradition in its representation of the emotion. Clearly, the suggestion that the sertão is an Edenic space involves a romanticization of the region and its history of social inequality and violence. We can recall here, from Chapter 3, my discussion of Hutcheon's ([1997] 2000) theorization of nostalgia as a 'complex projection' that often idealizes the past in order to express a dissatisfaction with the present. This complex projection, involving a temporal aspect but largely spatializing the idealized traditional (past) Brazil in the northeastern or northern regions, is something that Salles shares with an earlier road movie director, Cacá Diegues. However, Salles's more recent film recognizes less interpenetration between Rio de Janeiro (urban Brazil and its media) and the interior, more rural regions (especially the *sertão*) – and as a result he tends to idealize the latter even more in *Central do Brasil*. One specific example of this idealization of the backlands is that the assistant director Sérgio Machado filmed some locations in a deserted town in Ceará that had been the stage of a violent feud between two families, the Montes and the Feitosas (Almeida 2002: 55). This conflict would later inspire Salles's *Abril despedaçado* (*Behind the Sun*) ([2001] 2002), but all existence of such violence in the region is suppressed in favour of representing a heartland worthy of Josué – a redemptive 'desired country' or, in biblical terms, a promised land. Salles wished to critique what he deemed the 'Social Darwinism' of urban Brazil through his representation of Rio de Janeiro in the film, but he chose to ignore similar violence in the backlands for the purposes of his saudoso vision in the Romantic tradition (Almeida 2002: 44). In this sense he comes closer to the Humberto Mauro of the 1950s than Cacá Diegues did in the 1970s.

Nevertheless, the scene in which Dora reads a letter from Josué's father addressed to his sons Isaías and Moisés reveals, in a subtle manner, the hierarchy of lettered and oral, urban and rural cultures in Brazil. Dora edits the letter on behalf of Josué, pretending that it was also addressed to him in order to make him feel included in the family of the two half-brothers whom he has only just met. Essentially, she helps to maintain a more idyllic vision of their situation, mirroring Salles's representation of the northeastern sertão as a promised land. The power dynamics of the lettered elite with respect to the illiterate masses are maintained, even as a degree of emotional solidarity is called for between the classes and regions of Brazil. Salles's vision here thus also resonates with Mauro's on another level beyond its focus on national rural culture – *Central do Brasil* falls within the tradition of seigneurial nostalgia inherited from the plantation class and their perspective in the works of authors from the coastal sugar regions from northeast to southeast, from Gilberto Freyre and José Lins do Rego in the twentieth century back to Romantic authors like Casimiro de Abreu in the nineteenth. Authors in this vein tended to emphasize cordial patron-client relationships between the landed-elite families who owned the plantations on the one hand, and their employees, often subsistence farmers and day labourers, on the other.

In the period of slavery, the integrity of the enslaved workers' families was contingent upon the approval and support of the plantation masters. Even in the post-slavery latifundia system, as seen in the plot of Mauro's *Canto da saudade* discussed in Chapter 2, the local landowner would often serve the role of legitimizing marriages – Colonel Galdino must approve the marriage of Maria Fausta if she wishes to remain a member of the community living and working on his lands. We see a modern-day echo of this hierarchy of families in Dora's role as guarantor of the unity of Josué's family, symbolized most succinctly by her placement of Josué's mother's letter (in a pink envelope) next to his father's letter (in a blue envelope) on the mantle of his half-brothers' living room before she departs for the last time. Salles ([1998] 1999, DVD commentary) has indicated that Dora's placement of these letters together represents the reunion of their family for which Josué and his half-brothers are longing. Credit for this reunion is symbolically conferred upon Dora, who, as Salles stated, represents the Brazilian elite. This more modern, more urban elite is one which, the film laments, has become more distant from rural Brazil than the landed elite represented by Colonel Galdino in Mauro's film, who continues to keep close watch over his subalterns.

The idealization of the sertão in the film has received criticism for obscuring the lived realities of its populace. For instance, Saliba argues from a historical perspective that the sertão's poverty is portrayed without reference to the workings of political and economic power to marginalize or exclude the rural poor (2001: 254). This argument finds support in the fact that *Central* does not make obvious the reasons behind the displacement of the many migrating sertanejos represented in the film. Saliba goes too far in ascribing an 'empty universalism' ('universalismo vazio') to Salles's sertão, but it cannot be denied that the framing of the region is far more based on the expression of Dora and Josué's emotional and psychological development than any documentarian or politically critical motivations. This *Bildungsroman* aspect of the narrative, combined with the portrayal of the rural interior as the essence of the nation, place it firmly within the Romantic tradition first established in Brazilian cinema by Humberto Mauro. However, the narrative focus on a single woman's perspective adds an underrepresented viewpoint to a migration story, revising the typical male-centred, patriarchal vision of the region, and thus anticipating the works of Andrucha Waddington in the following decade such as *Eu tu eles* (*Me You Them*) ([2000] 2001) and *Casa de areia* (*House of Sand*) ([2005] 2006) (see also Draper 2011b for an analysis of the feminist perspective on the region in both these films). Another non-traditional, feminist aspect of Dora's character lies in the fact that she departs from the traditional association Orgeron identifies, common from the very origins of cinema, of masculinity with motion and action on the one hand, and femininity with stasis, domesticity and stability on the other (2008: 63). In order to restore Josué to his family, Dora must take bold action, break out of the confines of her everyday life and travel to a distant region she has never been to before. Further, a middle-aged female lead character represents a particular stage of life not often given extensive screen time in cinema.

Saliba makes the point that the many poor migrant workers that Dora encounters on her journey form a 'reserve army' that has existed for many years and remains marginalized in the Brazilian economy (2001: 252). In an economic sense this is true; however, the emotional logic of the film is to reveal a kind of affective wisdom in this same population. Dora's personal growth involves opening herself up to authentic emotions, especially saudade, which the poor migrants and pilgrims she encounters easily express. With the help of letter-writers such as Dora, many of the northeastern migrants are able to marshal these emotions in order to cement bonds over a distance that separates them from loved ones, in marked contrast with Dora, who describes herself being treated like a stranger by her own alcoholic, abusive father when she met him on the street. Dora's decision in the latter part of the film to finally send all of the letters she writes for illiterate migrants is an affirmation of their emotional wisdom. It is also, as Saliba writes, a 'transposition of the narrated oral world to the written world' ('transposição do mundo oral narrado para o mundo escrito') (2001: 255). As such, Dora serves as a mediator for the subaltern in a more privileged, dominant discourse, in much the same way that filmmaker Salles serves such a function on behalf of rural Brazil for his primarily urban, middle-class (Brazilian and international) cinematic audience. Via these diegetic and non-diegetic mediating figures, the audience is given a kind of sentimental education through the Romantically pure, authentic emotions of the common man and woman of the sertão.

Saliba rightly suggests that a 'certain infantilism' colours the sentimental education of Dora, and by extension the audience, in the narrative (2001: 257). Dora returns to her childhood in her memory and revives her desire for a father figure who sorely disappointed her in the past. The religious symbolism of the film, including a variety of images of the baby Jesus, suggests that all the characters are ultimately children of God, the heavenly father. Indeed, Dora in particular is positioned, unconscious and helpless, in Josué's arms in a shot towards the middle of the film. This now famous shot has been termed a 'reverse pietà' by the director, placing Dora in the position of the deceased Christ rather than in that of his mother, Mary. The idea that it is at least partially the Christ child, and not the adult Jesus as in the traditional pietà, being referenced in this shot is emphasized by the immediately preceding shot of a painting of the baby Jesus in his mother's arms. The infantilizing side to the narrative, encouraging identification with the main child character and also returning the main adult character to her childhood in memory and on a psychological and emotional level, is another clear example of the legacy of the Romantic tradition. The resonance with this tradition is strongest with respect to saudade, in a similar vein to works such as Casimiro de Abreu's seminal ode to his childhood years, 'Meus oito anos' ('When I Was Eight'), adapted to film by Humberto Mauro and analysed further in Chapter 7.

Saliba further comments that, for Dora and Josué, 'it is just mobility that teaches them some sense of belonging or of identity' ('só a mobilidade é que lhes ensina algum senso de pertencimento ou de identidade') (2001: 253). It overstates the case to claim that mobility alone produces an identity for these characters, since, independent of their journey across the country, they both represent different sectors of the Brazilian populace (broadly speaking, Josué the northeastern rural poor and working class and Dora the urban middle class and elite of Rio). Saliba's analysis is strongest here in its emphasis on the importance of mobility to produce *change* in the characters' identities, especially in Dora. Mobility helps Dora to see and feel her own displacement from her past and from her fellow Brazilians. In his writings on the road movie genre, Walter Salles has emphasized the importance for the characters of learning from the other, 'he who is different' ('aquele que é diferente'), while on the road (Strecker 2010: 255). The point here related to Dora and mobility is that her very sense of self becomes displaced and *othered* through her journey with Josué. In tandem with her body's movement through the Brazilian national landscape, Dora's psychological and emotional state moves much closer to the other, and now openly feels a saudade for close personal contact that mirrors that of some of the poor Brazilians she has been writing letters for. Something similar is apparent in the words of the Ernesto Guevara character (Gael García Bernal) in Salles's *Diarios de motocicleta* at the end of his journey: 'I am no longer myself – at least, I'm not the same self as before' ('Yo ya no soy yo – por lo menos, no soy el mismo yo anterior'). Guevara, too, meets many poor and working-class people who have a great impact on his personal development as he travels across various South American countries, and his character reveals his transformation in an intimate voice-over near the film's end just as Dora does. Salles continues a similar epistolary structure in *Diarios de motocicleta* as well, since Ernesto Guevara is shown writing his diary and letters to loved ones throughout his journey, and it is presumed that his comments about the othering of his self are being written into his diary, later to be published as a travel memoir. One could describe these pivotal moments of realization narrated by Ernesto and Dora in either film as sections of the narrative that move beyond representing 'film letters' to becoming 'letter films' in the sense that Hamid Naficy (2001) describes. The very structures of the films become epistles in these moments, intimately testifying to the discovery of authentic emotional connection and transformation.

Saliba (2001) criticizes *Central do Brasil* for not presenting a project for the future, in concordance with other critics who, especially in comparison with earlier Cinema Novo works, find the film politically retrograde or, at best, reformist (e.g. Nagib 2007; Oricchio 2003). Indeed, the film is not primarily oriented towards the future, and certainly presents no clear political project in the conventional sense. Dora's statement that she 'has saudade for everything' in the final film letter points towards an emotional relationship with the past as the primary focus. The ethics of the film are emotional as Saliba argues, but also *religious* in the broadest sense, that is, in the Latin root's sense of reconnecting (*religāre*) to history, community and nation, and to one's own childhood, emotions and humanity (in addition to the more conventional religious tie to one's spirituality, morality or God). Just as nostalgia represents a more universally recognized sentiment related to saudade, there is a universal side to Dora's emotional and psychological development, but the specific historical and cultural framework for saudade and the relationship to place have a genealogy very much rooted in the Brazilian Romantic tradition (with even deeper Lusophone roots as discussed in the Introduction). The film laments that the connection of the educated elite and middle class to popular cultural traditions and the authentic emotional and spiritual life of the people, valued so much in this Romantic tradition, has attenuated greatly. Thus, the film does indirectly suggest a path forward for the society, which involves reviving and strengthening this tradition of respect for the common folk and their (traditionally oral) culture.

The cinematography of the final scene of the film, including the manner in which it mirrors that of the opening scene, simultaneously highlights the varying mournful and joyful valences of saudade, and visually underlines the ethics of reuniting the social body of the nation. After Dora departs from the home in which she has newly established Josué with his half-brothers, the final scene depicts her writing a farewell letter to him synthesizing her emotions, including the confession that she 'feels saudade for everything', which are in fact her final words in the film. Upon her completion of the letter, the camera alternates between close-ups on Dora's and Josué's faces, the two now distant from each other but thinking and feeling in parallel as they both look at the same souvenir photo of themselves on their journey. The photo of the two was taken by a photographer selling pictures in front of a background of iconography related to popular culture and religiosity in the sertão, such as the sign referring to the regionally important festival of St. John, and a life-sized image of the revered northeastern religious figure of Padre Cícero. Thus, the saudade the two are clearly feeling for each other at this moment is firmly grounded in the popular culture of the rural backlands. What they miss most is who they became together as they travelled into this authentic heartland of the Brazilian nation, rather than who they were in the putatively alienated space of the southeastern urban metropolis where they first met and began their journey.

Their faces also depict, over the course of about a minute of screen time, a transition from tearful sadness to joy at the memory of being together, the transition between the two facial expressions occurring the moment after they simultaneously, coincidentally both look at the souvenir photos they have with them. The full range of saudade's valence is visible in their miens, which transform from pained to pleased within just a few seconds, overlapping somewhat in tears first produced out of sadness but in the end mixed with the joy of their smiles. The shifting valences of saudade are highlighted all the more moments later when the credits roll, since the song that begins playing is Cartola's samba 'I Need to Find Myself' ('Preciso me encontrar'). The very emotionally resonant, repeated lines in the chorus of this song are 'Let me go, I need to wander / I'll go afar seeking / To laugh in order not to cry' ('Deixo-me ir, preciso andar / Vou por aí a procurar / Rir pra não chorar'). These lines evoke not only the very mixed, in-between emotional state (named saudade in Portuguese) of Dora and Josué at the film's end, they also apply equally to the many other, poor northeastern migrants featured in the film from its opening scene. That first scene in particular is close to a graphic match of the closing scene, but rather than on the main characters, it focuses on the alternately joyous and mournful faces of migrants at Rio's central train station as they dictate letters to loved ones back home. The repetition of the close-ups of an emotional letter sender at the film's end, along with a close-up of the future receiver of that letter, serves to firmly restore Dora herself back into the heart of the Brazilian people. Despite her higher social class and regional difference from the people sending letters earlier in the film, Dora has achieved a deep solidarity with them on an affective, even *biopolitical* level. As defined by Hardt and Negri, biopolitics is 'the power of life to resist and determine an alternative production of subjectivity' (2009: 57). Dora has managed over the course of the film, with the help of her interactions with Josué and other poor and working-class Brazilians, to reorient her emotional disposition radically, producing a new subjectivity linked into a collective ethos that had become entirely foreign to her in her previous life.

Rossini argues astutely, in a historical vein, that the 'new Brazil' to which young Josué leads Dora is, paradoxically, 'the return to the old, to the central, internal, agrarian, rural Brazil' ('o retorno para o antigo, para o Brasil central, interno, agrário, rural') (2005: 102). She goes on to explain this paradox as typical in a moment of identity crisis for the Brazilian nation, during which the northeast is always raised up as the 'privileged space of the old struggle between the archaic and the modern, the poor and the rich, and of other binomials established, since Humberto Mauro, in Brazilian cinema' ('espaço privilegiado da velha luta entre o arcaico e o moderno, o pobre e o rico, e de outros binômios instaurados, desde Humberto Mauro, no cinema brasileiro') (2005: 103). I would add that it was Cinema Novo directors who first uniquely privileged the northeast as a representative national space in cinema in the way that Rossini describes (a good example analysed in Chapter 3 would be Anselmo Duarte's *O pagador de promessas*). As can be seen in Chapter 2, Mauro in the 1940s and 1950s had a more national, generic vision of the Brazilian rural landscape that he depicted utilizing location shooting in the environs of his family's lands in Volta Grande, Minas Gerais. The distinction is important in this context because Salles's vision of the northeast is closer to Mauro's more homogeneous, generic rural Brazil (and to Diegues's archaic Brazil discussed in Chapter 4) than it is to the cinemanovista representation of the sertão as a place of polar extremes. Luiz Zanin Oricchio (2003) suggests as much when he emphasizes that the sertão has become a place of reconciliation rather than conflict in Brazilian cinema of the 1990s and early 2000s – but the examples of *Bye Bye Brasil* and Mauro's films demonstrate that the more homogeneous, socially harmonious representation of the rural, too, has a deep genealogy in Brazilian cinema (older than the Cinema Novo approach in fact).

In the final years of the twentieth century, Salles once again reencounters the archaic Brazil that successive generations of filmmakers in the 1950s and 1970s had worried was being forgotten or fast disappearing. This recurring Brazilian Romantic tradition in Brazilian cinema bears out the theory of the fluctuating relevance of saudade as a resonant structure of feeling to successive generations (further developed in the Conclusion [Chapter 8]). The emotional common sense in the discourse of Brazilian cinema has periodically incorporated a greater degree of sentimentalism regarding rural Brazil and its popular culture, never fully departing from the Romantic notion that these are the keepers of the nation's authentic essence. More recent films by northeastern Brazilian directors such as *O som ao redor* (*Neighbouring Sounds*) (Mendonça Filho, [2012] 2013) and *Boa sorte, meu amor* (*Good Luck, My Sweetheart*) (Aragão, 2013) swing back in a direction that emphasizes conflict between social classes, and a clash between modernity and tradition, in their region. There is no reason to doubt that the pendulum will swing back again in a more Romantic, saudoso direction in the work of future generations. The intimist sensibility of a film like Marcelo Gomes and Karim Aïnouz's *Viajo porque preciso, volto porque te amo* (*I Travel Because I Have To, I Return Because I Love You*) ([2009] 2013) already points the way.

Note

1 'Walter Salles expressa o Brasil desejado, mas distante' (Strecker 2010: 17).

Chapter 6

Transnational and Postnational Emotional Vectors in Contemporary Brazilian Cinema

As we have already seen, the emotion of saudade has a long and storied history of representations in Brazilian art. Often the emotion has been expressed in a context of diaspora or exile, as in Gonçalves Dias's famous poem, 'Canção de Exílio' ('Song of Exile'). As in this poem, the emotion has typically been tied to nationalism in artistic representations, with the beloved object of saudade in large part represented as Brazil itself (whether it be the Brazilian people, climate, culture or something else perceived as distant from the artist/subject of narration). In a postmodern era characterized by the globalization of national economies and communication systems, one can see signs in cinema of the formation of new identities that are transnational and at times postnational. In concert with the shifting identities of filmic subjects, we find a shift in the objects towards which their emotions are directed, as well as in the intensity and malleability of those emotions.

I focus in this chapter on representations of subjects feeling saudade in two twenty-first-century films. The nation continues to be an important point of reference in the films *Budapeste* (*Budapest*) (Carvalho, 2009) and *Um passaporte húngaro* (*A Hungarian Passport*) (Kogut, 2001); however, the emotions of the films' protagonists with respect to Brazil, and their saudade for their home country in particular, seem to be far more fluid in terms of their object and intensity than past representations in film, literature or popular music. Barely a decade before, films such as *Central do Brasil* took a much more traditionalist perspective on the emotion, framing it as a longing for the rural, idyllic heartland of Brazil. In these more recent films by Sandra Kogut and Walter Carvalho, however, the real and imagined protagonists of the films essentially deconstruct their own nationalities and shift their sentiments of longing in the direction of a country that on first glance has very little in common with Brazil, namely, Hungary. I will seek to demonstrate how this reframing of saudade in both a documentary and a fictional film signals an opening to transnational, and at times postnational, subjectivity and affectivity in Brazilian cinema.

Since at least the time of the Renaissance and the works of Luís de Camões, saudade's most privileged object has been the lover left behind in one's home nation. Indeed, nation, lover, home and family have been strongly tied together as part of the affectively charged narratives of memory, love and loss that characterize the saudoso (saudade-feeling) subject's experience. At times in the last century, regional saudades in Brazil such as those expressed in northeastern as well as central-southern Brazilian country music (*forró* and *música sertaneja*) have focused the sentiment primarily on a subnational region, though the object of saudade is still focused in a specific home and territory connected with a lover and family left behind. Also, the saudade that *forrozeiros* (forró musicians) sing about in their songs, for instance, even as it tends to be focused on just one region of Brazil, is still very much tied to Brazilian national history and the large-scale internal migration that caused massive displacements of workers from rural regions, along with their related feelings of saudade for the countryside. Thus, the song 'Vida do viajante' ('Life of the Traveller') (cited in the Introduction), which is sung by famous northeastern accordionist Luiz Gonzaga, explains that the emotion of saudade serves to tie together all of the places the singer has travelled to in the country, effectively creating a cognitive-affective map of the nation (Draper 2010, 2014).

Geopolitical developments as well as economic globalization since the 1960s have doubtless created a new framework for cinema, and art in general. In the broadest sense, the very notion of 'home' itself has been more or less gradually displaced and fragmented by the acceleration of transnational flows of people, corporations, labour, capital markets, cultural production and information in general. As the idea of home splinters, expands or contracts, it is to be expected that saudade, an emotion that relies so much on a conception of returning home (as does its sister emotion nostalgia), will tend to undergo some transformations and find its affective charge being directed along new vectors with different levels of intensity. In terms of affect more generally, such a transformation has been theorized both as a waning and as a flattening of affect in our postmodern era (Jameson [1984] 2000; Probyn 1996). Jameson explains that the 'depth models' of modernity that relied so much upon notions of interiority of the subject are being replaced by surface or multiple surfaces. Saudade discourses in particular have until fairly recently – in Brazilian cinema up until the 1990s at least – depended upon a notion of the subject's affect as a bridge between the private, emotional interior and the desired element (saudado) in the exterior, social world. The depth of this desire in the subject's interior world, psyche or soul has been considered to largely determine the authenticity of the subject and that of his or her desire – as well as the authenticity of the privileged objects of desire/saudade such as home, nation, lover, family or childhood.

Beyond the Luso-Brazilian realm of saudade per se, a few scholars in this global postmodern era have considered contemporary manifestations of nostalgia within art and in a broader societal or international cultural context, most notably Fred Davis (1979) and Svetlana Boym (2001). Though saudade is not identical with nostalgia, especially due to the fact that the affective term saudade has an alternative cultural history that is several centuries longer than that of the term nostalgia, there are many helpful parallels that can be drawn between the evolution of the emotions of nostalgia and saudade in recent decades, along with the corresponding evolution in artistic/cinematic representations of these emotions. Firstly, Davis's study (1979) carries out a schematic sociological analysis of nostalgia in US popular/youth culture as well as US cinema of the 1970s. One of Davis's analytical strategies for discussing nostalgia is to divide the emotion into three distinct 'orders', essentially organized by the level of self-consciousness or ambivalence the nostalgic subject feels about his or her own nostalgia. First-order nostalgia is a more or less straightforward experience of longing for the past, while the second- and third-level orders of the emotion add layers of self-consciousness, doubt and/or irony about the specific context within which one feels nostalgia. Boym later independently developed a related, but perhaps more political schema of two opposing forms of nostalgia, restorative versus reflective. For Boym, restorative nostalgia tends to be more associated with ethno-nationalist and/or exclusive, traditionalist imaginaries of the lost home or homeland. On the other hand, reflective nostalgia is characterized by a more ambivalent longing for the lost home/era that can be critical of its flaws and focuses more on the potentialities of what this home 'could have been' rather than imagining it as an actual ideal place that one must return to or reconstruct, as restorative nostalgia does. Boym tends to associate reflective nostalgia with political exiles, in particular exiles or emigrants from the Soviet Union like herself. Thus, it seems that reflective nostalgics would tend to fall much more into Davis's third order of nostalgia, while restorative nostalgics relate more to the primal fears and desires associated with a first-order, uncritical vision of the lost, idealized home that envisions its immediate recovery as a real possibility and desired outcome. Overall, Davis tends to see nostalgia as a moderating rather than a reactionary force in politics, since he claims that the emotion 'defuses what could be a powerful, panic-prone reactivity to jarring change and uncertainty by turning it into tender musing and mutually appreciative self-regard over a shared past' (Davis 1979: 110). Boym's context of Soviet- and post-Soviet Europe is more explicitly politicized, and her two varieties of nostalgia reflect the political divide between a fascist or Stalinist nostalgia and some form of liberal, social-democratic nostalgia for certain aspects of socialist societies or lifestyles in the post-socialist era.

For the purposes of my analysis of these two twenty-first-century Brazilian films featuring saudade, the theoretical frameworks Davis and Boym have developed to analyse nostalgia are helpful in a number of ways, some of which will be developed further below. At this point, I would emphasize one of the most fundamental insights from these scholars of nostalgia – namely, that it is obvious in the context of both modernity and postmodernity, that the fact that an emotion is critically analysed, ironized or questioned in some way by the subject of the emotion herself does not mean that it is not a real emotion or that the emotion is reduced in some way. In the postmodern contexts of the production and narratives of *Um passaporte húngaro* and *Budapeste*, saudade is not usually expressed in an uncritical, first-order or restorative form. In fact, I will argue that a changing, transnational notion of home in the postmodern era makes it all the more likely that the diasporic subjects of these films and other migrants like them will demonstrate a more complex, shifting and reflective saudade. Nevertheless, we should consider this a postmodern form of the emotion rather than a disappearance of the emotion. Thus, the concept of a flattening or surfacing of saudade (more on 'surfacing' below) is more appropriate than the idea of a waning of nostalgia or saudade. According to Boym, this flattened, reflective nostalgia is very much associated with diaspora and what she calls 'diasporic intimacy'. Boym's description of diasporic intimacy characterizes the relationship with the other in exile or diaspora, and could well define many of the relationships of the characters and subjects of Kogut and Carvalho's films:

> [Diasporic intimacy] thrives on the hope of the possibilities of human understanding and survival, of unpredictable chance encounters, but this hope is not utopian. Diasporic

> intimacy is haunted by the images of home and homeland, yet it also discloses some of the furtive pleasures of exile. [...] The illusion of complete belonging has been shattered [for the exile/migrant]. Yet, one discovers that there is still a lot to share.
>
> (Boym 2001: 252, 255)

The importance for the diasporic subjects in these films of unpredictable chance encounters is highlighted by the very structure of the films' narratives, which often feature characters met in a bookstore or on the train as very pivotal in the formation of the migrant's relationship to specific places in the space of diaspora. These same chance encounters yield various 'furtive pleasures of exile' even as the migrant subjects struggle to define for themselves the degree and manner of their belonging in a new culture. One of these furtive pleasures, perhaps bittersweet, is the ability to feel and explore new forms of saudade directed at a widening variety of places, people and cultures.

The final relevant insight from these nostalgia analyses I will emphasize here relates to the commodification of emotion. Davis repeatedly emphasizes how nostalgia is increasingly tied to consumerism, while Boym acknowledges the increasing prevalence of 'ready-made' nostalgic consumer goods – both of these analyses place nostalgia within a postmodern context where the market tends to encroach on all aspects of life, including emotions. However, although a market responding to saudade certainly exists in Brazil and elsewhere, the phenomenon of saudade's commodification is markedly absent from either of the Brazilian films I will discuss below. The saudoso subjects' perspectives in both *Budapeste* and *Um passaporte húngaro* are much closer to Boym's notion of reflective nostalgia than to consumerist or conservative-nationalist remembrance. The filmmakers frame the emotion more as an evolving affective process that their main characters go through, a process that does not seem to be influenced primarily by economic transactions. Rather, the experience of migration is portrayed as the key influence on the development of saudade, more specifically the personal relationships with family, friends, lovers, colleagues or even government bureaucrats that are maintained, grow in intensity or dwindle along the path of migration. The one exception might be Kogut's Hungarian passport itself; the passport she pursues throughout her film might be considered the ultimate saudade-derived consumer good, since it will allow her easy access to the country of her ancestors and represents something that was forcibly taken away from her grandparents when they went into exile to escape the Holocaust. Yet, a passport is also undeniably tied to the legalistic side of migration, so even here the emphasis on the experience of migration remains pre-eminent – indeed, Kogut focuses on the extended migratory journey she must carry out simply to acquire this passport.

In developing her notion of reflective nostalgia, Boym demonstrates a healthy suspicion of the notion of belonging often tied to restorative nostalgia, which can take reactionary and exclusive forms in sundry ethno-nationalist or fundamentalist movements around the world. Yet, Probyn develops a theory of 'outside belonging' that allows us to imagine a different kind of relationship to the home sometimes longed for by nostalgic or saudoso subjects.

'Outside belonging' reflects the postmodern flattening of affect and imagines what a new notion of home might look like, one that does not depend on the sharp, modern distinction between the private and public spheres nor on exclusive narratives of authenticity. Desire in the postmodern, postcolonial era is defined as 'an intimate relation producing the social as outside, as a plurality of surfaces' (1996: 30). The desires to belong to a nation, to return home or to recover a lost love play out along the surface of the social, the social as surface. Perhaps the biggest transformation indicated by the theory of outside belonging – especially in terms of our discussion of saudade – is that the idea of a hierarchy of emotional objects has been jettisoned. No longer are saudade for a specific territory like one's nation of birth, or saudade for certain individuals like one's lover, parents or children, or even saudade for the Portuguese language itself that produced the very word saudade, privileged as the most acceptable and praiseworthy form of the emotion. Further, a 'surfacing' of affect and identity 'presupposes a rendering visible of the forces which constitute the outside and the inside as dichotomous' (1996: 12). There is no doubt that such forces are revealed, circumvented and/or struggled against in the films *Budapeste* and *Um passaporte húngaro*.

Um passaporte húngaro (2001)

To begin our close film analyses along these lines, we can consider Sandra Kogut's film. The forces that produce the dichotomy between inside and outside seem to be alternatively rigid, inconsistent and permissive and are primarily represented by governments and their bureaucracies in *Um passaporte húngaro*. Kogut makes these bureaucracies visible through a multiplicity of human faces and spaces in the film as she shoots footage from her own point of view to introduce the audience to the polyglot group of bureaucrats she must negotiate to attempt to acquire a Hungarian passport. It is these bureaucrats, along with the help of some average Hungarians and some members of Kogut's family, especially her grandmother Mathilde, that help her to explore where the line between the 'outside and inside' of Hungarian nationality and citizenship lies. As part of this exploration, we learn that national identity seems to be a far more shifting and ambiguous terrain than citizenship, even in the 1930s when Kogut's grandparents migrated to Brazil from Hungary. For the immigration officials in Brazilian ports, it appears from the logbooks of the era in Recife – shown on camera as Kogut interviews an archivist – that anyone of possibly Jewish descent/religion was considered an 'Israelite' ('Israelita') and would typically not be allowed to enter the country, regardless of their citizenship status (which in the case of Kogut's grandparents was Hungarian).

Kogut's efforts to become a Hungarian citizen diegetically represented in her film, as well as her exploration of her Jewish ancestry, in and of themselves position her as a kind of transnational and diasporic subject. In terms of discourses of saudade, diaspora and transnational displacement have been some of the most common factors contributing to the trauma of separation, which in turn causes the grief component of the emotion and the saudoso's typical longing to return to this beloved person, place or thing that has become distant. Although Hungary itself is not a very common object of saudade, countless Lusophone artists have expressed the sentiment of saudade in contexts that are very much analogous to the historical and contemporary situations of her grandparents and herself posed by Kogut in her film. Thus it is not surprising that Kogut's grandmother Mathilde, an Austrian migrant to Brazil who lost her Austrian citizenship when she married a Jewish Hungarian, raises the issue of this kind of longing near the end of the film when she offers up to her granddaughter the words of an old German song: 'Ask a traveler where are you going and he will say happily, "Home!" Ask him where he is coming from and he will say sadly, "Home!"'. Especially in a Brazilian, Lusophone context, this song epitomizes the traditional, dual affective valence of saudade, which involves both the love of the distant object of saudade, the joy derived from that love and the grief of having lost the object more or less permanently. Departure from home, the place one loves, is experienced with sadness or grief, while the return is experienced as a kind of joyful redemption. Generally though, these positive and negative affects are not cognitively or even discursively distinguished in the experience and artistic representations of saudade, rather the emotion is experienced and expressed more holistically as a kind of feeling blend of grief and love mediated through memory. Kogut emphasizes the saudoso tone set by some of her grandmother's musings through a klezmer-influenced score that is centred around two Jewish folk songs evoking 'the old country'. Further, the Yiddish and Hebrew lyrics of the specific folk songs chosen evoke the longing for a distant lover (in 'Papir Iz Dokh Vais ['Paper is Really White']) as well as Jewish exile and the desire to return home to Jerusalem (in 'Yah Ribon Olam' ['God, Master of the Universe']). At certain points in the film during her grandmother's narrative about migration, this music is played as Kogut cuts away to train station scenes and arrivals in ports like Recife that she shot in Super 8. This departure from the remainder of the film shot with digital camera adds all the more to the saudoso feeling of the music.

In fact, we can further explore Kogut's evocation of her grandmother's memories as an example of how cinema itself is capable of producing saudade. These memories belong neither to the filmmaker nor to her audience, yet using some of the strategies outlined above, Kogut is able to evoke, through film, a sentiment of saudade for her grandparents' past and her ethno-geographical roots. Kogut's cinematic production of emotion here corresponds to two of Davis's insights regarding nostalgia, which are equally applicable to saudade in this case. For one, Davis notes that nostalgia is not just a sentiment but an 'aesthetic modality in its own right' (1979: 73). Kogut's filmic combination of voice-overs of her grandmother's memories, folk melodies and Super 8 footage as well as digital footage of scenes evoking travel all combine to establish saudade as an important aesthetic modality in her film. A second key point that Davis makes regarding nostalgia is that, as it loses some of its 'biographically distinctive moorings', media products 'may now serve memory where once houses, streets, and persons did' (1979: 129). Through her own filmic media product, Kogut herself and her viewers are able to experience a (mediated, reflective) saudade for a home from which her grandparents were exiled long ago.

Considering that some version of the Jewish exilic subject has existed for millennia, to better establish a contemporary historical context it is also worth considering to what degree Sandra Kogut as a filmmaker and subject of her own film matches up with modern-day theoretical descriptions of the transnational subject and/or postnational subject. According to Bradatan et al., a transnational subject 'plays different roles in front of different audiences, [he or she is] a flexible social actor that internalized [*sic*] the rules and constraints of different social contexts' (2010: 177). On the other hand, postnationalism in cultural production consists of 'a creative reinterpretation of the diverse traditions of the past, not their liquidation' and a non-linear vision of history as collage (Kearney 1992: 585, 586). This latter definition of postnationalism, of course, sounds very close to a definition of postmodernism as an artistic style. In any case, by these definitions of transnational and postnational subjects, it is safe to say that Kogut would fit fairly easily into either category. In her film, she is shown to converse and maintain relaxed, friendly relations with many different people of different nationalities, speaking different languages, and ranging in role from family members to officials in various bureaucratic positions in Brazil, France and Hungary. Kogut seems to be able to move through these different environments with relative ease due to her flexibility in terms of the languages she speaks and her ability to internalize conflicting information from many different bureaucratic sources without expressing hostility, belligerence, exasperation or really any other aggression or negative affect. The narrative structure of *Um passaporte húngaro*, as well as Kogut's personal affect as filmmaker and first-person subject of the film, serve to produce a sense of diasporic intimacy in the film. The filmic narrative is haunted by overlapping images, sounds and discourses of home at the same time that the notion of belonging is flattened and scattered across several hemispheres. We discover that one of the 'furtive pleasures of exile' (see Boym 2001, cited above) is precisely the formation of these new affective ties that do not seek complete belonging; instead an outside belonging takes shape that does not forget but historicizes and ultimately undermines earlier exclusive notions of intimacy and home. Kogut's camera evokes a diasporic intimacy whether she is in her Austro-Brazilian grandmother's dining room, in the offices of the Hungarian embassy in Paris or speaking with a Brazilian archivist. Her ability to film so many scenes suffused with this diasporic intimacy highlights her identity as a flexible social actor, thus matching the definition of transnational subject noted above.

But it is also fair to say that Kogut's filmic style is postnational in the sense that it reinterprets traditions of the past (such as Yiddish and Hebrew music and German lyrics for example). Further, the film certainly takes a non-linear view of history, interweaving modern-day footage of Sandra Kogut's travels, bureaucratic travails and conversations seamlessly with her grandmother's and others' recollections of pre-World War II Hungary and Brazil. In the process, she not only reinterprets but redefines these memories in the context of her own experiences as a transnational filmmaker in an era of rapidly expanding economic globalization. To a large degree, this redefinition of the significance of Hungarian identity and citizenship comes about very simply through the director's silence – her resolute refusal, despite constantly being asked about them, to clarify her reasons for pursuing Hungarian nationality in terms of nationalist fervour, familial legacy or the economic and political advantages of potential European citizenship. Her silence is not only a negative refusal to conform to one kind of belonging though, it is also an ability to listen to the other across cultures, borders and even historical time without imposing a nationalist discourse on the other's narrative.

Sandra Kogut has said of *Um passaporte húngaro* that 'the story of the film is formed by the stories BETWEEN stories' ('a estória [do filme] é formada pelas estórias ENTRE estórias') (Kogut quoted in Lins 2004: 3). This comment can be tied to Fredric Jameson's description of the replacement of depth with surface in postmodern times: 'What replaces [...] depth models [in the postmodern era] is for the most part a conception of practices, discourses and textual play [...] depth is replaced by surface, or by multiple surfaces (what is often called intertextuality is in that sense no longer a matter of depth)' (Jameson [1984] 2000: 198). From Kogut's description of her film's story, one gets the sense of the film being an intertext that she develops through a process of textual play between and along some of the major modern narratives of European and Latin American national identity and citizenship. Kogut's conception of the 'camera as pen' underlines all the more that she thinks of her filmic process as a writing on the margins – or the surfaces – of hegemonic discourses (Kogut 2001). The impact of such a process upon the affective register of the narrative is largely to uproot the emotion of saudade, traditionally very much focused on a specific place or nation and often not one of the subject's conscious choosing, and to scatter it across a multitude of places and times. There is a related shift in the intensity of the emotion as it is refracted through Jewish folk melodies, Mathilde's memories and Kogut's own present-day travels, shuttling back and forth across Europe and Brazil. It is difficult to situate saudade clearly within the authentic, passionate interior of any individual in this film due to such a flattening of affect. It should also be noted that her use of the camera as pen adds a personal touch to the film – shaping her production process into one that both represents and reproduces a feeling of diasporic intimacy.

We can consider an example of the transformation of saudade that Kogut effects in the same scene where one can hear the audio of Mathilde telling her granddaughter the lyric from the old German song about the desire to return home and the sadness of leaving it. Immediately before we hear Mathilde's voice, the scene depicts a uniformed Hungarian official on a train taking Kogut's new Hungarian passport to inspect it. He seems confused as to why someone would have a Hungarian passport but not be able to speak the Hungarian language, and abruptly disappears down the train corridor, taking Kogut's passport with him. As Kogut continues the take without cuts in the man's absence, the imagery on screen is of the train window on the other side of the empty corridor in front of her compartment, as the train moves along through the Hungarian countryside. It is at this point that Mathilde's non-diegetic voice is heard quoting the saudoso German song discussed above. Thereafter, the Hungarian official returns and hands back Kogut's passport without further comment. Thus, the way that Kogut deploys her grandmother's voice here, on a moving train without even clearly establishing where the train is headed, and within the dramatic tension of whether her newly acquired Hungarian citizenship will seem authentic to the official with her passport, pulls the affective force of saudade out along several vectors that stretch from Budapest to Paris to Recife to Rio de Janeiro. It is really any point along these vectors that could be considered a 'home', which could be affectively charged for Kogut more negatively as being left behind, or more positively as a place to which the traveller is returning – or even more likely, as somewhere in between. This affective in-between space shot through with past memories can be called saudade, but its trajectories, depths and general spatio-temporal orientation are decidedly transnational and postmodern.

Budapeste (2009)

Much the same can be said of saudade as expressed and felt by the protagonist of Walter Carvalho's *Budapeste*, a 2009 filmic adaptation of the eponymous 2003 novel by Chico Buarque. In this case the protagonist is an entirely fictional Brazilian man named José Costa (Leonardo Medeiros) who travels to Hungary and develops a fascination for the city of Budapest, the language of Hungarian, Hungarian literature and poetry and last but certainly not least, a Hungarian woman named Kriszta (Gabriella Hámori). José Costa's profession is that of a ghost writer, and associated with this profession in the film's narrative come the key themes of alienation and doubling. Costa quite obviously serves as a secret authorly double to several other characters in the film who are the nominal authors of books written in both Portuguese and Hungarian. But it is not far into the film that Costa also starts to develop a secret, second life in Hungary where he seeks the authentic integration into a family, language and country that he does not quite seem to have found in his native Rio de Janeiro. Costa clearly feels alienated in Brazil despite all the trappings of a seemingly very successful middle-class lifestyle, with a steady income, a nice apartment and a beautiful newscaster wife and young son that he lives with there.

Yet, the life that Costa builds for himself in Budapest is very much a mirror image of his life in Rio, rather than an escape from it. He becomes involved with a Hungarian woman of about the same age as his wife, who has a young boy about the same age as his own son. As he learns Hungarian, Costa quickly becomes interested in ghost writing for a Hungarian poet. However, Costa does not immediately run away from his life in Brazil. At first he has feelings of saudade for his wife and home country, as evidenced by a scene in which he makes a phone call back home from a telephone booth in Hungary. As usual, Costa's wife Vanda (Giovanna Antonelli) does not answer the phone, but he proceeds to leave a long message in which he says 'Vanda…Eu…estou com saudade (I feel saudade)' and then speaks a string of Portuguese words to assuage his feelings of saudade, including the very word saudade itself: 'saudade – Pão de Açucar – Maracanã – Guanabara – avenida (avenue) – casa (house/home) – saudade – marimbondo (wasp; also a nickname given to the Brazilians by the Portuguese around the time of Independence according to Michaelis) – adstringência (astringency)'. Aside from evoking the emotion of saudade itself by repeating the word, Costa also says other words that reference home (*casa*) along with specific famous places in his native city of Rio de Janeiro, as well as the African influence in the Brazilian Portuguese language (the word *marimbondo* derives from the Bantu language of Kimbundo) – an influence that certainly seems far removed from the reality of life in Hungary that he is currently situated in.

Appropriately, the word that ends this string of associations is a synonym of 'severity', namely 'astringency'. Onomatopoeically, the word *adstringência* sounds quite severe when spoken in Brazilian Portuguese, especially in contrast with the previous words Costa speaks, words like 'saudade' and 'Guanabara' that would be much more at home in Brazilian lyrics or poetry. Anatomically speaking, according to the Oxford English Dictionary, something that is 'astringent' has the 'power to draw together or contract the soft organic tissues'. There is a clear association here with a contraction back to Hungary – that is, the end of Costa's attempt to 'reach out and touch someone' (to paraphrase the old AT&T ad) as he pulls himself back into his immediate reality of life in a country that is still quite foreign to him. The theme of doubling is emphasized here by a bad phone line that echoes Costa's words back to him, and in the following scene all the more stressed with a greater emphasis on alienation when Costa returns home to Rio to find his own message waiting for him, unlistened to, and proceeds to play it back to himself as he walks through his apartment alone and suspects his wife of infidelity.

Emphasizing doubling and alienation all the more, Costa finds a copy of the novel that he ghost wrote and that his wife has been reading – the copy is signed by the nominal author, Kaspar Krabbe (Antonie Kamerling), with a warm message to Costa's own wife. If we think back to the film letters of *Central do Brasil*, Costa's phone message is the equivalent of the letters that are never received, representing a failure to communicate. The additional element here is that he himself receives his own letter, representing a kind of solipsistic loop within which the character is caught. There is no one else who can truly identify with saudade exactly as he feels it, caught between two cultures as he is, except perhaps someone who is his own double, another ghost writer – a character in the film who fittingly remains anonymous, without a name other than Costa's own. Costa's novel *O ginógrafo* (*The Gynographer*), representing his work as a ghost writer but signed by the nominal author to his wife, is another kind of message; it is equivalent to a letter that Costa wrote but is signed by someone else, someone he jealously imagines to be his wife's lover. With regard to the emotion of saudade itself, there is an abrupt shift here from the scene in the phonebooth where his wife and Brazil had been the objects of an emotion that is very much tied to familiar and beloved people and places that are missed, to the subsequent scene where his wife, son and apartment in Brazil are *made alien* or better yet, *unheimlich* (German for 'uncanny', but literally 'unhomely'), by his realization that life in Rio has continued on without him as he has pursued his fascination with Hungary. His feeling of saudade has certainly not been reciprocated by anyone else.

Yet, the film goes even further than demonstrating the alienation of the protagonist's saudade to really emphasize the *replaceability* of the objects of saudade, even those related to national origin and identity like the references Costa makes to places in Rio de Janeiro. It is this aspect of the film that most closely echoes the transnational and postnational vectors of saudade discussed above as represented in *Um passaporte húngaro*. This treatment of saudade also marks a significant departure from traditional saudade discourse, which has a strong tendency to privilege the object of saudade as having its own intrinsic, unique, enchanting qualities that quite naturally evoke saudade, rather than an emphasis on the emotion as a projection of positive qualities by the saudoso (subject) upon his or her saudado (object). In Costa's case, *Budapeste*'s narrative makes it clear that the initial objects of his saudade in Brazil are very much replaceable. One scene in particular, after Costa has a dramatic and public fight with his Brazilian wife Vanda, demonstrates the very conscious effort he makes to substitute his saudade for Brazil and the Portuguese language with a new love for Hungary, its language and Kriszta, his new love interest. Feeling angry with and jealous of his wife, and all the more alienated from his home country, Costa announces in a voice-over as he returns to Hungary that he is planning to 'substitute in his head one language for the other' in order to forget what he has said in Portuguese to his wife Vanda. Costa likens his mind to 'a house being remodeled' ('uma casa em obras') with one language being built up (Hungarian) and the other (Portuguese) being disassembled and hauled away. This idea of uprooting from one's national origins and identity, as well as one's mother tongue, and replacing them with another is not only postnational and made possible by an already transnational mindset in Costa, but also entirely at odds with the traditional expression of saudade that is tied so strongly to love of *pátria* (homeland) and one's loved ones who live there.

Yet, this is not to say that Costa is somehow opposed to the love of country – he simply, and radically, wants to choose a substitute for the object of his patriotic love, at the same time substituting his native language, family and wife. This idea of leaving the Portuguese language behind is actually foreshadowed earlier in the film when we see the image of a woman washing off Portuguese words written across her body as a voice-over narrates a scene from the novel *The Gynographer*, which José Costa ghost wrote. (The protagonist of this novel does all of his writing on women's bodies.) Later in the film, as Costa returns to Brazil one last time, he is unable even to find this formerly best-selling novel in a bookstore and its very existence is questioned – thus reinforcing the idea that Costa's Brazilian past has been entirely dismantled. During this same final visit to Brazil, we see José Costa walking down the sidewalk next to Leblon beach and passing by a group of street musicians on the beach playing Chico Buarque's samba, 'Feijoada completa' (a very nationalist topic since *feijoada*, or black bean stew, is a typically Brazilian dish). Suddenly, instead of the musicians' voices Costa hears a man's voice in Hungarian singing to the same tune. At first he seems disoriented but then a smile spreads across his face as he starts to enjoy the sound of the new, Hungarian lyrics. This scene can be read as the realization of Costa's earlier expressed desire to replace his native language with Hungarian – the remodelling of his house of language and national identity is complete.

The replaceability of saudados emphasized in this film, which we can connect to the general postmodern phenomenon of the surfacing of affect discussed at the beginning of this chapter, is represented in the city of Budapest through Costa's observance of two public statues. These public statues in Budapest also serve to address the historical and political context of Hungary in the post-socialist era, as Costa first briefly travels to the country in 1991 and then he returns there for an indefinite stay around the turn of the twenty-first century. Further, the fact that the two statues Costa sees have antithetical historico-political associations reiterates the theme of doubling and alienation in the film. The first public statue seen in the film is one of the first things that Costa encounters upon his decision to return to Hungary, just as he arrives in central Budapest by taxi. Driving along the bank of the river Danube that divides the city, Costa tells his driver to stop as he becomes interested in the cargo of a barge that is floating downriver. He proceeds to get out of the taxi and stands on the riverbank as the barge passes by. The camera first emphasizes a bemused expression on Costa's face with an extreme close-up, and then the viewer is shown the barge with an enormous statue of Lenin tied to its deck. The statue has clearly been junked, as it is broken into seven segments and is being hauled away on a rusty barge to an unknown destination (presumably the dustbin of history!). The statue's finger is shown to be pointing in one direction and Costa markedly walks in the opposite direction after seeing the statue, though perhaps his expression has become more wistful than bemused by the time the statue floats away downriver. Costa's bemused, then wistful facial expressions immediately establish a political orientation that deems the Soviet past quaint, kitschy and irrelevant. This is not so far from the attitude of Hungarians themselves towards their socialist past in the immediate post-socialist period, according to Maya Nadkarni (2010). With this scene featuring a junked Lenin statue, we find an interesting cross-pollination of Hungarian and Brazilian nostalgia/saudade. It is clear that the director Carvalho wants Costa to be associated with saudade for a national culture and folk-linguistic-artistic history rather than an older form of politics or social organization like socialism. Costa's attitude towards the socialist past foreshadows his approach to Hungarian history and culture, which focuses on folk-national culture, including neo-Romantic Hungarian poetry and the Hungarian language itself.

Costa's saudade is framed within the context of a Hungarian society that tore down its old Lenin statues and then proceeded to privilege other objects of nostalgia, including figures from folk-national history that have their own representative statues. Thus, there is a parallel between Costa's attempt to replace his own personal, Brazilian history with Hungary's attempt to replace, or at least establish a distanced relationship to, its socialist history. The example of a post-socialist national monument highlighted in the film is the statue of 'Anonymus', the anonymous chronicler of the Hungarian king Béla III in the late twelfth century. At one point in the film, in fact in the scene immediately following Costa's phone call in which he expresses his saudade for Brazilian culture and language, he visits the statue of Anonymus in Budapest's City Park. On one level, there is an obvious relationship between the statue itself and the story of Costa since he too writes as an anonymous author. This was a fortuitous coincidence discovered by the filmmakers as they prepared to shoot *Budapeste*, since the author of the original novel, Chico Buarque, was unaware of the existence of this statue in Budapest when he wrote his novel (having never visited the city himself before his novel was adapted to film). The idea that Hungary has a national hero who is an anonymous author made the country seem, ex post facto, to be the perfect place for a man of José Costa's profession to migrate and reshape his identity. Yet in a contemporary political context, this statue takes on another significance in opposition to the statue of Lenin depicted earlier in the film, a return to pre-socialist folk history, especially the nationalist history of the Magyars to whom Hungarians trace their ethnic roots.[1] This historico-political relationship between the two statues again serves to emphasize the postmodern (and post-socialist) replaceability of saudados or objects of nostalgia.

Costa's visit to the Anonymus statue thus presents us with a complex cross-pollination of Hungarian nostalgia and Brazilian saudade. His rather traditionalist Brazilian saudade, presumably inculcated in him from an early age within the context of Brazilian culture and society, paradoxically inclines him to identify with the national, folk history of Hungary and to pursue an intimate knowledge of the literature and language of that people as he seeks to run away from his Brazilian life and the Brazilian Portuguese language and culture that he associates with it. Thus, we can associate the doubling of the statues with a doubling of Costa's own saudade. This doubling yields another paradoxical effect of making saudade seem more universal and everlasting despite the replaceability of its objects. Through the discarding of one constellation of saudados, just as the Lenin statue was discarded, saudade reveals itself in an abstract, more transnational form that can exist independently of Brazilian culture and then attach itself to new saudados in an entirely distinct, non-Lusophone culture.

Echoes of the José Costa character can be found in other postmodern Brazilian novels. Consider, for example, the following description of the narrator and protagonist of João Gilberto Noll's *Hotel Atlântico* (1989): 'The narrator of *Hotel Atlântico* precisely exemplifies these new zones of urban experience, always between inertia and migration, the masked desire to escape oneself and egocentrism, amnesiac uprooting and the nostalgic impulse to return to a volatile concept of home' ('El narrador de *Hotel Atlântico* justamente ejemplifica estas nuevas zonas de la experiencia urbana, siempre entre la inercia y la trashumancia, el deseo enmascarado de salir de sí y el egocentrismo, el desarraigo amnésico y el impulso nostálgico de regreso a un volátil concepto de casa') (Zambrana 2009: 151). It would be difficult to invent a better description of José Costa himself, and like *Budapeste*, the novel *Hotel Atlântico* was adapted to film in 2009 – though the latter film's notion of migration/displacement is more restricted since the travels of *Hotel Atlântico*'s protagonist are within Brazil's borders (Amaral). Generally speaking, Moriconi describes the postmodern imaginary in Brazil as one that emphasizes 'the notion of multiple and fragmentary identities as well as the fragmentation of meaning' (2005: 356). Thus, Costa's deconstruction and reconstruction of his national identity and language, as well as the fragmenting and reorientation of his affective attachments to nation, family and lover, fit into a general trend of Brazilian postmodernism. Kogut's *Um passaporte húngaro* certainly fits squarely within this trend as well, since one of the film's main themes is the multiple and fragmentary (not to mention shifting, evolving) nature of transnational identities. Along with these identities, Kogut demonstrates the flattening or 'surfacing' of affective attachments to places and people met in one's home nation as well as in the process of transnational migration and travel. In this way, her work fragments the traditional, 'deep' meanings ascribed to nation, family and home into a multiplicity of potential nations, families and homes to which the postnational subject might ascribe some sort of personal significance or attachment.

Conclusion

Before my final consideration of the forms of saudade presented in these two films, it is worth emphasizing the distinction between what I have been calling the transnational, postnational and postmodern characteristics of Kogut and Carvalho's films on the one hand, and what Santiago (2001) has more broadly termed the 'in-between space of Latin American discourse' on the other. Santiago and others have argued that at least since the advent of Brazilian Modernismo and other Latin American modernist avant gardes in the early twentieth century, if not before, Latin American artists have been developing notions of national identity that are hybrid and 'impure' by European standards. Taking European (transnational) influence and cannibalizing it for their own purposes, Brazilians and other Latin American artists of the last century have helped to decolonize and decentre the very notions of literature and civilization, thus opening up space for further international exchange between artists on more equal terms than in the colonial and neocolonial past. The same could certainly be said of Cinema Novo and New Cinema in general across Latin America, as well as the various 'Third Cinemas' developed across the globe in the last 50 years. However, when focusing on the affective register and representations of emotions like saudade, today there does seem to be a clear distinction from even Brazilian films made in the 1990s like *Central do Brasil* in terms of the flattening of affect. Saudade, one of the emotions with the most specific and profound connotations in Lusophone cultures, and a related history of thought and literary history going back hundreds of years, has not been reshaped by past filmmakers to nearly the degree to which it is rethought and refelt here in these films of the twenty-first century.

Simply put, it means something quite different when José Costa says 'I feel saudade' ('estou com saudade') to his answering machine than it did when Dora wrote 'I feel saudade for my father, I feel saudade for everything' ('eu tenho saudade de meu pai, eu tenho saudade de tudo') in her letter at the end of Salles's *Central do Brasil*. In the context of the latter film, Dora's statement not only ties her saudade to her intimate personal and familial history, but by association to her personal experience of the national geography. Thus, there is a traditional focus on the authenticity of affective interiority/depth and a grounding of this experience within national identity (indeed, within the nation's interior or heartland in the northeastern *sertão*). As argued in Chapter 5, this representation falls within the Brazilian Romantic tradition and is likewise very much akin to the twentieth-century understanding of saudade expounded by anthropologist Roberto DaMatta, when he writes that saudade is a national 'ideological and cultural focus' that 'is centred in a temporality of the home' ('se centra numa temporalidade da casa') (DaMatta 1993: 21, 32). There is a sense of permanence and self-evidence, of profound intimacy combined with national-popular authenticity, to Dora's saudade that does not hold true for the shifting vectors and intensities of this emotion in *Um passaporte húngaro* and *Budapeste*. This evolution is all the more striking in that some of the very same filmmakers are involved in the films contrasted here – namely, the director of *Budapeste* (Carvalho) was the cinematographer of *Central do Brasil* and also of *Terra estrangeira*, another 1990s film with a more traditional, Lusophone-oriented representation of saudade even while that story takes place in a transnational context between Brazil and Portugal. On the other hand, the recent flattening of affect in cinema is by no means anti-emotional or rationalist in nature, thus departing from earlier, especially realist eras in Brazilian and Portuguese literature and cinema when affect was repressed or subordinated to cognitivist logic and ideological rigidity (cf. Podalsky 2011 on the framing of affect in New Latin American Cinema of the 1960s). What is taking place in contemporary Brazilian cinema is by no means the death of saudade, but rather its coming to terms with an increasingly volatile, transnational concept of home. Taken together, Walter Carvalho and Sandra Kogut's films are vivid examples of the emotional experiences common to many contemporary transnational migrants, lending credence to the belief that reflective subjects of saudade and nostalgia 'can create a global diasporic solidarity based on the experience of immigration and internal multiculturalism' (Boym 2001: 342). These filmmakers imagine/model psychologically internalized multicultural identities, as well as socially multicultural spaces of solidarity and understanding, that are made more possible through the complex, evolving emotional ties of postmodern saudades.

Note

1 Svetlana Boym (2001) demonstrates in her discussion of statues of Peter the Great in St. Petersburg that this renewed interest in regional/national folk heroes is a larger phenomenon throughout the former Eastern Bloc. In fact, there is a striking parallel in terms of the local mythology developed around the new Peter the Great statue in St. Petersburg as described by Boym on the one hand, and the Anonymus statue depicted in the Budapest of Carvalho's film on the other. Boym relates the popular superstition in St. Petersburg that one will become rich if one touches the index finger of this 1991 monument to Peter the Great, while in the film *Budapeste* a Francophone tour guide tells tourists that one will have luck if one touches Anonymus's pencil. Both superstitions demonstrate a personal, emotional and physical connection to the statues that vivifies them and literally establishes a direct contact between the people and their newly valued monuments, clearly distinguishing them from the destroyed and discarded statues of the Soviet era.

Chapter 7

Haptic and Optical Cinematic Approaches to Childhood Memories

From classic Brazilian cinema of the 1950s to the films of the current decade, representations of the child and childhood have been a common theme. Often, saudade has been evoked by filmmakers in their attempts to present an adult perspective on a childhood left behind. Yet, it should be clear, in the wake of the preceding chapters, that it is always important to historicize representations of emotion, even those that may seem timeless like saudade or nostalgia.

The filmic representation of childhood in the 1950s as epitomized by the 'grandfather of Brazilian cinema', director Humberto Mauro, follows the lead of Brazilian Romantic poetry in its nostalgic emphasis on an idyllic, rural youth. Mauro's pedagogical, nationalist framing of various narratives invoking childhood on the ranch/plantation utilizes a filmic style that I term optical cinema (following Marks 2000). Childhood is laid out like a landscape that is easily perceived and thus (re)mastered and possessed by the adult subject, even if only in memory. Narrative identification with the imagined child is facilitated by evocation of the visual plenitude of childhood in the rural landscape.

More recent, haptic cinematic approaches question the very possibility of visual plenitude with respect to childhood memories. I argue that this is a fetishistic approach to childhood that refuses to possess the figure of the child or gain mastery of a childhood narrative, for nationalistic purposes or otherwise. We can see a haptic cinematic style in recent years in the work of director Petra Costa. Costa explores memories of her own childhood with a far greater emphasis on sensory experience beyond vision, especially touch and kinesthetics. Her work explores the surface of the image, and by extension the past itself, as a mysterious fetish, or radioactive fossil, that cannot be easily penetrated or mastered.

Humberto Mauro ([1945, 1954–56] 2002) explores the past as landscape in his *Brasilianas* series of short films in the mid-1950s (esp. *Meus oito anos* [*When I was Eight*] in 1956, *Engenhos e usinas* [*Sugar Mills and Factories*] and *Cantos de trabalho* [*Work Songs*] in 1955 and *Aboios e cantigas* [*Cattle Calls and Ballads*] in 1954) as well as his feature film *O canto da saudade* (1952), discussed in Chapter 2. His framing of this landscape falls for the most part very much within the realm of optical visuality as first described by art historian Aloïs Riegl at the turn of the twentieth century. Laura Marks explains that '[o]ptical visuality [...] assumes that all the resources the viewer requires are available in the image. Accordingly, the optical image in Riegl's sense corresponds to Deleuze's movement-image, as it affords the illusion of completeness that lends itself to narrative' (2000: 163). Mauro invokes memory not so much for the purpose of thematizing recollection itself but rather as the narrative framework through which he will recover the bucolic past of rural Minas Gerais for the benefit of a larger, national narrative.

This is a narrative critical of developmentalism in Brazil to the extent that the imperative of economic growth via industrialization and urbanization forgets the continued importance of the agricultural economy and regional cultures of Brazil in the 1950s. In the face of the hegemonic and utopian ideology of economic development, Mauro's films of this era propose a pedagogical project to promote the preservation of regional culture, itself understood to include the sugar plantation and cattle economies and associated traditional rural social relations, in addition to the regional folk tales, songs, dances and music that are produced within these rural economies.

In various scenes from both the feature film *O canto da saudade* and some of the short films from the same era like *Meus oito anos*, Mauro's camera establishes a commanding view of the landscape of rural Minas Gerais. Both the *Brasilianas* series of short films as well as the 1952 feature film were shot on location in and around Volta Grande, the small, rural municipality where Mauro had founded and established his independent film studio Rancho Alegre in the early 1950s. In two different scenes early in the films *Meus oito anos* and *O canto da saudade*, the characters are positioned on hilltops that are somewhat protected from the elements by groves of trees, at the same time that the trees are distant enough from each other in spots

Figure 6: Director/producer Humberto Mauro (r), musician/actor Mário Mascarenhas (m) and playwright Silveira Sampaio (l) on set at the Rancho Alegre Studios (Volta Grande, Minas Gerais) for the shooting of *O canto da saudade* (Courtesy Museu de Imagem e Som, Rio de Janeiro).

to allow for panoramic views of the surrounding grassy hills and pastures. The tree groves allow for a kind of seclusion and create a space for the quiet reflection of the characters on the landscape, which itself soon becomes a metaphor for not only the past of the region itself, but also for the whole way of life of rural Brazilian culture.

We should consider the opening sequences more specifically in either film that feature such commanding hilltop views, in order to get a sense of both the artistic tradition in which Mauro is working as well as the nostalgic pedagogical frame of cultural rescue (*resgate*) that shapes the filmmaker's narratives, cinematography and *mise-en-scène*. Firstly, I will analyse *Meus oito anos* since the film itself hearkens back to a much earlier era by adapting Casimiro de Abreu's Romantic-era poem of the same title. Although the film is an adaptation of a poem from a century before, Mauro only emphasizes continuity between the rural Brazil of Rio de Janeiro province that Abreu celebrated in the 1850s and Mauro's contemporaneous (1950s) shooting location of Volta Grande, Minas Gerais. The lack of differentiation between different regions and centuries highlights the timelessness of a utopian rural-national landscape that Mauro wishes to convey.

Mauro shares with the Romantics of the nineteenth century a nostalgic vision, but rather than being one of childhood in the rural landscape as in the original poem, Mauro's nostalgia (or saudade, to cite the specific language of Abreu's poem) expands to become a saudade for Brazilian rurality itself. The director even goes so far as to account for a reference to the ocean in the original poem (since the area Abreu describes was coastal) by having his boy protagonist dream of the ocean while sleeping in a hammock in land-locked Minas Gerais. In this way the generic ruralism of this short, and of the other films in the series, departs somewhat from Romantic poets like Abreu, who tended to find a virtue in capturing a specific place or moment in time, and thus to avoid generalization (Candido [1975] 2014: 509). Randal Johnson (1999) has referred to the emotional framework for much of the *Brasilianas* series as a 'cultural nostalgia' for rural Brazil, noting the 'nostalgic gaze' of various characters including the protagonist of *Meus oito anos*, as he looks out from a hilltop onto the Volta Grande landscape. A guiding preoccupation of the *Brasilianas* series of films is clearly to transfer to, or evoke in, the viewer this emotional perspective on rural Brazil, a perspective that naturally supports the preservation of ways of life found in the geographic and economic landscapes of rural agriculture still so important in most regions of the country.

Returning to a specific analysis of the *mise-en-scène* of *Meus oito anos*, the film begins with a middle-aged man walking into an area on a hilltop, within a copse of trees as noted before. This man, it is soon revealed, is to be the subject of reminiscence who thinks back to his childhood years in this rural area in the same vein as the remembrances of Abreu in the original poem. With respect to our discussion of optical visuality, the vantage point established for this male protagonist at the start of this film is paramount. The man is shown in a wide shot within the grove, taking a position where he can look through a gap in the trees out into the landscape. He assumes a thoughtful expression as Mauro's camera focuses on him in successive medium and extreme close-ups while Abreu's poem begins to be sung on the soundtrack. One should note here the appropriateness of setting Abreu's poetry to music, since 'his verses seek out the most song-like rhythm' ('os seus versos buscam o ritmo mais cantante') (Candido [1975] 2014: 512). The final extreme close-up highlights the man's gaze above all, filling the frame with just the upper half of his face, with his left eye well-lit and located centre-screen. The protagonist settles himself beneath a flowering tree, whose blooms begin to cascade down around the man in the breeze just before the camera turns to contemplate the landscape in a point-of-view shot from the man's perspective. This sequence of shots is meant to set the stage for a transition back into the past, presumably to the childhood of the protagonist, in parallel with the verses of Abreu's poem.

The man's view of the rural Minas Gerais landscape, represented by the camera, is unobstructed and clear, and would not be unfitting as the subject of a Romantic-era painting. A painting of this kind, and not coincidentally Mauro's shot as well, serves up a visual plenitude to the viewer and draws his/her gaze into the depths of this fullness, penetrating the imaginary three-dimensional space that is created by the optical perspective, a legacy of the western Renaissance tradition in the visual arts. Mauro's sequence of shots leading up to the landscape imagery underscores this optics through the establishment of the setting and the specific point of view of the character on the hill. The symbolism of this landscape with respect to childhood memories becomes clear as the film seamlessly transitions to the past with a series of shots depicting the protagonist's pre-adolescent life in an idyllic rural environment.

A boy runs through a wooded area replete with banana trees and other flowering, tropical plants. The boy sets a trap to catch a songbird for a pet. This boyhood sequence begins to be intercut with the image of the older man looking out into the landscape, re-emphasizing the nostalgic gaze framing these memories. As the story returns to the past, the boy is shown with a girl of similar age, to whom he gives an orange blossom as a gift, having shot it out of a tall tree with his slingshot. This falling flower finds its graphic match with the petals falling around the reminiscing man as Mauro cuts back yet again to the older protagonist in his solitary reverie. Flowers, of course, are frequently associated with love in Romantic poetry and the whiteness of the petals in both past and present also underscores the purity of young love.

Beyond some melodramatic orchestral music arranged by composer Aldo Taranto, and the voice-over of musician José Mauro alternately reading and singing Abreu's poem, the flower-images are the most non-visual sensorial element in the film. They invoke scent and the strong neural pathways between the olfactory receptors and the amygdala, a section of the brain's limbic system that has a pivotal role in shaping emotional memories (Ledoux 1996; of course Proust most famously emphasized the scent-memory link with his character Marcel's reminiscence about his own past, catalysed by the tastes and smells of tea with madeleine crumbs). The graphic match of descending white petals in scenes set in both past and present hints that it is the scent of flowers that forms the most powerful connection between the present and past selves of the protagonist. The evocation of scent is not strictly a haptic element in the film, but like haptic visuality, it does depart somewhat from the hegemonic western focus on visual plenitude lending itself to narrative. It is evidence that Mauro's film form certainly allows room for non-visual components of the sensorium at certain moments. Flower images do indeed evoke a Romantic narrative framework; however, they also participate in a different form of sensorial epistemology that joins together present and past via the olfactory system rather than the symbolic rationality of narrative.

Meus oito anos culminates with one final scene of boy and girl together, then cuts to the last shot of the older man, who slowly walks away from his hilltop refuge, presumably to return to his quotidian life after his mental and emotional voyage to the past. The final scene for boy and girl re-emphasizes the innocence of their love and friendship, as they hold hands and approach a small chapel in the countryside. In the context of romance, the chapel suggests marriage, and thus a kind of limit point for child-like affections. Boy and girl, along with a third friend who joins them, walk away from Mauro's stationary camera and approach the church, thus symbolically leaving their innocent childhood years behind and drawing the older man's reminiscence on his youth to a close. As the film cuts back to the final shot of the man departing the hilltop, flower petals continue to cascade down from above and the rural landscape spread out beneath the hillside is again on display for the viewer. Thus, the entirety of the film is bookended by the initial object of the protagonist's gaze, a rural-regional scene of lush, grassy hillsides and fields laid out from a commanding perspective for the nostalgic, middle-aged, Euro-Brazilian man.

Both the framing of this landscape itself and the representation of the memories and saudade of the protagonist strive towards the national resonance achieved by the poem 'Meus oito anos'. By the time this film was shot in 1956, Casimiro de Abreu's work had been consecrated as part of the Brazilian literary canon and had become part of the standard school curriculum such that the subtitle of this film refers to the poem as a 'canto escolar' or school song. To get a sense of the broad emotional appeal and relevance that Mauro is trying to tap into in this film, we must recall that saudade is uniquely privileged as a structure of feeling in Lusophone cultures (Orico 1940; DaMatta 1993; Lourenço 1999). Casimiro de Abreu's poem is representative of a central emotional theme of Romantic poetry in both Brazil and Portugal, which privileged saudade as one of the most authentic and pure passions. As explored by Abreu and many other authors from Gonçalves Dias and José Alencar in Brazil to Almeida Garrett in Portugal, saudade can be directed at a lover far away, at a childhood left behind or at one's own nation or region, among other pivotal individual and more collective, social objects of love. Humberto Mauro, in *Meus oito anos* and various other works of the same era, seeks to tie this universally understood and often celebrated emotion to his vision of rural Brazil and a cinematic project that traces Brazil's rural, regional roots. It is no accident that such a nationalist project would have primary recourse to optical visuality and its 'illusion of completeness that lends itself to narrative' noted by Marks. Traditionalist representations of nostalgia, with their roots in the Romantic era, have more often than not harnessed and narrativized the shifting affective blend of saudade on behalf of a universal subject coded as (Luso-)Brazilian male and elite. The protagonist of *Meus oito anos* occupies this privileged position and Mauro's film seeks to encourage continued identification of a national Brazilian audience with the gaze of the seigneurial class. Yet, the purpose of identification with this gaze and the object of its desire, rural Brazil, is far less to reinstate the pre-eminence of rural plantation elites than to promote continued respect for rural regions, especially rural workers and their popular culture or folklore, but also their native flora and fauna, and to highlight them as a legitimate object of the cinematic gaze in an era when Brazilian *chanchadas* set in Rio de Janeiro were far more common.

The boy and girl protagonists of the childhood memories in *Meus oito anos* and a few of Mauro's other films in the *Brasilianas* series are perhaps the most ideal universal subjects for his project, in that their youth and innocence pre-empt questions of class and/or racial conflict in rural Brazil. *Brasilianas Vol. 1: Canções populares* (*Brasilianas Vol. 1: Popular Songs*) (1945) includes verses from a song called 'A casinha pequenina' ('The Tiny Little House') that associate a coconut tree with the young, innocent love of a girl and boy. The coconut tree is said to have died due to its own saudade for the childhood romance that the singer himself is remembering. Thus, this folk song, played in its entirety as part of a film on representative popular music, resonates with a perspective of nature as perfectly mirroring the emotional memories of the singer or filmmaker. Through the soundtrack, Mauro provides an aural echo of the optical visuality once again on display with various scenes of a boy and girl by turns gathering kindling, sitting side-by-side on a riverbank and finally embracing, thereby acting out the young, child-like love for which the singer feels nostalgia. Everything in the audio-visual environment builds a clear, direct link to past memories and their unproblematic association with nature as present in the cattle-raising culture and economy of Minas Gerais. The chasteness of the first love represented by the child actors is only magnified by the pure, isolated and bucolic landscape whose only human dwelling is a humble little one-room house that gives the film its name. Once again Mauro presents us with a *mise-en-scène* defined by passions at the same time authentic and transparent, a setting that could fit quite well in a Romantic poem or painting of the nineteenth century. The two children in the film appear to dwell in an Edenic environment free not only of class and racial difference, but even of any adults who might seek to limit their freedom.

In a similar vein, let us consider briefly the opening and ending sequences of Mauro's fictional feature film from the same era, *Canto da saudade*. This film was actually released in 1952 a few years before the *Brasilianas* series of shorts, but was also produced by Mauro's Rancho Alegre Studios and shot on location in the same rural region of Volta Grande, Minas Gerais. Although the film was not funded by INCE, the National Institute of Educational Cinema, as the later *Brasilianas* series would be, it is clear from the beginning that *Canto da saudade* shares a pedagogical, nationalist narrative with the *Brasilianas* films. The film begins with the director Mauro himself on-screen, explaining that on land that used to be the seat of his grandparents' Santa Cruz Ranch there stands today a school that is a 'poor little country school but in the end a *Brazilian* school' ('uma escolinha pobre e de fazenda mas ao final das contas uma escola *brasileira*'). This introduction, along with the fact that Mauro later also plays the part of the local 'Colonel' or cacique, emphasizes his family's membership in the seigneurial class in this rural community, former owners of the land the school is built on.

After introducing the school, Mauro introduces the schoolteacher who works there and the camera cuts to a scene with her and the students in the school house. The teacher begins a respectful telling of the region's history and its folklore, becoming a modern-day proponent of the social hierarchy in a setting that has become nationalized through its generalization as a representative of Brazilian rurality and the state system of elementary education. Shortly after being introduced in the schoolhouse, the teacher and her class go on an excursion to a hilltop with views of the rural landscape, akin to the one featured in *Meus oito anos*. Thus, the children, who begin to listen to a folk tale told by their teacher, are seated in a natural environment that becomes a kind of proscenium to the staging of this story, said to have taken place in the same countryside setting. The viewer is put in the position of the schoolchildren, listening to the teacher's voice on the soundtrack along with them as the film cuts to the diegetic world of the story itself. Again, as in the short film *Meus oito anos* analysed above, Mauro creates a *mise-en-scène* with a commanding view of the landscape in order to establish an optic visual framework through which to explore memory unproblematically. The infantilization of the viewer in saudoso, rural narratives would later be taken up again in Walter Salles's *Central do Brasil*, as discussed in Chapter 5.

However, in this case, rather than evoking memories of the protagonist's childhood, we see the educational system striving to inculcate a cultural nostalgia in the children themselves. It is no coincidence that the children are being taken to a similar location to that of the saudoso (nostalgic) man of *Meus oito anos*. This diverse group of children of various races and genders are being encouraged as feeling subjects to develop an appreciation, indeed a love, for not only their local folklore and landscape, but simultaneously for the emotion of saudade itself. This sentimental education mirrors sociologist Roberto DaMatta's (1993) analysis of his own schooling in twentieth-century Brazil. The film encourages from the outset, as do most of Mauro's films in the *Brasilianas* series, that the viewer consider Volta Grande as a symbol of Brazilian rurality in general. For this reason, we can consider this opening sequence of *Canto da saudade* as a model for how all Brazilian children should feel about and remember the traditionally very significant contributions of Brazil's rural regions to the country's economy, society and cultural history.

The schoolchildren sit in rapt attention as their teacher tells the folk story that is the main narrative of the film, until the final sequence in which their own emotional responses to the tale's end are foregrounded. The protagonist Galdino (Mário Mascarenhas), a ranchhand and accordion player who had fallen in love with a local laundress named Maria Fausta (Cláudia Montenegro), ends up with a broken heart because Maria Fausta marries another man with the Colonel's blessing. As the schoolteacher explains, the story goes that Galdino disappeared on Maria Fausta's wedding day, never to be seen again in those parts. The camera, rather than assuming a commanding hilltop position, in this ending sequence takes positions in the bottom of various valleys or on empty country roads, as we hear the Colonel shouting 'Gaaaaaaldiiiino!' repeatedly in his attempt to find the missing ranchhand. The camera thus shows us, via its less commanding perspective on the landscape, the subordinate position of Galdino on this ranch dominated by the Colonel. But Galdino himself is never shown again; thus, while his name, perspective and social position are evoked, it is only in order to highlight his absence. The absent Galdino and his music become the object of the children's own saudade in the final images of the film, thus bringing to fruition the tale's intended sentimental education of the students. The teacher's final, languorous words are that while Galdino has never been seen again, 'They say that still today one hears [his] accordion music: in the early mornings, on the peaks struck by the light of the afternoon sun, at dusk…' ('dizem que ainda hoje ouve-se a música da sanfona: nas madrugadas, nas lombas batidas pelo sol da tarde, ao anoitecer…'). As she finishes her tale, Mauro's camera cuts to the smiling faces of the children, ultimately pulling into an extreme close-up on a boy's face and eyes through a series of jump cuts. This shot then fades into some landscape shots that mirror the imagery in the words of the schoolteacher, showing the local landscape and hills in the afternoon and then darkening to dusk. As the fade-away from the boy into the late-afternoon landscape occurs, for a moment the upper half of his face, including eyes, nose and forehead, is transposed over the landscape itself. This striking yet fleeting image suggests that the landscape of the story, and by association the popular culture and emotional yearning for the way of life it represents, have imprinted themselves in the boy's mind. Presumably, from the huge smile on his face, they have also found their way into his heart. Thus, Mauro closes his film with imagery suggesting a thorough interpenetration of the child's psyche, landscape and rural culture, driven home by the bittersweet notes of Galdino's accordion on the soundtrack.

In a general sense, the haptic visuality of Petra Costa's *Elena* ([2013] 2014) consists of an exploration of surfaces, such as the textures of clothing, of bodies floating across water and of water itself, of broken yet reflective glass, of the windows of a train, airplane or apartment, and of the various media of filmic imagery themselves, including VHS, Super 8 and digital. I will consider one childhood memory, related in the film by its director/narrator, as a pathway through which to consider some of this imagery in its full sensual, symbolic and associative richness. Before doing so, let us consider as a theoretical guide the following description of haptic perception and visuality:

> Haptic *perception* is usually defined by psychologists as the combination of tactile, kinesthetic, and proprioceptive functions, the way we experience touch both on the surface of and inside our bodies […] In haptic *visuality*, the eyes themselves function like organs of touch.
>
> (Marks 2000: 162, original emphasis)

As regards the impact of haptic imagery in film, Marks emphasizes that '[t]he haptic image forces the viewer to contemplate the image itself instead of being pulled into narrative' (2000: 163). It is my contention that Brazilian cinema in recent years has participated in an international trend towards haptic visuality (see for instance Filho 2012), and Petra Costa's work is an excellent example of how this kind of visuality does indeed focus the viewer on the image, in its seemingly infinite layers and textures, not just through the gaze but by repeatedly evoking the sense of touch, kinesthetics and other non-visual sensory systems. This haptic visuality actually hearkens back to the early silent era of cinema as described by Lant (1995), the initial, experimental cinematic era contemporaneous with the spatial aesthetic theories of Riegl, and historically preceding the Classical Hollywood era of film after 1917, during which optical visuality would achieve a certain hegemonic status.

In terms of its narrative structure, *Elena* shows a clear mystery-genre influence. The director-protagonist Petra Costa's investigation of her sister Elena's life is carried out over the course of the film, and the mystery of the Costa family's past is explored through objects like a large, souvenir conch given to her by her sister Elena, a letter and other documents related to Elena's 1990 suicide, and a collection of VHS home videos as well as audio tapes, all of which function as radioactive fossils. As Marks describes this Deleuzian term, the '"radioactive" aspect of these objects is that they may arouse other memories, causing inert presences on the most recent layer of history to set off chains of associations that had been forgotten' (Marks 2000: 91). Costa[1] explores the present as the surface of memory, and finds various fossils that, rather than helping her to penetrate this surface, instead help to bring other memories to the surface, still very much in the mediated context of the present. This is a process that Marks describes as common in the works of diasporic artists, the result of which is to transform 'fossil-images' into 'recollection-images' (2000: 124).

The international diaspora of Brazilians is certainly an important theme in the film, and the distance between Elena as migrant in New York City on the one hand and her family including seven-year-old sister Petra in Brazil on the other is thematized in various ways including the particularly radioactive fossil of the conch, an object that also resonates with water- and ocean-imagery in the film. The viewer is introduced to this fossil in a voice-over from Petra, who describes the moment when her sister gifted the conch to her little sister, explaining its power to connect the two sisters across the distance between São Paulo and New York. Thus, Petra's beloved sister, in a situation of imminent departure whose emotional tone we might call one of anticipatory saudade, imports magical powers to this fetish associated with the sound of the ocean. In the narrative of the film, the conch-image functions as a conveyor of remembrance, a saudade machine producing recollection-images. This machinic, affective-tactile assemblage of touch, sound, memory and love is also the perfect symbol of the emphasis on the non-optical and even the non-visual in the film. The sound of the sea in the conch even synesthetically evokes the movement of waves, resonating with the physiology of the senses of sound and balance, as they are produced in the liquid of the inner ear.

In the same year in which she was given the conch on her seventh birthday, Petra's sister Elena committed suicide. In the wake of this tragedy, souvenir objects such as the conch of course took on a new level of significance. The magical or radioactive properties of this fossil now needed to pierce not only distance but time, and to reach across what Costa reveals to be a Stygian, watery border between the living and the dead. Aesthetic representations of female suicide later enter into the film's narrative, particularly that of Shakespeare's Ophelia, to whom Petra was introduced when first reading Hamlet at age seventeen. She would later interpret the role of Ophelia, and images of Petra in this role too become part of the water-imagery in *Elena*. In the wake of Ophelia's entrance into the film as theme, the conch now becomes a vehicle that must transport Petra to the land of the dead and back again, bringing her memories of her sister with her and transforming their significance in the present through an artistic alchemy.

To begin this alchemy, which will involve several sequences of haptic imagery, Petra stages a scene of herself in the present, in which she puts her ear to the conch and in voice-over says 'I drown in you… in Ophelias' ('Me afogo em você… em Ofélias'). Regarding the Shakespearean character of Ophelia, it should be noted that Costa was influenced more broadly by Gaston Bachelard's identification of an 'Ophelia complex' of artistic and folkloric imagery associating water, femininity and death (Costa 2014, personal interview). According to Bachelard, '[d]eath in calm water has maternal features' ([1942] 2006: 89). Bachelard cites a Rainer Maria Rilke poem in which 'water mixes its ambivalent images of life and death' in order to illustrate how water 'is a substance full of reminiscences and prescient reveries' ([1942] 2006: 89). Water can have a Stygian association with death, carrying away the deceased into the afterlife or dissolving the body into the infinite depths of the ocean, but also can have life-giving properties if provided to a seed, to an infant as mother's milk or even as amniotic fluid in the womb. As such it is also multi-temporal, carrying along memories in its depths but also providing a reflective surface in which to contemplate the future and from which to receive sustenance in the present. The conch as radioactive fossil in this scene evokes Petra's personal memories of her sister within the allegorical constellation of the Ophelia complex. At the moment when her voice-over says she drowns in her sister, now revealed as part of a longer history of Ophelias, the conch is featured in close-up against Petra's ear, emphasizing its pinkish-whitish surface, by turns smooth and ridged. Petra is then shown yelling in what appears to be a dance studio, followed by rapid cuts to images from different eras of her bursting forth from water, or the air bubbles of her underwater shout bursting up to surface. The close-ups on her face underwater are haptic, emphasizing the texture and bubbly surface of the water as well as its distortions of the colour and surface of Petra's face and thus taking the viewer into an otherworldly realm between living and dead. A younger Petra is also shown in video footage performing on stage as Ophelia in this sequence. Jumping to digital footage in a well-lit room, we see hands on a white, embroidered lace dress or cloth. Petra's face also appears momentarily in extreme close-up, obscured behind a white veil of the same cloth. Costa periodically uses such haptic bodily imagery that invokes the texture of the skin and the sense of touch. As viewers, we remain throughout this sequence in an ambiguous space between a less-narrative, more directly sensorial experience, and the film's overall narrative progress towards a transformation of Petra's sorrow. There is a mirroring of the grieving process here, which can shuttle back and forth between physical souvenirs of the dead and memories of their past interactions with the living. This kind of grieving, a multi-sensory experience in dialogue with memory and an enduring connection to the deceased (saudade), does not follow a clear, linear narrative logic of cause and effect, and for this reason neither does Costa's film.

Petra's hand exploring the textures of white lace foreshadows the textures of the dresses on various Ophelian images of women that soon begin to appear in this sequence. The transition into a constellation of Ophelia images begins with some footage of Petra performing as Ophelia on stage, emerging from a small pool of water. She says in voice-over: 'And I act out, I act out our death. To find air, to be able to breathe' ('E enceno, enceno a nossa morte. Pra encontrar ar, pra poder viver'). This paradoxical reference to life and death sets the tone for the staging of a sequence of ambivalent, protean imagery – establishing a perspective that Deleuze ([1983] 2013) would call *liquid perception*. Inspired by the Ophelia complex and Petra's own performance of that role, this liquid perception achieves a grace in continuous movement and transformation that allows for a gradual transition from becoming Ophelia/death to becoming water, becoming air, becoming life and becoming dance. One of the first images to appear is of Petra in a flowery summer-dress, floating in a body of water. First we see a shot of her body from below, the camera underwater. Her body is less well defined here, diminishing in size as the camera moves away and dissipating into the water due to a golden-yellow wash effect from a light source above. The camera cuts to a position beside her body, and we now see her more clearly, floating with the current just beneath the surface of the water, the flower pattern of her dress now clear as her form slides over a shallow bank of sand. The film then cuts to a shot from above, as a close-up reveals Petra's hand and then slides upward over her arm, upper body and face, which looks peaceful. Her closed eyes and pale skin still bear connotations of lifelessness, yet the flow of her body across the water and the screen begins a movement that will eventually pull this Ophelia back into the realm of the living. A song performed by musician Maggie Hastings Clifford (which she co-wrote with Petra Costa herself and Fil Pinheiro) begins on the soundtrack at this point, with the lyrics: 'I'm sick, I'm sick / with love / Touch me, touch me / I turn to, I turn to / I turn to water'. These lyrics describing suffering, love and liquid transformation are accompanied by notes played on Waldorf and Korg synthesizers that evoke an eerie soundscape. This instrumentation is more atmospheric than melodic, echoing the non-narrative aspect of haptic visuality. Clifford's lyrics are broadly evocative but not a detailed narrative, and she also sings very slowly, emphasizing single words and notes rather than the linearity of melody and lyrical syntax.

The sense of touch named in the song finds its partner in an image of Petra, in a room that will be revealed as a dance studio, slowly inverting her hands and running their backs across both of her cheeks. In this same *mise-en-scène* of the dance studio, the sound of Petra's living breath has already been emphasized, underlining her quest to dance with death and then return to the living. The Ophelia images then continue to reappear, as Petra is framed again on the surface of the water from above, this time with her mother. But now even more movement is introduced as she begins to kick and actively move herself across the water, as do other Ophelias who appear and begin to float across the surface, appearing more animated and sometimes kicking themselves along from the top to the bottom of the frame. The water here has become black, outlining them in sharp relief, as their skin tones are very pale and all wear flower- or summer-dresses. A series of shots alternates

Figure 7: Playing the part of herself, but within a series of Ophelian images associated with the life and death of her sister Elena, Petra Costa develops a liquid perception to explore the fluidity of memory and the transformation of melancholy grief into a more joyful saudade (Courtesy Busca Vida Filmes, São Paulo).

between close-ups framing only parts of bodies floating across the surface of water, and more distant shots from above or below, typically about two body lengths in height and width. In the close-up shots, tactile, haptic images abound and the water and bodies seem more in flux, more animated, more alive. In contrast, the distant, more optical viewpoint of these floating Ophelias gives them an appearance closer to pale corpses, suggesting the continued presence of death (see Figure 7).

At a certain point (beginning at 1:14:07), Petra says in voice-over 'little by little the pain becomes water, becomes memory' ('pouco a pouco as dores viram água, viram memória') as we continue to see more 'Ophelias' with Petra and her mother. The Bachelardian, paradoxical associations of water with both life (amniotic fluid, womb) and death (dissolution, Stygian travel to the beyond, Ophelian suicide) are very evident here. The flowery summer-dresses also contrast with the at-times deathly bodies. Flowers are usually associated with life and spring/summer, but are also fragile and when immersed in water emphasize an imminent dissolution. The water surface itself continues to go back and forth between opaque, dark and more translucent, light, yellowish-green tones. The lack of resolution into clearly illuminated water here reemphasizes the slippery, sometimes opaque nature of both memory and emotion.

Beyond just the periodic opacity of the water in this Ophelia sequence, darkness itself is treated in a very nuanced way by the film. It is fitting that the film's various sequences in

Figure 8: Director Petra Costa behind the lens of a Nikon R10 Super 8 camera while shooting *Elena* (Courtesy Busca Vida Filmes, São Paulo).

past and present explore darkness to a great degree, given the noir-mystery genre in which the filmmaker frames the narrative. In Petra's investigation of the mystery of her sister's life up to her suicide in 1990, various scenes depict her roaming around Manhattan's streets at night. Darkness in this New York City *mise-en-scène* is emphasized at least as much as light, most tragically when a shot – with the grainier texture of a Super 8 camera – slides down following a shadow towards a gutter and across a sewer drain, haptically reenacting the movement and unclean, shameful feeling of a line from Elena's suicide letter, read in voice-over: 'I will degrade myself and go down this drain. Now I'm entering it. Good' ('Eu vou me degradar e escorrer por esse ralo. Agora tô entrando dentro dele. Que bom'). The noir influence continues to make itself felt over the course of the film as the camera follows Petra's dark silhouette around the city, often backlit by traffic lights and car headlights.

These night scenes are also echoes of Elena's home videos, including the narrative darkness of a horror/suspense plot she filmed in her own home as a teenager. The extreme contrast of darkness and light further recalls the *mise-en-scène* of the video clip in which Elena holds a bright light, pretending she is dancing with the moon. This latter scene itself is placed in stark contrast with an image immediately preceding it, which had filled the frame, namely the word 'suicide' typed in black ink on a starkly white piece of paper.

Even before this imagery, the hospital where Elena died is not entered by the camera, but presented in extreme relief as a whited-out limit, mirroring not only the whiteness of the autopsy report but that of Elena's own suicide letter. Thus immediately following the revelation of the cold facts of her sister's suicide, Costa returns to the yard at night in which Elena dances with the moon in order to demonstrate that this dark atmosphere represents her life and personality far better than the brutally blunt language and imagery associated with the manner of her death in an autopsy report. Regarding the significant amount of home video (much of it Elena's own directorial work, since she was an avid videographer as a teen), Mark's commentary on Sami Alkassim's work is relevant: '[T]he decaying image makes the viewer reflect on how much of perception is generated by memory and longing, rather than engagement with a crisply available visual object' (Marks 2000: 156). Darkness or obscurity of the image can thus be associated with saudade, with love and longing, just as much as with death, fear or isolation.

Towards the end of the film, Petra herself begins to twirl in the darkness of the streets of New York, no longer tracking her sister's path across the same city in the past but dancing her own steps. This final sequence after the choreography of floating Ophelias features Petra in the present, dancing in the streets and in a dance studio, twirling like her sister did. From the camera's perspective she in fact dances with her sister by intercutting her own dance with some home video of Elena twirling again, to the tune of a more joyful, polkaesque piano accompaniment by Alexandre Desplat on the soundtrack. Petra's voice-over in this sequence emphasizes the undoing of traumatic memories that has come about through the film's assumption of a liquid perception in its processing of all the Ophelia-imagery, allowing room for an aesthetic transformation of mourning:

> Memories go with time [...] they are unmade. But some find no consolation, just some relief, in the small openings of poetry. You are my inconsolable memory, made of stone and shadow. And it is from it that everything is born – and dances (As memórias vão com tempo [...] se desfazem. Mas algumas não encontram consolo, só algum alívio, nas pequenas brechas da poesia. Você é minha memória inconsolável, feita de pedra e de sombra. E é dela que tudo nasce – e dança).

Thus, the narrative of the film consists of a mystery without a resolution other than the aesthetic practice as exemplified by the film itself. Costa ends the film with Petra in the present, dancing with the camera along with a voice-over that privileges the aesthetic as the lens through which to explore the mysteries of the past, of memory. Rather than floating along a liquid surface symbolizing a current of trauma, we now see the protagonist in a series of more active movements, even as the camera continues through close-ups to explore a tactile relationship with the dancer's body. This final dance evokes an embodied visuality, one that, as Marks defines the term, 'acknowledges[s] the presence of the body in the act of seeing, at the same time that [it] relinquish[es] the (illusory) unity of the self'

(2000: 151). Petra dances along with not only her sister, but with her own younger selves and memories of childhood, and along with anyone who has had a similar brush with childhood trauma.

Note

1 Here and below, for purposes of clarity I will refer to the director by last name, while referring to her protagonist-self in the film as Petra.

Chapter 8

Conclusion - The Waxing and Waning of Saudade in Cinematic Skies

E às vez, recordando a feliz mocidade,
Canto uma sôdade que mora em meu peito.[1]

Patativa do Assaré

In his recent memoirs, Carlos Diegues contemplates the significance of the moon in his work and in Brazilian cinema as a whole. His musings serve well as a point of departure to consider the fluctuating sentimentality of Brazilian cinema and its cyclical focus on the longing for past experiences and identities of various levels including the personal, national and cinematic. Diegues recalls, during the making of *Bye Bye Brasil*, and while he was filming in the sertão,

> I wanted to film the moon, an unthinkable shot for the orthodoxy of Cinema Novo, an affront to our political films glued to the human face and to the geography of misery which surrounded it. It was as if, filming the moon, I was leaving behind the shots of my previous films [...] Filming the moon shining in the sky was for me opening a door to contemplation and dreaming, the concrete becoming enchantment, a break with the obligation that our films had to save the world (Eu queria filmar a lua, plano impensável para a ortodoxia do Cinema Novo, uma afronta a nossos filmes políticos colados ao rosto humano e à geografia da miséria que o cerca. Era como se, filmando a lua, estivesse deixando para trás os planos de meus filmes anteriores [...] Filmar a lua brilhando no céu era para mim abrir uma porta para a contemplação e o sonho, o concreto tornado encanto, um rompimento com a obrigação que nossos filmes tinham de salvar o mundo). (2014: 441–42)

Diegues's comments demonstrate several essential characteristics of saudade in cinema, which have been explored in this book: the seminal relationship between nature and desire (especially as represented in rural, interior Brazil) inherited from the Romantics, the concern for the representation of the common people, their needs and desires, in dialogue with a focus on the profundity of individual experience and affect, and lastly the shifting emotional common sense among Brazilian filmmakers with the passing of the generations. With regard to one of the films analysed in Chapter 7, it is worth noting that Humberto Mauro includes a shot of the moon in *Meus oito anos*. This is part of the dream sequence of the boy in the film, who is peacefully sleeping in a hammock on the plantation veranda. The shot captures the full moon in the sky for a few moments, then cuts to images of the waves gently lapping on the beach. Here we have entered the realm of enchantment, since the boy's dream fantasies, along with the lines from Casimiro de Abreu's poem, carry him far away from his home in rural Minas Gerais to the ocean. Clearly Diegues's association of the moon with 'contemplation and dreaming' is one that continues in the Brazilian Romantic tradition that Mauro had consolidated in Brazilian cinema in the 1950s.

While Diegues conceived his shot of the moon as a break from the previous generation, it was also a cycling back to an earlier emotional discourse in cinema and literature. A repetition with a difference in the same lineage is evident in Walter Salles's *Central do Brasil*. In a scene from the latter part of the film, after they have become true friends, Dora and Josué contemplate the night sky of the sertão together silently, gazing at the stars. This constellation of lights recalls the earlier pivotal scene in the film in a religious festival, during which hundreds of candles could be seen in a single shot while the pilgrims worshiped the Virgin Mary of the Apparition. At that time, Dora was running frantically amongst the pilgrims looking for Josué after quarrelling with him, but in the later stargazing scene, the two are finally able to stop and contemplate the beauty of their destination together. One final film that must be mentioned in this beautiful lineage of moon and stars is Petra Costa's *Elena*. One of the most striking home-video images from the documentary is of Elena holding a large, over-exposed light outside at night. As she moves the glowing, circular orb around, she proclaims she is 'dancing with the moon'. The moon's association with the oceanic tides fits not only with the Bachelardian Ophelia complex explored in Costa's film, but even recalls Mauro's dream sequence from sixty years before. Elena's dance with the moon becomes an inspiration for Petra Costa's own cinematic and corporeal dance with the memory of her sister. The moon represents a night-time longing, a desire that can be dark and melancholy, but also beautifully replete with love – a saudade.

The associations with this celestial body are even more diverse than this, though – the moon represents nature and longing, but it is also a face, a window or a screen in the night sky. These various visual-metaphorical aspects of the moon unite my arguments on emotion, neo-Romantic rurality, liminality and the function of the saudado as fetish developed in this book. The films, analysed as (re)producers of saudade, can be understood together in terms of: (1) the face as fetishized representation of affect, (2) the window as a liminal frame between spaces or eras and (3) the screen as virtual, televisual and cinematic frame or mirror. Firstly, in films such as *O canto da saudade*, *Sinhá moça*, *O pagador de promessas*, *Bye Bye Brasil* and *Central do Brasil*, we have seen the fetishization of marginalized/national-popular figures like enslaved peoples, rural peasants or migrants, often emphasized with the facial close-up shot. These fetishes mark the meeting-point of heterogeneous forces of tradition and modernization, of rural life and urban development, and of local, national and international cultural influences in Brazil. Secondly, in Humberto Mauro's films of the 1950s, and also in *O passaporte húngaro*, *Budapeste* and *Elena*, a variety of imagery and shots related to windows and glass frames evoke liminal spaces and times, and the desire to contemplate them, or gaze through them, and to maintain a connection across space and time best expressed emotionally through saudade. In Mauro's films as well as *Terra estrangeira*, these liminal 'window frames' tend more towards those of natural landscapes, shorelines or seascapes that become liminal spaces through which the characters and viewers can contemplate the colonial or plantation past, and their legacy in national society or postcolonial relations (the latter especially thematized in *Terra*). Thirdly, in *O caminho das nuvens*, *Bye Bye Brasil* and *Macunaíma*, the thematization of televisual and cinematic screens sheds light on the increasing mediatization (and virtualization) of rural, interior spaces of Brazil that traditionally had been considered undisturbed repositories of authentic folk culture associated with the national-popular, peasant subject. After the ironic saudade for Brazilian cinema and the self-cannibalizing national 'screen' of the bloody river in *Macunaíma*'s final shot, a transitional phase is highlighted in *Bye Bye Brasil* with the emphasis on contact and exchange between traditional culture (northern Brazil and the circus) and (inter)national culture (Rio de Janeiro and the TV) before *O caminho das nuvens* reveals a fully mediatized interior that sees itself through the TV screen and sings itself in the pop-culture narratives of Roberto Carlos. Finally, regarding the kinds of visuality involved in this constellation of moon-images, as a face, the moon is a more haptic image, as window it is more optical, while as a screen it could be either. We commonly see a combination of haptic and optical imagery to evoke memory in these films, but the more recent emphasis on haptic visuality and the problematization of easy access to (and mastery of) memory is most evident in *Elena*'s treatment of the saudado as a mysterious fetish.

Despite the continuing resonance of a cinematic-affective tradition with roots in rural Brazil, this study has also revealed that saudoso narratives, increasingly, cannot be limited to rural or even Brazilian spaces. Dreaming and contemplation can take filmmakers and viewers virtually anywhere, to the moon and back, and there are many more moons than any one tradition can contemplate. We can recall, in various chapters of this book, the alternative saudades of the twenty-first century, connected to diverse urban and international spaces from Rio to New York to Budapest, and sometimes expressed and experienced via the urban culture industry and television among other media. As a final object of contemplation, it is fitting to take inspiration from the verses of Patativa do Assaré that begin this chapter, in light of the variety of emotional discourses presented in Brazilian cinema since the 1950s. Every saudade, in its perspective, has its own window on space and time; in its expression, its own accent.

Note

1 'And at times, recalling happy youth / I sing a saudade that lives in my breast'. The spellings of 'vez' (instead of 'vezes') and 'sôdade' (instead of 'saudade') emphasize a northeastern sertanejo accent.

References

Abreu, G. de ([1946] 2006), *O ébrio* (*The Drunkard*), DVD, São Paulo: Versátil.

Abu-Lughod, L. and Lutz, C. ([1990] 2009), 'Emotion, discourse, and the politics of everyday life', in J. Harding and E. D. Pribram (eds), *Emotions: A Cultural Studies Reader*, London: Routledge, pp. 100–12.

Ahmed, S. (2004), *The Cultural Politics of Emotion*, New York: Routledge.

Almeida, C. H. d. (2002), *Walter Salles: Uma entrevista (Walter Salles: An Interview)*, Santa Maria da Feira, Portugal: Festival de Cinema Luso-Brasileiro de Santa Maria da Feira.

Amaral, S. (2009), *Hotel Atlântico*, DVD, Rio de Janeiro: Lume Filmes.

Amorim, V. ([2003] 2004), *O caminho das nuvens* (*The Middle of the World*), DVD, New York: Film Movement.

Anderson, B. (1983), *Imagined Communities: Reflections on the Origin and Spread of Nationalism*, London: Verso.

Andrade, M. d. ([1928] 1988), *Macunaíma: O herói sem nenhum caráter/Macunaíma: The Hero Without Any Character*, Florianópolis, Brazil: UFSC.

Andrade, J. P. d. ([1967] 2006), *Brasília: Contradições de uma cidade nova/Brasília: Contradictions of a New City*, DVD, Rio de Janeiro: Videofilmes.

——— ([1969] 2006), *Macunaíma*, DVD, Rio de Janeiro: Videofilmes.

Andries, A. L. F. (2001), *O cinema de Humberto Mauro* (*The Cinema of Humberto Mauro*), Rio de Janeiro: Ministério da Cultura, Fundação Nacional de Arte.

Antonioni, M. ([1970] 2009), *Zabriskie Point*, DVD, Burbank, CA: Warner Home Video.

Antunes, A. (1983), *Saudade e profetismo em Fernando Pessoa: Elementos para uma antropologia filosófica* (*Saudade and Prophetism in Fernando Pessoa: Elements for a Philosophical Anthropology*), Braga, Portugal: Faculdade de Filosofia.

Aragão, D. (2013), *Boa sorte, meu amor* (*Good Luck, Sweetheart*), Recife, Brazil: Cicatrix Filmes.

Bachelard, G. ([1942] 2006), *Water and Dreams: An Essay on the Imagination of Matter* (trans. E. R. Farrell), Dallas: Pegasus Foundation/Dallas Institute of Humanities and Culture.

Bacon, L. ([1933] 2006), *Footlight Parade*, DVD, Burbank, CA: Warner Home Video.

Barreto, B. ([1976] 2008), *Dona Flor e seus dois maridos* (*Dona Flor and Her Two Husbands*), DVD, New York: New Yorker Video.

Barreto, L. ([1953] 2011), *O cangaceiro* (*The Bandit*), DVD, São Paulo: Versátil.

Bayman, L. and Pinazza, N. (2013), *Directory of World Cinema: Brazil*, Bristol, UK: Intellect.

Benjamin, W. (1999), *The Arcades Project* (trans. H. Eiland), Cambridge: Harvard University Press.

Bodanzky, J. and Senna, O. ([1974] 2015), *Iracema*, DVD, Rio de Janeiro: Instituto Moreira Salles.

Boym, S. (2001), *The Future of Nostalgia*, New York: Basic Books.

Bradatan, C. P., Popan, A. and Melton, R. (2010), 'Transnationality as a fluid social identity', *Social Identities: Journal for the Study of Race, Nation and Culture,* 16:2, pp. 169–78.

Brandellero, S. (2013), '*Bye Bye Brasil* and the quest for the nation', in S. Brandellero (ed.), *The Brazilian Road Movie: Journeys of (Self) Discovery*, Cardiff: University of Wales Press, pp. 49–68.

Brennan, T. (2004), *The Transmission of Affect*, Ithaca: Cornell University Press.

Burle, J. C. ([1952] 2007), *Carnaval Atlântida*, DVD, Barueri, Brazil: Europa Filmes.

Butler, J. (1987), *Subjects of Desire: Hegelian Reflections in Twentieth-Century France*, New York: Columbia University Press.

——— (1997), *The Psychic Life of Power: Theories in Subjection*, Stanford: Stanford University Press.

——— (2004), 'Violence, mourning, politics', in J. Harding and E. D. Pribram (eds), *Emotions: A Cultural Studies Reader*, London: Routledge, pp. 387–402.

Câmara, A. d. S., Bezerra, G., Miranda, R. S., Lessa, R. and Vital, T. (2006), 'O Caminho das Nuvens: Representação da vida no nordeste ou saga urbana?' ('The road in the clouds: Representation of life in the northeast or urban saga?'), *O olho da história* (*The Gaze of History*), 12:9, http://oolhodahistoria.ufba.br/wp-content/uploads/2016/03/antoniocamara.pdf. Accessed 5 January 2016.

Candido, A. ([1975] 2014), *Formação da literatura brasileira: Momentos decisivos* (*Formation of Brazilian Literature: Decisive Moments*), Rio de Janeiro: Ouro Sobre Azul.

Carlos, R. (1969), 'As curvas da estrada de Santos' ('The curves of Santos highway'), http://www.robertocarlos.com/br/music/roberto-carlos-1969. Accessed 12 January 2016.

Carvalho, J. ([1951] 1998), 'Problemática da saudade' ('Problematic of Saudade'), in C. Henrique (ed.), *Elementos constitutivos da consciência saudosa e problemática da saudade* (*Constitutive Elements of the Saudoso Consciousness and Problematic of Saudade*), Lisbon: Lisboa Editora, pp. 66–75.

Carvalho, W. (2007), 'De Muybridge a Matrix' ('From Muybridge to Matrix'), in E. Ades and M. Kaufman (eds), *Luz em movimento: A fotografia no cinema brasileiro* (*Light in Movement: Photography in Brazilian Cinema*), exhibition catalogue, Rio de Janeiro: CAIXA Cultural, pp. 17–18.

——— (2009), *Budapeste*, DVD, Rio de Janeiro: Nexus/Imagem/Eurofilm.

Código Criminal do Império do Brasil (*Criminal Code of the Empire of Brazil*) (1830), Article 14, Section 6, http://www.planalto.gov.br/ccivil_03/Leis/LIM/LIM-16-12-1830.htm. Accessed 15 October 2014.

Cohen, V. (2003), 'Retirantes no Alvorada' ('Refugees in the presidential palace'), *Istoé Gente*, 18 August, www.terra.com.br/istoegente/211/reportagens/vicente_amorim.htm. Accessed 31 January 2007.

Costa, D. L. P. d. and Gomes, P. (eds) (1976), *Introdução à saudade: Antologia teórica e aproximação crítica* (*Introduction to Saudade: Theoretical Anthology and Critical Approximation*), Porto, Portugal: Lello & Irmão Editores.

Costa, P. (2009), *Olhos de ressaca* (*Undertow Eyes*), DVD, São Paulo: Buscavida Filmes.

——— (2014), Personal interview with author, 11 April.

——— ([2013] 2014), *Elena*, DVD, Rio de Janeiro: Instituto Moreira Salles.

Cunha, E. da ([1902] 1957), *Rebellion in the Backlands* (trans. S. Putnam), Chicago: University of Chicago Press.

DaMatta, R. (1993), *Conta de mentiroso: Sete ensaios de antropologia brasileira* (*Tale of a Liar: Seven Essays of Brazilian Anthropology*), Rio de Janeiro: Rocco.

Darwin, C. R. (1872), *The Expression of the Emotions in Man and Animals*, London: John Murray, http://darwin-online.org.uk/content/frameset?pageseq=1&itemID=F1142&viewtype=text. Accessed 9 June 2015.

Davis, F. (1979), *Yearning for Yesterday: A Sociology of Nostalgia*, New York: Free Press.

Debord, G. ([1967] 1994), *The Society of the Spectacle* (trans. D. Nicholson-Smith), New York: Zone Books.

Deleuze, G. ([1983] 2013), *Cinema 1: The Movement Image* (trans. H. Tomlinson and B. Habberjam), Minneapolis, MN: University of Minnesota Press.

Dennison, S. and Shaw, L. (2004), *Popular Cinema in Brazil, 1930–2001*, Manchester, UK: Manchester University Press.

——— (2007), *Brazilian National Cinema*, London: Routledge.

Diegues, C. ([1976] 2014), *Xica da Silva*, DVD, New York: New Yorker Video.

——— ([1978] 2007), *Bye Bye Brasil*, DVD, New York: New Yorker Video.

——— ([2000] 2003), 'The cinema that Brazil deserves', in L. Nagib (ed.), *The New Brazilian Cinema*, London: I.B. Tauris, pp. 23–35.

——— (2014), *Vida de Cinema: Antes, Durante e Depois do Cinema Novo* (*Life of Cinema: Before, During and After Cinema Novo*), Rio de Janeiro: Editora Objetiva.

Diegues, C. and Oroz, S. (1984), *Os filmes que não filmei* (*The Films I Didn't Film*) (trans. S. Barros), Rio de Janeiro: Editora Rocco.

Draper, J. A., III (2008), 'Renovation and conservation in Brazilian literature and music', *Journal of Latin American Cultural Studies*, 17:2, pp. 167–84.

——— (2010), *Forró and Redemptive Regionalism from the Brazilian Northeast: Popular Music in a Culture of Migration*, New York: Peter Lang Publishing.

——— (2011a), 'Forró's wars of maneuver and position: Popular northeastern music, critical regionalism, and a culture of migration', *Latin American Research Review*, 46:1, pp. 80–101.

——— (2011b), 'Reimagining Rosinha with Andrucha Waddington and Elena Soarez: Nature, woman and sexuality in the Brazilian northeast from popular music to cinema', in C. Rêgo and C. Rocha (eds), *New Trends in Argentine and Brazilian Cinema*, Bristol, UK: Intellect Books, pp. 243–56.

——— (2014), *Forró e o regionalismo redentor do nordeste brasileiro: Música popular em uma cultura de migração* (*Forró and Redemptive Regionalism from the Brazilian Northeast: Popular Music in a Culture of Migration*) (trans. N. Milanez), São Paulo: Editora Intermeios/University of Missouri Research Council.

Duarte, A. ([1957] 2009), *Absolutamente certo!* (*Absolutely Correct!*), DVD, São Paulo: Dynafilmes/Cinedistri.

——— ([1962] 2005), *O pagador de promessas* (*The Given Word*), DVD, São Paulo: Dynafilmes/Cinedistri.

Duarte, D. ([1438] 1976), 'Leal conselheiro/Loyal Councillor', in D. L. P. d. Costa and P. Gomes (eds), *Introdução à saudade*, Porto, Portugal: Lello & Irmão Editores, pp. 17–19.

Eng, D. and Kazanjian, D. (2003), *Loss: The Politics of Mourning*, Berkeley: University of California Press.

Fernandes, M. d. Z. P. (1950), *Sinhá moça* (*The Landowner's Daughter*), São Paulo: Editora Cupolo.

Ferreira, C. O. (2012), *Identity and Difference: Postcoloniality and Transnationality in Lusophone Films*, Berlin: Verlag.

Filho, O. G. d. R. (2012), 'Reconfigurações do olhar: O háptico na cultura visual contemporânea' ('Reconfigurations of the gaze: The haptic in contemporary visual culture'), *Visualidades* 10:2, pp. 75–89.

Fleming, V. ([1939] 2009), *Gone with the Wind*, DVD, Burbank, CA: Warner Home Video.

Ford, J. ([1956] 2007), *The Searchers*, DVD, Burbank, CA: Warner Home Video.

Freud, S. ([1917] 1957), 'Mourning and melancholia', in J. Strachey (ed. and trans.), *The Standard Edition of the Complete Psychological Works of Sigmund Freud*, vol. 14, London: Hogarth Press, pp. 238–58.

Freyre, G. ([1933] 1986), *The Masters and the Slaves: A Study in the Development of Brazilian Civilization* (trans. S. Putnam), Berkeley: University of California Press.

——— (1962–63), 'On the Iberian concept of time', *The American Scholar*, 32:1, pp. 415–30.

Galvão, M. R. and Bernardet, J. (1983), *Cinema: Repercussões em caixa de eco ideológica: As idéias de 'nacional' e 'popular' no pensamento cinematográfico brasileiro* (*Cinema: Repercussions in an Ideological Echo Chamber: The Ideas of 'National' and 'Popular' in Brazilian Cinematographic Thought*), São Paulo: Brasiliense/Embrafilme.

Ginway, E. (2004), *Brazilian Science Fiction: Cultural Myths and Nationhood in the Land of the Future*, Lewisburg: Bucknell University Press.

Gomes, M. and Aïnouz, K. ([2009] 2013), *Viajo porque preciso, volto porque te amo* (*I Travel Because I Have To, I Return Because I Love You*), DVD, Caldas de São Jorge, Portugal: Nitrato Filmes.

Gomes, P. (1976), 'Saudade: ou do mesmo ou do outro' ('Saudade: Either for the Self or the Other'), in D. L. P. d. Costa and P. Gomes (eds), *Introdução à saudade* (*Introduction to Saudade*), Porto, Portugal: Lello & Irmão Editores, pp. 158–215.

Gonzaga, L. and Cordovil, H. ([1953] 2000), 'A vida do viajante' ('Life of the Traveller'), in E. B. Ramalho (ed.), *Luiz Gonzaga: a síntese poética e musical do sertão* (*Luiz Gonzaga: The Poetic and Musical Synthesis of the Sertão*), São Paulo: Terceira Margem, p. 127.

Grossberg, L. (1992), *We Gotta Get Out of this Place: Popular Conservatism and Postmodern Culture*, New York: Routledge.

Harding, J. and Pribram, E. D. (2004), 'Losing our cool?: Following Williams and Grossberg on emotions', *Cultural Studies*, 18:6, pp. 863–83.

——— (2009), *Emotions: A Cultural Studies Reader*, London: Routledge.

Hardt, M. and Negri, A. (2009), *Commonwealth*, Cambridge: Harvard University Press.

Hatzimoysis, A. (ed.) (2003), *Philosophy and the Emotions*, Cambridge: Cambridge University Press.

Henrique, C. (ed.) (1998), *Elementos constitutivos da consciência saudosa e problemática da saudade* (*Constitutive Elements of the Saudoso Consciousness and Problematic of Saudade*), Lisbon: Lisboa Editora.

Hobsbawm, E. and Ranger, T. (eds) (1983), *The Invention of Tradition*, New York: Cambridge University Press.

Hutcheon, L. ([1997] 2000), 'Irony, nostalgia and the postmodern', in T. d. Haen, R. Vervliet and A. Estor (eds), *Methods for the Study of Literature as Cultural Memory*, Amsterdam: Editions Rodopi, pp. 189–207.

Jaggar, A. ([1989] 2009), 'Love and knowledge: Emotion in feminist epistemology', in J. Harding and E. D. Pribram (eds), *Emotions: A Cultural Studies Reader*, New York: Routledge, pp. 50–68.

Jameson, F. (1989), 'Nostalgia for the present', *South Atlantic Quarterly*, 88:2, pp. 517–37.

——— ([1984] 2000), 'Postmodernism, or the cultural logic of late capitalism', in M. Hardt and K. Weeks (eds), *The Jameson Reader*, Oxford: Blackwell, pp. 188–232.

Jesus, S. d. (2015), *Saudade: Da poesia medieval à fotografia contemporânea, o percurso de um sentimento ambíguo* (*Saudade: From Medieval Poetry to Contemporary Photography, The Way of an Ambiguous Sentiment*), Belo Horizonte, Brazil: Autêntica Editora.

Johnson, R. (1984a), *Cinema Novo x 5: Masters of Contemporary Brazilian Film*, Austin: University of Texas Press.

——— (1984b), 'Film, television and traditional folk culture in *Bye Bye Brasil*', *Journal of Popular Culture*, 18:1, pp. 121–32.

——— (1998), 'Documentary discourses and national identity: Humberto Mauro's *Brasiliana* Series and Linduarte Noronha's *Aruanda*', *Nuevo Texto Crítico*, 11:21&22, pp. 193–206.

Kearney, R. (1992), 'Postmodernity and nationalism: A European perspective', *Modern Fiction Studies*, 38:3, pp. 581–94.

Klass, D., Silverman, P. R. and Nickman, S. (eds) (1996), *Continuing Bonds: New Understandings of Grief*, New York: Routledge.

Kogut, S. (2001), *Um passporte húngaro* (*A Hungarian Passport*), DVD, Rio de Janeiro: Videofilmes/Riofilme.

Laclau, E. (1996), *Emancipation(s)*, London: Verso.

Lant, A. (1995), 'Haptical Cinema', *October*, 74:Autumn, pp. 45–73.

Ledoux, J. (1996), *The Emotional Brain: The Mysterious Underpinnings of Emotional Life*, New York: Simon & Schuster.

Lima, A. A. (1955), 'Saudade', in A. A. Lima, *Meditação sobre o mundo interior* (*Meditation on the Interior World*), Rio de Janeiro: Livraria Agir Editora, pp. 115–19.

Lins, C. (2004), '*Passaporte húngaro*: Cinema político e intimidade', *Galáxia, Revista Transdisciplinar de Comunicação, Semiótica e Cultura*, 7, pp. 75–84.

Lopez, A. (1998), 'The São Paulo connection: The Companhia Cinematográfica Vera Cruz and *O Cangaceiro*', *Nuevo Texto Crítico*, 11:21&22, pp. 127–54.

Lourenço, E. (1999), *Mitologia da saudade seguido de Portugal como destino* (*Mythology of Saudade followed by Portugal as Destiny*), São Paulo: Companhia das Letras.

Lupton, D. (1998), *The Emotional Self: A Sociocultural Exploration*, London: Sage.

Mamoulian, R. ([1940] 2005), *The Mark of Zorro*, DVD, Los Angeles: Twentieth Century Fox Home Entertainment.

Marks, L. (2000), *The Skin of the Film: Intercultural Cinema, Embodiment, and the Senses*, Durham: Duke University Press.

Martinez, M. (1984), *Por uma questão de saudade/Due to a Question of Saudade*, Rio de Janeiro: Nova Fronteira.

Massumi, B. (2002), *Parables for the Virtual: Movement, Affect, Sensation*, Durham: Duke University Press.

Mauad, A. M. (2001), '*Bye Bye Brasil* e as fronteiras do nacional-popular' ('*Bye Bye Brasil* and the borders of the national-popular'), in M. d. C. Soares (ed.), *A história vai ao cinema* (*History Goes to the Cinema*), Rio de Janeiro: Editora Record, pp. 75–86.

Mauro, H. (1935), *Favela dos meus amores* (*Favela of My Loves*), Rio de Janeiro: Brasil Vox Filme.

——— (1942), *Argila* (*Clay*), Rio de Janeiro: Brasil Vita Filmes S.A.

——— ([1952] 2000), *O canto da saudade: Lenda do carreiro* (*The Song of Saudade: Legend of the Ox Cart Driver*), Rio de Janeiro: Ministério da Cultura, FUNARTE, Decine CtaV.

——— ([1945, 1954–56] 2002), *Brasilianas*, DVD, Rio de Janeiro: FUNARTE.

Memória Vera Cruz: Depoimentos sobre a Vera Cruz (n.d.), DVD, São Paulo: Museu de Imagem e Som.

Mendonça Filho, K. ([2012] 2013), *O som ao redor* (*Neighbouring Sounds*), DVD, New York: Cinema Guild.

Merten, L. C. (2004), *Anselmo Duarte: O homem da palma de ouro* (*Anselmo Duarte: The Man of the Palme D'Or*), São Paulo: Imprensa Oficial.

Moriconi, I. (2005), 'The postmodern debate: Brazilian force fields – An introductory overview', *Journal of Latin American Cultural Studies*, 14:3, pp. 355–70.

Nabuco, J. (1909), 'Camões: The lyric poet', Digital Archive of the Fundação Joaquim Nabuco, http://digitalização.fundaj.gov.br/fundaj/. Accessed 10 August 2009.

Nadkarni, M. (2010), '"But it's ours": Nostalgia and the politics of authenticity in post-socialist Hungary', in M. Todorova and Z. Gille (eds), *Post-Communist Nostalgia*, New York: Berghahn Books, pp. 190–214.

Naficy, H. (2001), *An Accented Cinema: Exilic and Diasporic Filmmaking*, Princeton: Princeton University Press.

Nagib, L. (ed.) (2003), *The New Brazilian Cinema*, London: I.B. Tauris.

——— (2007), *Brazil on Screen: Cinema Novo, New Cinema and Utopia*, London: I.B. Tauris.

——— (2013), 'Back to the margins in search of the core: *Foreign Land's* geography of exclusion', in S. Brandellero (ed.), *The Brazilian Road Movie: Journeys of (Self) Discovery*, Cardiff: University of Wales, pp. 162–83.

Orgeron, D. (2008), *Road Movies: From Muybridge and Méliès to Lynch and Kiarostami*, New York: Palgrave Macmillan.

Oricchio, L. Z. (2003), 'The Sertão in the Brazilian imaginary at the end of the millennium', in L. Nagib (ed.), *The New Brazilian Cinema*, London: I.B. Tauris, pp. 139–56.

Orico, O. (1940), *A saudade brasileira* (*Brazilian Saudade*), Rio de Janeiro: Editora S.A. A Noite.

Panelas, T. (1982), 'Yearning for yesterday: The sociology of nostalgia', *American Journal of Sociology*, 87:6, pp. 1425–27.

Pascoaes, T. ([1913] 1976), 'O gênio português' ('The Portuguese Genius'), in D. L. P. d. Costa and P. Gomes (eds), *Introdução à saudade: Antologia teórica e aproximação crítica*, Porto, Portugal: Lello & Irmão Editores, p. 64.

Payne, T. ([1953] 2005), *Sinhá moça* (*The Landowner's Daughter*), DVD, Cult Classic/Coleção Vera Cruz.

Pietz, W. (1985), 'The problem of the fetish, I', *RES: Anthropology and Aesthetics*, 9, pp. 5–17.

——— (1987), 'The problem of the fetish, II', *RES: Anthropology and Aesthetics*, 13, pp. 23–45.

——— (1988), 'The problem of the fetish, IIIa', *RES: Anthropology and Aesthetics*, 16, pp. 105–24.

Pinazza, N. (2015), *The Journey in Argentine and Brazilian Cinema*, New York: Palgrave Macmillan.

Pinto, L. d. A. C. ([1953] 1998), *O negro no Rio de Janeiro* (*Blacks in Rio de Janeiro*), Rio de Janeiro: Editora UFRJ.

Podalsky, L. (2011), *The Politics of Affect and Emotion in Contemporary Latin American Cinema: Argentina, Brazil, Cuba, and Mexico*, New York: Palgrave Macmillan.

Portes, E. A. and Santos, A. M. X. d. (2009), 'Aspectos da educação e do êxodo rural em Minas Gerais (1950–1970)' ('Aspects of Education and Rural Exodus in Minas Gerais [1950–1970])', Paper delivered at the V. Congresso de Ensino e Pesquisa de História de Educação em Minas Gerais (V. Congress of Historical Instruction and Research in Minas Gerais), http://www.congressods.com.br/vcopehe/images/trabalhos/8.estado_e_politicas_educacionais/2.Ecio%20Antonio%20Portes.pdf. Accessed 11 October 2014.

Probyn, E. (1996), *Outside Belongings*, New York: Routledge.

Ray, Nicholas ([1961] 2009), *King of Kings*, DVD, Burbank, CA: Warner Home Video.

Ribeiro, D. ([1995] 2000), *The Brazilian People: The Formation and Meaning of Brazil* (trans. G. Rabassa), Gainesville: University Press of Florida.

Rocha, G. ([1964] 2010), *Deus e diabo na terra do sol* (*Black God, White Devil*), DVD, Brighton, UK: Mr. Bongo Films.

——— (2003), *Revisão crítica do cinema brasileiro* (*Critical Review of Brazilian Cinema*), São Paulo: Cosac Naify.

——— (2004), *Revolução do cinema novo: Glauber Rocha* (*Revolution of Cinema Novo: Glauber Rocha*), São Paulo: Cosac Naify.

Rosenblatt, P. C. (1999), 'Grief', in D. Levinson, J. Ponzetti and P. Jorgensen *Encyclopedia of Human Emotions*, vol. 1, New York: Macmillan, pp. 301–7.

Rossini, M. d. S. (2005), 'O cinema da busca: Discursos sobre identidades culturais no cinema brasileiro dos anos 90' ('Cinema of the Search: Discourses About Cultural Identities in Brazilian Cinema of the 90s'), *FAMECOS*, 27:Aug, pp. 96–104.

Sadlier, D. J. (2007), 'Leaving home in three films by Walter Salles', *symploke*, 15:1&2, pp. 125–39.

Saliba, E. T. (2001), 'História e mobilidade em *Central do Brasil*' ('History and Mobility in *Central Station*'), in M. d. C. Soares (ed.), *A história vai ao cinema* (*History Goes to the Cinema*), Rio de Janeiro: Editora Record, pp. 247–58.

Salles, W. (1996), *Socorro Nobre*, Rio de Janeiro: Videofilmes.

——— ([1998] 1999), *Central do Brasil* (*Central Station*), DVD, Culver City, CA: Videofilmes/Sony Pictures/Columbia TriStar Home Video.

——— ([2001] 2002), *Abril despedaçado* (*Behind the Sun*), DVD, Burbank, CA: Buena Vista Home Entertainment.

——— ([2004] 2005), *Diarios de motocicleta* (*The Motorcycle Diaries*), DVD, New York: Universal Studios.

——— (2007), 'Notes for a theory of the road movie', *The New York Times Magazine*, 11 November, http://www.nytimes.com/2007/11/11/magazine/11roadtrip-t.html?p.&_r=0, Accessed 23 February 2016.

Salles, W. and Thomas, D. ([1995] 2005), *Terra Estrangeira* (*Foreign Land*), DVD, Rio de Janeiro: Videofilmes.

Sampaio, J. S. ([1949] 1961), 'Da necessidade de ser polígamo: Sátira em três atos' ('On the Necessity of Being Polygamist: Satire in Three Acts'), in *Trilogia do herói grotesco* (*Trilogy of the Grotesque Hero*), Rio de Janeiro: Editora Civilização Brasileira, pp. 57–102.

Santiago, S. (2001), *The Space In-Between: Essays on Latin American Culture* (ed. and trans. A. L. Gazzola), Durham: Duke University Press.

Santos, N. P. d. ([1963] 2005), *Vidas Secas/Barren Lives*, DVD, New York: New Yorker Video.

Sedgwick, E. K. (2003), *Touching Feeling: Affect, Pedagogy, Performativity*, Durham: Duke University Press.

Skidmore, T. (1992), *Black into White: Race and Nationality in Brazilian Thought*, Durham: Duke University Press.

Soares, M. d. C. (ed.) (2001), *A história vai ao cinema* (*History Goes to the Cinema*), Rio de Janeiro: Editora Record.

Solomon, R. C. (ed.) (2004), *Thinking About Feeling: Contemporary Philosophers on Emotions*, Oxford: Oxford University Press.

Stam, R. (1997), *Tropical Multiculturalism: A Comparative History of Race in Brazilian Cinema and Culture*, Durham: Duke University Press.

Standing, G. (2011), *The Precariat*, London: Bloomsbury Academic.

Starobinski, J. (1966), 'The idea of nostalgia' (trans. William S. Kemp), *Diogenes*, 14:54, pp. 81–103.

Stowe, H. B. ([1852] 2007), *Uncle Tom's Cabin* (ed. H. L. Gates Jr. and H. Robbins), New York: W. W. Norton.

Strecker, M. (2010), *Na estrada: O cinema de Walter Salles* (*On the Road: The Cinema of Walter Salles*), São Paulo: Publifolha.

Terada, R. (2001), *Feeling in Theory: Emotion After the 'Death of the Subject'*, Cambridge: Harvard University Press.

Tolentino, C. A. F. (2001), *O rural no cinema brasileiro* (*The Rural in Brazilian Cinema*), São Paulo: UNESP.

Tomkins, S. (1995), *Shame and Its Sisters: A Sylvan Tomkins Reader* (ed. E. K. Sedgwick and A. Frank), Durham: Duke University Press.

Viany, A. (1980), *A noiva da cidade* (*The Town's Fiancée*), Rio de Janeiro: Catavento Produções Cinematográficas Ltda/Embrafilme.

Waddington, A. ([2000] 2001) *Eu tu eles* (*Me You Them*), DVD, Culver City, CA: Columbia TriStar Home Entertainment.

——— ([2005] 2006) *Casa de areia* (*House of Sand*), DVD, Culver City, CA: Sony Pictures Home Entertainment.

Webcine (n.d.), 'Notas da produção: *Caminho das Nuvens*' ('Production Notes: *Caminho das Nuvens*'), http://www.webcine.com.br/notaspro/npcamnuv.htm. Accessed 8 January 2016.

Wenders, W. ([1974] 2016), *Alice in den Städten* (*Alice in the Cities*), DVD, New York: Criterion Collection.

——— ([1976] 2016), *Im Lauf der Zeit* (*Kings of the Road*), DVD, New York: Criterion Collection.

Williams, R. (1977), *Marxism and Literature*, Oxford: Oxford University Press.

——— ([1979] 2009), 'On structure of feeling', in J. Harding and E. D. Pribram (eds), *Emotions: A Cultural Studies Reader*, New York: Routledge, pp. 35–49.

Viany, A. (ed.) (1978), *Humberto Mauro: Sua vida, sua arte, sua trajetória no cinema*, Rio de Janeiro: Artenova/Embrafilme.

Vieira, J. L. (2003), '*Bye Bye Brasil*', in A. Elena and M. Díaz Lopez (eds), *The Cinema of Latin America*, New York: Wallflower Press, pp. 161–67.

Xavier, I. (1997), *Allegories of Underdevelopment: Aesthetics and Politics in Modern Brazilian Cinema*, Minneapolis: University of Minneapolis Press.

Zambrana, R. D. (2009), 'Memoria, sentido trágico y el viaje de aniquilación en *Hotel Atlântico* de João Gilberto Noll' ('Memory, tragic meaning and the journey of annihilation in *Hotel Atlântico* by João Gilberto Noll'), *Romance Quarterly*, 56:2, pp. 142–52.

Žižek, S. ([1989] 2008), *The Sublime Object of Ideology*, London: Verso.

Zwingmann, C. (1959), '*Heimweh' or 'Nostalgic Reaction': A Conceptual Analysis and Interpretation of a Medico-psychological Phenomenon*, Stanford: Ph.D. dissertation, Stanford University.

Index

Italic numbers denote reference to illustrations.

www.ingramcontent.com/pod-product-compliance
Lightning Source LLC
LaVergne TN
LVHW060728310826
846742LV00016B/55

* 9 7 8 1 7 8 3 2 0 7 6 3 3 *